TEXTILE COLLECTIONS OF THE WORLD: VOLUME 1 UNITED STATES & CANADA

AMERICA. Marriage quilt, 1785. Pieced and stitched for Anna Tuels by her mother. *Wadsworth Atheneum—1967.75 (140 C).*

TEXTILE COLLECTIONS OF THE WORLD:
VOLUME I

AMERICA. "Bed Rugg," dated 1790. *Brooklyn Museum—49.189a.*

UNITED STATES & CANADA

AN ILLUSTRATED GUIDE TO TEXTILE COLLECTIONS
IN UNITED STATES AND CANADIAN MUSEUMS

EDITOR : CECIL LUBELL

WITH ESSAYS ON THE TRADITIONS
OF NORTH AMERICAN TEXTILE DESIGN BY
ANDREW HUNTER WHITEFORD (NORTH AMERICAN INDIANS)
ROBERT RILEY (UNITED STATES)
DOROTHY K. BURNHAM (CANADA)

 VAN NOSTRAND REINHOLD COMPANY
NEW YORK   CINCINNATI   TORONTO   LONDON   MELBOURNE

AMERICA. Detail of "Boston Town" coverlet, Steubenville, O., c. 1840. Gift of Bernice Sweet. *Cleveland Museum—71.138 (41400).*

Van Nostrand Reinhold Company Regional Offices: New York   Cincinnati   Chicago   Millbrae   Dallas.

Van Nostrand Reinhold Company International Offices: London   Toronto   Melbourne.

Copyright © 1976 by Cecil Lubell. Library of Congress Catalog Card Number 75-30412. ISBN 0-442-24896-2.

Book design by Cecil Lubell. Manufactured in the United States of America.

Published by Van Nostrand Reinhold Company, 450 West 33rd Street, New York, N.Y. 10001. Printed in the U.S.A.

16 15 14 13 12 11 10 9 8 7 6 5 4 3 2

Library of Congress Cataloging in Publication Data
Main entry under title:

United States & Canada.

(Textile collections of the world ; v. 1)
Includes bibliographical references.
1. Textile fabrics—United States. 2. Textile fabrics—Canada. 3. Indians of North America—Textile industry and fabrics. 4. Art—United States—Galleries and museums. 5. Art—Canada—Galleries and museums. I. Lubell, Cecil. II. Whiteford, Andrew Hunter. Fabrics of the North American Indians. 1976. III. Riley, Robert. The traditions of American textile design. 1976. IV. Burnham, Dorothy K. Canadian textile traditions. 1976. V. Series.
NK8812.U54   746'.074'013   75-30412
ISBN 0-442-24896-2

AMERICA. Detail of applique-stitched quilt, c. 1852.
Gift of Mrs. C. I. Wagner. *Newark Museum—47.127 (13301a).*

PHOTO CREDITS: All photographs are courtesy of the collections, except these by Freda Rubin: 114 (bot. left); 116 (bot. right); 118; 119 (top right); 121 (bot. left); 127 (bot. left & right); 128. Museum names are abbreviated; full names on pages 10–11. Captions list accession number and negative (in parentheses) where available.

Baker 3/80 10478

AMERICA. Detail of coverlet woven by Abram William VanDoren, 1847 (Avon, Mich.). *Cranbrook—Temp. 1034.*

Plan and Purpose

The *Textile Collections of the World* series combines resource information with design ideas.

As such it is chiefly directed to professional textile designers, to producers of textiles, to craft workers in thread, and to students of textile design.

Resource information is given in reviews of the textile collections. Textile-design ideas are shown in color and B/W photographs of pieces in the collections reviewed.

Photographs are arranged by national origin. But the intent is not to present a picture history of textile design with all phases represented. That would have meant showing many designs for their historical import rather than for their visual impact on contemporary designers. It would also have involved the repetition of basic design themes which surface at different times in many places.

This I have sought to avoid. My aim has been to select pictures which show graphic ideas that I consider adaptable for today's textiles. The pictures thus reflect a personal view of the collections.

My hope is that these reviews and this photographic sampling will prod designers into visiting the museums and exploring the source material for themselves.—C. L.

Contents   Vol. 1   U.S.—Canada

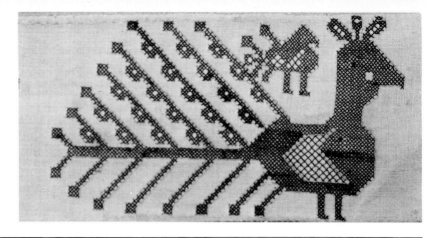

FINLAND. Fragment of embroidered linen in black thread, made in Finland about 1680. *Montreal Museum of Fine Arts—56.Dt.8.*

BOKHARA. Section of a woven ikat, 18th Century, from Turkestan, Bokhara. Gift of the Carnegie Corporation, New York, 1930. *Metropolitan Museum—30.10.13 (178543 tf).*

BOKHARA. Another ikat from Turkestan, also from the 18th Century. This one is done in scarlet silk. *Brooklyn Museum—19.176.*

INTRODUCTION

North America is rich in resources for textile design.

The region has wealth, and donors of textile collections have been generous. This wealth and this private generosity have often made up for the advantages of time and place which are on the side of European and Asian museums.

The result is that more than 70 museums in the United States and Canada hold textile collections that are worthy of note. This is possibly the largest regional count for such collections in the world. Not all are extensive, but all have holdings either specialized enough or important enough to interest professional textile designers and students of decorative art.

Equally noteworthy in a region so huge is the distribution of these collections from the East to the West Coast. Representative pieces from the world's major textile cultures can be found in most of the larger collections, and this puts rich source material within easy reach of designers who live and work far from the extraordinary resources of New York City.

New Yorkers, myself included, tend to be provincial. Many of us think of New York museums as the exclusive American repositories of the world's textile heritage. How wrong we are! For me it was something of a revelation to find so many and such fine sources of textile design far removed from New York City.

Resources in these many cities are detailed in this volume. I estimate that among the museums reviewed there are over half a million pieces of textile treasure available for research and study, not including the many thousands of swatches in old sample books nor the impressive range of museum publications in the field.

In this volume, wherever possible, I have sought to emphasize the distinctively American and Canadian textile holdings in the museums under review. The majority of these collections are international in scope, but almost all have made an effort to preserve the record of North America's textile past.

ECUADOR. Embroidered wool blanket from Rio Bamba, 1930 (detail). Yarns of white, red, orange, turquoise, lavender on dark bluish-brown ground. *The American Museum of Natural History, New York—AMNH (322364).*

This record is presented in larger detail through the three essays which form an essential part of this work—*Fabrics of the North American Indians* by Andrew Hunter Whiteford, *United States Textile Traditions* by Robert Riley, and *Canadian Textile Traditions* by Dorothy K. Burnham. To each of these creative specialists I owe a large debt of gratitude for the knowledge and perceptiveness they were able to pack into a pre-determined space.

*   *   *

For myself, I emerge from this extensive research with a feeling of great humility. As one who has been closely involved with the design and production of contemporary textiles, the achievements of the past—in fabric aesthetics—put most of our contemporary efforts to shame, except occasionally for some of our prints.

There are exceptions to this dictum. The new growth of handweaving as a cultural expression, the evolution of contemporary wall hangings and art fabrics, the new fascination with macramé and lace, the interest of young artists in batik and tie-dyeing and ikat—all these are helping to revive an ancient concept of textiles as art.

But these are largely handcrafts. In the mass production which flows from our ingenious modern machines we do not match the art of handweaving in ancient Peru or Coptic Egypt. We produce little that compares with the luxury of Venetian velvets, the silk brocades of Lucca, the batik panels of Indonesia, or the printed and painted palampores of India. Nor have we conceived anything as moving in its roseate splendor as that masterpiece of 16th-Century tapestry work, *La Dame à la Licorne* at the Cluny Museum in Paris.

The examples could be multiplied many times.

This is not to derogate our modern achievements—which are substantial—but to raise our sights. These earlier cultures had time, much time, cheap labor, and elite markets. They served the wealthy and the powerful few. We have achieved speed and the ability to serve the vast proliferating populations of an industrialized society. I would not want to minimize that achievement.

ABYSSINIA. Hanging from Gondar, probably 18th Century, card-woven of heavy silk in three widths. Gift of Col. George A. Sweny Estate. *Royal Ontario Museum—922.26.1 (62AA422).*

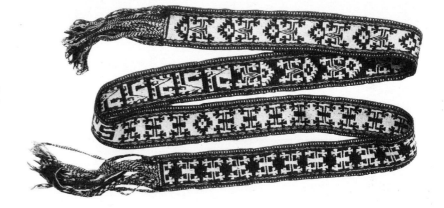

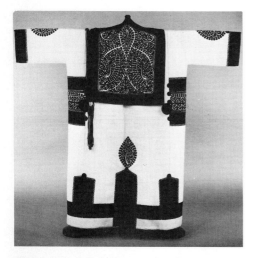

INTRODUCTION Cont'd

But in the process of gaining speed and productive capacity we are losing the enviable skills of hand and eye. Worse still, we are losing the desire to reach high and hard for excellence, for beauty. It is my hope that this volume and those to follow will help to revive that desire among those who design and make our mass-production textiles.

This basic aim is well expressed in the words of an earlier laborer in this same vineyard. He was M. D. C. Crawford—perceptive scholar, ethnologist, advisor to the Brooklyn Museum, and Research Editor of Fairchild Publications. He was the moving force behind a 1946 textile exhibition at the Brooklyn Museum, a pioneering exhibition in this field. In his handbook to that exhibition, Crawford wrote:

"We hope to demonstrate not only the sources of original ideas in cloth construction but also to indicate how these ideas were diffused through both the geographical and chronological patterns of civilization. In this exhibition . . . we hope to reach a common ground of understanding and interest for both the scholar and the industrial craftsman; and to add something to the present and the future achievements in the great realm of textiles. The actual specimens included in this exhibition are presented not as unattainable goals of achievement, but rather as inspiration for contemporary craftsmen. . . . The continuity of ideas is of more importance than the rarity or antiquity of the materials on display."

And he concluded his introduction with this evaluation, obviously based on long personal experience:

"It seems to me that the most satisfactory results from the association I am suggesting between the mill and the museum will be accomplished where each group performs the functions for which it is best qualified. The museums may offer certain canons of taste, but they should not attempt to unduly influence current fashion. The function of the museum is amply performed when inspiring and provocative material is placed at the disposal of industrial designers and technicians with adequate opportunities for critical analysis.

"The museum should not encourage the slavish copying of ancient documents but should rather use its collections to inspire creative effort both in design and the structure of cloth. On the other hand, the

CANADA. Detail of braided woolen sash with white beads. Made by Huron Indians, Quebec, early 19th Century. Gift of J. H. Crang. *Royal Ontario Museum—967.148 (67TEX342).*

industrial designer and the laboratory expert should bring to this new form of research a recognition of the gifts of the ages and a deep respect for the achievements of the past, and the same honesty and intensity of purpose, the same highly trained skills, which are now devoted to the more immediate physical and chemical problems of mass production."

Unfortunately I did not know Morris Crawford or see his groundbreaking exhibition, but it is obviously the unconscious prototype for my own efforts in this volume and the others of this series.

I have another aim—equally important for the future of textile design. I am hopeful that museum directors will be sufficiently impressed by the resources reviewed in this volume and will begin to give more exhibit space to the historic textiles in their care. Collections of fabrics are often treated as orphans in the museum world. They are given little exhibit space, and their facilities are sometimes relegated to remote corners of a museum. This is not always the case: the notable exceptions are recorded in this volume.

But it is generally true that the design of textiles is regarded by museum professionals as a very minor art and therefore can seldom compete with the other arts for scarce exhibition space. Unfortunate, because museums play a most important role in raising the level of public taste. If the riches of our textile heritage were given more public exposure, this might help to create more public demand for contemporary fabrics which match the excellence of those preserved from the past. And this in turn could help to influence the producers and designers of textiles today.

As for designers themselves, the photographs in this volume can stimulate ideas—but they cannot hope to replace the originals. The outline, the form, even the color, can be transmitted through a picture, but never the "feeling" of the original. Only the textile itself will move the designer to act creatively. The idea comes alive in the hand.

And for that you must go to the museums.

Cecil Lubell
Croton-on-Hudson, N.Y.
August, 1975

MADAGASCAR. Detail of woven mosquito netting from Kaudreo, Sakalava, Madagascar. *Field Museum of Natural History—186447 (96058).*

PERU. Detail of a woven alpaca-wool poncho from Tiahuanaco, c. 1000 A.D. *Museum of the American Indian—23/8338 (34192).*

UNITED STATES COLLECTIONS

Baltimore—Museum of Art—**NK**

Baltimore—Walters Art Gallery—**600+**

Bloomfield Hills—Cranbrook—**2,100**

Boston—Museum of Fine Arts—**27,000+**

Boston—Society for the Preservation of New England Antiquities—**5,000+**

Cambridge—Busch-Reisinger Museum—**400**

Cambridge—Fogg Art Museum—**100 (?)**

Cambridge—Peabody Museum—**10,000+**

Chicago—Art Institute—**8,000**

Chicago—Field Museum—**10,000+**

Cleveland—Museum of Art—**3,500+**

Cooperstown, N.Y.—Farmers' Museum & Fenimore House—**4,000+**

Dearborn—Henry Ford Museum—**1,000+**

Deerfield—Historic Deerfield—**1,500**

Denver—Art Museum—**6,000**

Detroit—Institute of Arts—**3,000**

Durham—Duke Museum of Art—**200**

Granville—Dennison Museum—**400+**

Hartford—Wadsworth Atheneum—**5,000+**

Indianapolis—Museum of Art—**7,000+**

Kansas City—Nelson Gallery of Art—**1,000**

Lawrence—University Museum—**500**

AND THE SIZE OF THEIR HOLDINGS

Los Angeles—County Museum of Art—**9,000**

Minneapolis—Institute of Arts—**400**

Newark—Newark Museum—**4,000**

New Haven—Yale Art Gallery—**3,000+**

New York—American Museum
of Natural History—**10,000 (?)**

New York—Artweave Textile Gallery—**NK**

New York—Brooklyn Museum—**28,000 (?)**

New York—Cooper-Hewitt Museum—**21,000**

New York—Design Lab, Fashion Institute
of Technology—**50,000 + 3,000,000 (?) samples.**

New York—Hispanic Society—**200 (?)**

New York—Metropolitan Museum of Art—**55,000**

New York—Museum of the American
Indian—**125,000**

New York—Museum of the City of New York—**NK**

New York—Museum of Contemporary Crafts—**NK**

New York—Museum of Modern Art—**250**

New York—Museum of Primitive Art—**100**

North Andover—Merrimack Valley
Textile Museum—**2,500+**

Palm Beach—Flagler Museum—**280**

Philadelphia—Museum of Art—**15,000+**

Philadelphia—University Museum—**5,000**

Providence—Rhode Island School
of Design/Museum—**5,000+**

Richmond—Valentine Museum—**14,500**

St. Louis—Art Museum—**900**

San Francisco—De Young Memorial Museum—**1,000**

Santa Fe—Museum of Navajo Ceremonial Art—**500**

Santa Fe—Museum of New Mexico—**3,000**

Seattle—Art Museum—**450**

Seattle—Costume/Textile Study Center—**5,000**

Shelburne—Shelburne Museum—**300+**

Sturbridge—Old Sturbridge Village—**4,000**

Washington, D.C.—Dumbarton Oaks—**250**

Washington, D.C.—Smithsonian: National Museum
of History & Technology—**23,000**

Washington, D.C.—Smithsonian: National Museum
of Natural History—**10,000+**

Washington, D.C.—Textile Museum—**8,000**

Williamsburg—Colonial Williamsburg—**10,000+**

Winterthur—DuPont Winterthur Museum—**4,000+**

CANADIAN COLLECTIONS

Montreal—McCord Museum—**5,000+**

Montreal—Museum of Fine Arts—**1,250**

Ottawa—National Museum of Man—**5,000**

Saint John—New Brunswick Museum—**7,000**

Saskatoon—Ukrainian Arts/Crafts Museum—**40,000**

Toronto—Royal Ontario Museum—**13,000**

Victoria—Art Gallery of Greater Victoria—**300**

Winnipeg—Ukrainian Cultural & Educational
Centre—**900**

NK—Size Not Known

UNITED STATES COLLECTIONS

PERU. Tapestry-woven hanging, cotton-wool. Crest, Viceroy of Peru (1622–9). *Textile Museum—1965.4.1.*

RIGHT. Walters Art Gallery, Centre Street building. Part of the original 1905 gallery is visible at right.

BELOW. One section of the handsome Cranbrook Academy of Art/Museum, set in its parklike grounds.

BALTIMORE, MD.

The Baltimore Museum of Art
Art Museum Drive
ZIP: 21218   TEL: (301) 889-1735

Dena S. Katzenberg, Curator, Textiles

At this point in time, the Baltimore Museum considers itself to have a textile collection which is still "in the making." It owns a good but small collection of American textiles, principally quilts and household furnishings which are on exhibit in the American Wing Textile Room. It also owns modest collections of West European and Near Eastern fabrics, as well as some examples of Coptic and ancient Peruvian work.

The museum has mounted two extensive textile exhibits, each of which was accompanied by a catalog. The first of these was *The Great American Cover-Up* in 1971. It was devoted to the quilt collection. The second, with a more extensive illustrated catalog, was an exhibit of blue resist textiles titled *Blue Traditions*.

BALTIMORE, MD.

The Walters Art Gallery
600 North Charles Street
ZIP: 21201   TEL: (301) 547-9000

Richard H. Randall, Director

The Walters Art Gallery has a modest textile collection of just over 600 pieces. Its strongest areas are early pieces from Egypt, Italy, France, Turkey, and Persia.

A more detailed listing of these and other holdings follows.

Egypt.   173 pieces in all. The larger group of 145 textiles is of Islamic origin, dating from the 9th through the 14th Century. These are chiefly linen fabrics with decorative bands of Kufic inscriptions. A smaller group of 28 pieces is Coptic, covering a pe-

riod from the 4th through the 9th Century and illustrating traditional Coptic tapestry-weaving skill with designs of human figures, animals, birds, floral motifs, and hunting scenes.

Italy.   139 pieces, of which 84 are secular and consist chiefly of velvets dating from the 16th through the 18th Century. The remaining 55 Italian fabrics are ecclesiastical vestments and embroideries dating from the 14th through the 17th Century, but concentrated mainly in the 16th Century.

France.   110 pieces. Of these, 75 are mostly 18th-Century satins, brocades, and velvets. An additional 35 examples are predominantly 18th-Century ecclesiastical work, with two pieces from the 16th Century.

Turkey.   55 pieces dating from the 16th through the 19th Century. They include embroidered linen kerchiefs, velvet hangings and covers, silk sashes, and other decorative work. The patterning is largely floral.

Persia.   29 pieces dating from the 17th through the 19th Century. Most are silks, sometimes with embroidery. There are also several gold and silver brocades, as well as one silk pall dating from about 1000 A.D.

Among other smaller groupings in the collection are the following.

Nineteen 18th-Century Near Eastern textiles, including a number of pile fabrics.

Seventeen early Spanish pieces, one from the 13th Century, others from the 16th Century.

Fourteen Japanese examples, including robes and tobacco pouches.

Ten Chinese examples, two of which are imperial robes.

Nine fabrics from Greece, including several from the 15th and others from the 17th Century.

Seven pieces from India, 17–19th Century.

Six from England, 16–19th Century.

Six from Mesopotamia, including four 10th-Century linen fabrics with tapestry-woven, embroidered, or painted Kufic inscriptions. Also one Seljuk and one Sassanian piece.

Five examples of early German ecclesiastical work, mostly from the 15th Century.

BLOOMFIELD HILLS, MI.

Cranbrook Academy of Art/Museum
Cranbrook Institute of Science
500 Lone Pine Road—P.O. Box 806
ZIP: 48103   TEL: (313) 644-1600

Mary Riordan, Museum Curator
Robert N. Bowen, Institute Director

Cranbrook has two collections of textiles, and though neither one is large, each is remarkably rich and varied for its size. This is not surprising since the Cranbrook Academy of Art is the leading graduate school

LEFT. Another view of Cranbrook with the *Orpheus* fountain by Carl Milles.

BELOW. Prayer rug, woven by Loja Saarinen at Cranbrook in 1928. *1955.4.*

CRANBROOK cont'd

in America for the study of fabric design. Thus, in the lush green landscape of Bloomfield Hills—with its winding lanes and its elegant re-creation of English squire country—you will find examples of textiles as diversified as those held by major museums.

The smaller collection belongs to the Academy of Art/Museum. It is historic in scope and numbers slightly less than 400 pieces.

The larger collection is held by the Institute of Science and is ethnological in content, with about 1,700 pieces.

Cranbrook Academy of Art/Museum

This collection is notable for its relatively large groups of fabrics from Coptic Egypt and ancient Peru, as well as for distinctive examples of Art Deco weaving design by Loja and Eliel Saarinen.

Cranbrook Textiles. About 50 pieces of American fabrics designed and made at Cranbrook chiefly within the second quarter of this century. The group includes 18 works by the Saarinens in Art Deco style. Eliel Saarinen, a leading architect, designer, and teacher, was the father of architect Eero Saarinen and the Academy's first president (1932). He designed many of Cranbrook's handsome buildings in a style quite different and more traditional than the avant-garde work of his famous son. His wife Loja was also a designer and headed the Cranbrook Weaving Studio. Most of the pieces they designed are carpets and wall hangings woven in the Studio between 1927 and 1940 and made to be used in Cranbrook buildings.

In addition to these unique pieces there are a small number of upholstery and casement lengths by Marianne Strengell, who headed the Art Fabric Design Department at Cranbrook from 1942 to 1961. Also about 20 art fabrics by Academy students.

Africa. Three 19th-Century raffia mats with strong geometric patternings from Central Congo.

Egypt. Exactly 36 fragments of Coptic tapestry weaving dating from the 3rd to the 6th Century. Several of these are quite as fine and representative as those found in the major U.S. collections of Coptic textiles.

Peru. About 40 examples of ancient Peruvian weaving skill, dating from the Early Nazca to the Ica cultures (B.C. to 1400 A.D.). Again, as with the Coptic material, there are many fine pieces in an excellent state of repair.

Perugia. Seven examples of the traditional blue-and-white towel borders woven in Perugia (Italy) during the 15th and 16th Centuries.

Fragments. Over 150 pieces in all, many of them dating from the 15th and 16th Centuries and others from the 18th and 19th Centuries. Of this group some 75 pieces are Italian, 18 French, 9 East Indian,

and 6 Persian. Most pieces are silk. There is also a varied group of about 50 early vestment ornaments and other later fragments of weaving and embroidery.

Lace. A group of about 40 pieces, including examples of Brussels point, Flemish bobbin, Valenciennes, Italian reticella, and English lace border tape.

Tapestries. Two Flemish pieces, one Gothic, one 19th-Century Chinese silk k'o-ssu, three woven by Herter in England, and one 16th-Century work from Brussels.

Cranbrook Institute of Science

The ethnological collection owned by the Institute numbers about 1,700 pieces of textiles and costume and represents more than a dozen regions of the world.

The largest category of about 600 pieces is a fairly complete illustration of textile work by the North American Indians. There is good representation from the Plains Indians, the peoples of the Central and Western regions, the Southwest, the Northwest Coast, Canada, and the Eskimo lands. Especially strong groups come from the Southwest (190 pieces), the Plains (150), and the Eskimo (100).

The next largest categories represent South America with some 320 pieces, Central America (140), Africa (130), the Pacific region (120), the Philippines (100), and Japan (80), including work of the Ainu people. There are smaller holdings from the peasant peoples of Europe (65), China (55), and Ceylon (50), and token representation of Indochina and Australia.

Publication. *Historic Fiberworks/Cranbrook.* A handsome catalog of the 1974 exhibition, which showed textiles from the two Cranbrook collections covering a time span from the 3rd to the 20th Century. Particularly illuminating are the printed comments by Cranbrook students, who selected and researched all the pieces in the exhibit.

RIGHT. One of the two Textile Galleries at Boston's Museum of Fine Arts.

BELOW. The second Textile Gallery at Boston's Museum of Fine Arts. Together the two galleries cover 2,500 sq. ft.

BOSTON, MASS.

Museum of Fine Arts

465 Huntington Avenue
ZIP: 02115   TEL: (617) 267-9300

Larry Salmon, Curator of Textiles

The international collection of historic textiles at Boston's Museum of Fine Arts is probably the second largest in the United States, next to that of the Metropolitan Museum in New York.

Boston holds an estimated 22,000–25,000 flat textiles, plus about 5,000 costumes and accessories. The numbers may be even larger, but the inability to conduct an inventory and incomplete cataloging have so far defied an accurate count.

Aside from size the Boston collection is unquestionably one of the richest in the country. It holds examples of textiles produced by most known techniques, from most parts of the world, and dating from the first millennium B.C. to the present.

The museum's Textile Department—which houses most of the fabrics and all of the costumes—is also one of the best equipped in the country. Its storage areas are large and climate-controlled, with facilities designed by the former curator Adolph S. Cavallo and the designer Duncan Smith. It has an extensive area for conservation work. Its study area is spacious and book-lined, holding over 5000 volumes on the textile arts. Best of all, the department has the use of two public galleries occupying some 2,500 square feet of space and devoted to frequently changed displays of fabrics and costumes from the collections. Three public exhibits showing different facets of the collection are scheduled each year, some of them accompanied by handsome and informative catalogs and picture books. Between Spring 1971, when the exhibit program was inaugurated, and early 1977 the museum had sponsored 25 important textile shows.

The museum's facilities for the research and display of historic textiles are thus perhaps the most extensive in the country. The fact that these facilities are insufficiently used by professional designers and researchers is not entirely the fault of the museum. It is partly due to the insular character of the textile-design profession, which tends to concentrate in New York and is generally unaware of Boston's impressive resources. It is of course also due to the historic movement of the textile industry away from its traditional New England base.

During much of the 19th Century and into the early decades of the 20th Century New England was the center of U.S. textile manufacturing and Boston was its hub. When the Boston Museum of Fine Arts was founded in 1870, one of its major objectives was "to be of great service to all students of design and manufacture." The founders were motivated by much the same considerations as those which launched the great collections at the Victoria & Albert Museum in London about twenty years

earlier. They hoped to raise the level of design among manufacturers in the region and thus to improve the marketability of their products. The chief of these products at that time was textiles.

In line with this objective the second work of art to receive a registration number at the new museum in Boston was a tapestry. It is also worth noting that among the early objects loaned to the museum in 1876 by the Boston Atheneum were silk weavings, embroideries, ecclesiastical vestments, and tapestries. The attempt to be of practical service to the textile industry was an important factor in the museum's development, and before the turn of the century it had opened a permanent facility for the study of textiles.

During the last decades of the 19th Century only limited funds were available for the purchase of historic textiles, but the museum was fortunate in its private donors. Many of its most important textile groups were acquired through such private gifts. Typical of such acquisitions is the museum's notable collection of early Peruvian textiles. The first gift of 47 pieces was made by Edward W. Hooper in 1876. Between 1897 and 1922 Dr. Denman Waldo Ross added to this collection a group of eight Peruvian tapestries of the Colonial period. In 1930 Edward Jackson Holmes gave the museum 27 important pre-Inca textiles. Textiles of the Nazca period were acquired in 1931, and pre-Columbian feather work in 1960. Today, expanded by other gifts and purchases (through the Charles Potter Kling Fund), the museum owns one of the world's finest collections of Peruvian fabrics from all periods.

The Textile Department was set up as a separate entity in 1930. Its first curator was Gertrude Townsend, succeeded in 1960 by Adolph S. Cavallo.

Larry Salmon, the present curator, took charge of the department in 1969.

LEFT. Fragment of a tapestry-woven wool Kashmir shawl, late 18th or early 19th Century. Ross Collection. *Boston Museum of Fine Arts—00.582 (C14664).*

BELOW. Silk warp ikat, India, 18–20th C. Gift of Ananda K. Comaraswamy. *Boston Mus. of Fine Arts—25.547 (C2168).*

BOSTON FINE ARTS cont'd

The Major Collections

Excluding Chinese and Japanese textiles (which are held by the Asiatic Department and described separately), the museum's Department of Textiles holds important collections of historic textiles in at least 13 areas. In each of these areas the museum is internationally known for the high quality and rarity of many individual pieces and also for its comprehensive coverage of cultures and periods. Its holdings include woven and printed fabrics of all types, embroidery, lace, costume, and costume accessories.

A breakdown of these holdings follows.

1. Eastern Mediterranean. Coptic and Egypto-Arabic tapestry weavings from the Eastern Mediterranean area dating from the 4th through the 12th Century. No accurate count of these holdings is available, but it probably numbers several thousand fragments in addition to a number of larger tapestry pieces. One of these is the famous arch curtain with a near life-size figure.

2. European & Asiatic Silks. A large and very representative collection of woven silks, compound weaves, brocades, velvets, double cloths, and damasks dating from the 12th through the 19th Century. Countries of origin include England, France, Italy, Sicily, Spain, Turkey, and Persia. Among the more important groupings are a large collection of Rennaissance velvets and an important group of damasks dating from the 16th to the 18th Century.

3. European Embroidery. England, France, Italy, and Spain are the chief sources of this notable collection dating from the 14th through the 18th Century. Many of these pieces came to the museum in the 1938 bequest of Philip Lehman in memory of his wife. Another large group was part of the Elizabeth Day McCormick Collection acquired from 1943–53.

4. Greek Island Embroidery. Also Turkish embroideries. One of the country's leading collections of this kind, dating from the 17th through the 19th Century. These Greek embroideries were the theme of an outstanding exhibit in 1974.

5. American Embroidery. Chiefly New England embroidery from about 1700 to 1850. A large and distinguished collection, including numerous examples of crewel-embroidered bed furnishings.

6. Lace. Bobbin and needle lace of all types dating from the 16th through the 19th Century and originating in England and continental Europe. The nucleus of this large collection also came to the museum in the McCormick bequests.

7. Printed Fabrics. The great upsurge of English and French textile printing during the 18th and 19th Centuries is well represented in the collection. Block prints and copperplate printing are included, with many fine examples of both English and French toiles.

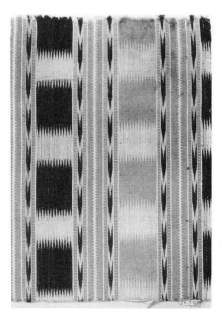

8. Tapestry. In addition to the Coptic tapestry weavings owned by the museum, it also holds a major and internationally famous collection of European tapestries made during the 14th, 15th, and 16th Centuries. They come from the important tapestry centers of France, Flanders, and Germany. Among them is one of the world's most renowned and lyrical mille-fleurs tapestries—the *Narcissus* from 15th or 16th Century France or the Franco-Flemish territories.

9. Peruvian Textiles. The collection of Peruvian fabrics, as already noted, is one of the finest and most representative in existence today. One of its strongest sections consists of tapestries made during the Colonial period, dating from the second half of the 16th Century through the 18th Century. Earlier Peruvian weavings and embroideries date from pre-Christian times up to the mid-16th Century. They include a group of embroidered mantles and breechcloths from the Paracas culture of 500–200 B.C.

10. Textiles of India. The textile arts of India are remarkably well represented in the museum. There are fine examples of woven textiles, embroideries, printed-and-painted cottons, Kashmir shawls, and many other types dating from the 17th Century to the early 20th Century.

11. Indonesian Batiks & Ikats. The collection of traditional textiles from Indonesia is outstanding. The museum holds some 300–400 pieces, most of them dating from the 19th and early 20th Centuries. The Indonesian group has been the source of two much-admired exhibits, one on ikats in 1972 and the other on batiks in 1974.

12. Rugs. The rug collection is not large, consisting of about 100 pieces which are representative of several rug-producing regions in the Near East. The most celebrated of this group is the Boston Hunting Carpet, made in Persia between 1525 and 1550.

RIGHT. Section of an embroidered Chaddar from India (Bikanir, Rajputana), 19th C. Cotton yarns on wool-cotton. Gift of Mrs. Samuel H. Waldstein. *Boston Museum of Fine Arts—62.627 (C21124).*

BELOW. Silk double ikat, India, 18–20th C. Gift of Ananda K. Coomaraswamy. *Boston Mus. of Fine Arts—25.547 (C2168).*

13. Costumes & Accessories. Complete women's costumes from the 18th through the 20th Century and accessories for both women and men dating from the 16th through the 20th Century, based on the Lehman and McCormick Collections.

The Asiatic Collection

Textiles and costumes from China and Japan are kept by the museum's Asiatic Department. The curator is Jan Fontein.

In all, this department holds about 2,200 costumes and textiles and maintains its own storage facilities in a separate part of the museum.

I mention the storage facilities because they seem to me quite remarkable and worthy of a special note. Two large, vaultlike rooms, entered through locked steel doors, hold a literal treasure house of oriental robes—one of the most spectacular collections of this type in the country. One vault holds 144 Chinese robes. The second vault holds 146 Japanese garments, including imperial robes, priest's robes, Nō drama costumes, and elaborately embroidered kimonos. The largest single unit is made up of 116 Nō costumes.

In each vault the garments are hung from numbered poles which can be drawn out to view the piece in full splendor. Even with inadequate lighting the vaults are filled with fabled magnificence. You feel as though you have penetrated the imperial treasure chambers of a legendary Empire long dead. These vaults are opened for visitors by appointment, and eight or nine of the robes are always on public view as part of the department's revolving permanent exhibition.

These two storage rooms are the high point of the Asiatic Textile collection. The rest of the collection is not as spectacular, but it may be even more important to the professional textile designer. Here too are treasures galore.

Among art fabrics from China are 63 brocades, 101 woven-silk tapestries (k'o-ssu), 20 pieces of velvet, 20 rugs, and 126 examples of fine embroidery work. Two large drawers are filled with an unusual collection of small wrist bags covered with intricate embroidery. In all there are over 400 pieces of Chinese work in the room.

The Japanese group stored in the same cabinets is almost three times as large and perhaps even richer as a source of design inspiration. It contains close to 1,200 pieces. The largest category consists of some 600 brocades. Next in size is a group of about 275 painted and printed silks. There are also about 80 pieces of embroidery work, some 50 gift covers (fukusa) and smaller groups of damasks, cottons, and velvets.

Research Facilities & Library

Due to limited staff time the textile collections are open to researchers by appointment only. More accessible is the Textile Department library, which holds a fine collection of 5,000 volumes on the textile arts as well as more than 500 pamphlets, exhi-

bition catalogs, and monographs. Among the major works are the following:

1. Julius Lessing's 11 volumes of superb plates on the textile collection of the Königlichen Kunstgewerbemuseum.

2. Ephraim Chambers' *Cyclopoedia*, London, 1786–89.

3. M. Paulet's *L'Art du Fabriquant d'Etoffes de Soie*, 1773–8.

4. Philemon-Louis Savary's *Dictionnaire Universel de Commerce*, Copenhagen, 1759.

5. Diderot's *L'Encyclopédie*, Paris, 1751–80.

6. *Ackerman's Repository* for the years 1809–1828. (English publication with embroidery designs and fabric swatches).

7. J. Forbes Watson's *The Textile Manufactures of India*, London, 1866.

Publications. Museum publications related to textiles include the following:

1. *A Study of Peruvian Textiles.* By Philip Ainsworth Means. 1932 (out of print).

2. *A Study of Some Early Islamic Textiles.* By Nancy Britton. 1938 (out of print).

3. *She Walks in Splendor.* By Adolph S. Cavallo. 1963 (out of print).

4. *A Devotional Miscellany.* By Margaret H. Swain. 1966.

5. *Tapestries of Europe and of Colonial Peru.* By Adolph S. Cavallo. 1967.

6. *The Boston Hunting Carpet.* By Stuart C. Welch, Jr. et al. 1971. *Boston Museum Bulletin*, LXIX, 355–356.

7. *Nancy Graves Cabot: In Memoriam, Sources of Design for Textiles and Decorative Arts.* By Susan L. MacMillan. 1973.

8. *Crewel Embroidered Bed Hangings in Old and New England.* By Ann Pollard Rowe. 1973. *Boston Museum Bulletin* LXXI, 365–366.

9. *Greek Islands Embroideries.* By Susan L. MacMillan. 1974.

10. *Batiks of Java.* By Susan L. MacMillan (in preparation).

LEFT. Deutsche Werkstätten print by Josef Hillerbrand, c. 1928. Gift of Bertha Schaeffer, 1961. *Metropolitan Museum of Art—61.223.2 (173666tf).*

BELOW. Woven bedspread by Anni Albers, 1949. *Busch-Reisinger—1967.20.*

BOSTON, MASS.

SPNEA—Harrison Gray Otis House
141 Cambridge Street
ZIP: 02114   TEL: (617) 227-3956
Richard C. Nylander, Curator

SPNEA stands for The Society for the Preservation of New England Antiquities. It is the largest regional preservation organization in the United States, with some 60 historic house museums in its care spread over Massachusetts, Connecticut, Rhode Island, New Hampshire, and Maine. Among them is the Harrison Gray Otis House (1796) in Boston. Here the Society has its headquarters, library, and museum. Here too is housed SPNEA's notable collections of textiles and wallpaper. The museum also owns study collections of ceramics, silverware, pewter, dolls, toys, glass, and fans.

The textile collection in the Otis House numbers about 5,000 pieces and represents a wide range of materials either made or used in New England. It includes costume as well as flat textiles, and its strongest groups are in the area of house furnishings. Many of the other SPNEA historic houses contain textiles appropriate to their period so that several thousand additional furnishings can be added to the 5,000 total kept in the museum.

The collection of wallpapers is an outstanding one, numbering some 3,000 pieces and including a large group of hatboxes covered with wallpaper.

The time range covered by the Otis House Collection is predominantly 18th Century, but some pieces go back to the 17th Century and forward to 1890. All pieces have been carefully documented as to the houses they came from and the families who originally owned them.

Among pieces I noted in the collection were the following:

Bed valances in herrateen (or moreen) in which a background pattern has been pressed into the fabric with a hot roller.

Wool blankets decorated with embroidered "Rose Wheel" sunburst designs, popular up to about 1830.

A large and handsome collection of woven coverlets and patchwork quilts—both pieced and appliquéd.

A representative collection of Kashmir and Paisley shawls.

Stencil and stamped designs on linen window curtains. These are the type made by itinerant stampers who traveled the countryside.

A number of ornate lambrequins used to decorate mantle shelves and pieces of furniture.

"Theorem" paintings on velvet, often in rose designs which may have been partly applied by stencil.

Copperplate prints from England, used for bed curtains.

Painted window shades.

Silk-embroidered pictures.

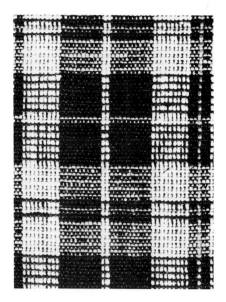

Hooked rugs. The Otis House contains only a few, but a large and important collection of hooked rugs is owned by the SPNEA Beauport House in Gloucester, Mass.

This is no more than a small sampling of an extensive collection which provides an excellent picture of the decor prevalent in early New England homes.

Publication. *Bed Hangings.* Compiled by Abbott Lowell Cummings. Boston, 1961. 60 pages, 61 illustrations. A treatise on the fabrics and styles of bed curtaining from 1650 to 1850.

CAMBRIDGE, MASS.

Busch-Reisinger Museum
Harvard University
29 Kirkland Street
ZIP: 02138   TEL: (617) 495-2338
Linda V. Seidel, Acting Curator

This small and elegant museum has been known to generations of Harvard students as the "Germanic." Less known—both to students and to those concerned with textiles—is the fact that it owns perhaps the most important collections of Bauhaus fabrics in the United States, as well as examples of textile work from the Wiener Werkstaette, which was approximately contemporary with the Bauhaus in the 1920s.

The Busch-Reisinger's textile holdings represent only one facet of the much larger Bauhaus research collection which covers all aspects of Bauhaus work—painting, sculpture, the graphic arts, wallpaper, furniture, work in metal, wood, glass, typography, photography, and architectural designs. There are also many class notes, student exercises, and pamphlets related to the work of the school. In short, the museum holds a complete record of the theory and practice which became a seminal influence on 20th-Century art and design.

RIGHT. The Peabody Museum, Cambridge, Mass. Entrance is at right.

BELOW. Illustration from Peabody brochure announcing opening of a new and enlarged Northwest Coast Indian exhibit.

The collection of textiles is not on exhibit but is easily accessible to researchers. It contains about 100 large examples of woven work and several hundred smaller samples of woven and printed designs, some in fabric, others on paper. These are kept in the museum library art files. Among them are many sample weavings by Anni Albers and Gunta Stölzl. In addition, there are about 15 large pieces which are either wall hangings or bedspreads. These are kept in storage.

The Wiener Werkstaette is represented by a small but no less interesting collection of mounted textile designs, chiefly for prints.

The museum library owns a collection of some 1,200 volumes and includes many works specifically related to the Bauhaus.

Publication. *Concepts of the Bauhaus.* By John David Farmer & Geraldine Weiss. 1971. This is an illustrated handlist and exhibition catalog prepared for the museum's definitive Bauhaus exhibit held in 1971. It contains an excellent short history of the school, its famous teachers, and its concepts. 136 pages with many fine illustrations.

CAMBRIDGE, MASS.

Fogg Art Museum
Harvard University—Quincy Street
ZIP: 02138   TEL: (617) 495-2378

Seymour Slive, Director

The Fogg Art Museum owns only a very small collection of textiles which consists chiefly of tapestries and rugs. The more important rugs are of Islamic origin. There are also a few 19th-Century Chinese robes, several Turkish silks of early date, and a miscellaneous group of textiles from various sources.

The Fogg, it should be noted, has jurisdiction over the Busch-Reisinger Musuem at Harvard.

CAMBRIDGE, MASS.

Peabody Museum of Archaeology & Ethnology—Harvard University
11 Divinity Avenue
ZIP: 02138   TEL: (617) 495-2248

Joanne S. Brandford, Textiles
Katherine Edsall, Chief Archivist

The Peabody Museum—like other major museums of archaeology and ethnology—can exhibit only a fraction of the vast resources it holds in its storerooms. Yet such collections tend to have a revelatory effect on the people of industrialized societies. When we come face to face with the unfamiliar artifacts of a preindustrial culture, the experience can only be humbling. We

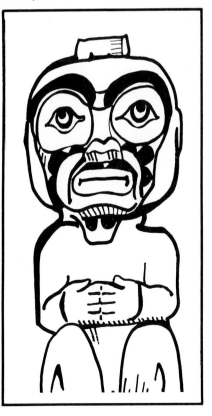

can then see at first hand the beauty and technical skill achieved in the textile arts by men and women of preindustrial societies—with only the simplest of materials and equipment. And we cannot help comparing these handcrafted pieces with the inferior products of our technological age.

For me this has always been especially apparent during my visits to the Peabody over a span of some 35 years. I have long felt this museum to be one of the most stimulating resources I could recommend to any textile designer and researcher. Each gallery and each exhibit case seems to me to hold a treasury of ideas for contemporary textile design.

How large is the Peabody textile collection? This is almost impossible to determine. Textiles are cataloged and arranged with the other artifacts of any given culture. All I can say with some assurance is that there are well over 10,000 pieces of flat textile and costume in the collection and that it is especially strong in examples from ancient Peru, modern Guatemala, the North American Indians, Southeast Asia, and Polynesia.

To say only this, however, is too general to convey the richness of the collection. Since no organized inventory of the textile holdings has ever been made, I will resort to a brief descriptive tour of what the "textile" visitor can hope to see.

But first I should say that a great deal of textile material is on display in the public galleries and even more in the nonpublic study areas. To explore the collection in any depth, it is essential to visit this study area. It is reserved for students, but visitors can gain admission by prearrangement. It contains a series of study alcoves created by the placement of large glass-fronted display cases. Each case contains an exhibit of artifacts and textiles from one or more preindustrial cultures. And there are many. For any professional textile designer the ex-

19

The forty-yard-long Textile Gallery at the Art Institute of Chicago, with an exhibit of American coverlets.

PEABODY MUSEUM cont'd

ploration of this dusty treasure house will in itself become a memorable adventure.

What, then, can the visitor expect to see in the Peabody exhibits? Here is a sampling:

Ikats. A small but choice collection of about 25 weft ikats (silk) from Thailand. Some of these were court saris. This group has been given special attention and study by Joanne S. Brandford, a Research Fellow in the Textile Arts. These and other ikats in the collection have also been studied by Monni Adams, an anthropologist now working at Harvard and a specialist in ikats from the Indonesian island of Sumba.

Batik. A fine display of Javanese batik work, including a demonstration panel showing twelve stages in the preparation of a batik.

Africa. A group of raffia pile weaves. Also indigo-striped cottons from West Africa.

American Indian. Strong in Navajo blankets and textiles from the Pueblo region of the Southwest. A good representative collection of Chilkat and Salish blankets. Superb examples of Alaskan porcupine-quill embroidery. Belts, sashes, and bags of the Plains and Woodland Indians. Extraordinarily fine examples of Seminole patchwork.

Argentine. Araucanian warp ikats in wool fiber.

Bolivia. Bags and belts of the postoccupation period, chiefly from the Titicaca region but also some pieces from nearby regions in Peru.

Burma. A very interesting group of woven pieces, chiely from the Kachin tribes of Upper Burma.

Guatemala. A very large collection, grouped by the villages where the fabrics were produced. Most of the work is from the late 19th and early 20th Centuries.

Hawaii. A good display of the rare Hawaiian feather cape.

India. A representative group of cottons.

Japan. A splendid collection of appliqué work by the Ainu people of Japan.

Mexico. A small but representative exhibit—ponchos, garments, etc.

New Zealand. Twined capes of the Maori.

Pakistan. A good range of cotton and silk weaves as well as embroideries.

Panama. A group of very fine early molas (appliqué) from the San Blas Islands. They are part of the Louis Hoover Collection.

Peru. The collection of textiles from ancient Peru ranges over the whole pre-Columbian time span and has fine examples of both woven and embroidered fabrics, as well as painted cottons and knotless netting. There are also contemporary weavings by the Quechua Indians of the Andes region.

Philippines. A very strong group with good representation from the important Philippine textile crafts—embroidery, beadwork, and ikat. The work is dominantly from Mindanao (Bagobo).

Polynesia. A special hall in the museum is devoted to work from the Pacific Islands. On public display here is one of the largest and most representative collections of tapa cloth I have yet seen anywhere.

Siberia. Some memorable examples of the sophisticated fish-skin appliqué designs made by the people of Southeast Siberia.

Thailand. Rich weavings in gold and silk yarns.

Tibet. A modest but stimulating collection, one of the few in American museums.

This listing is no more than a sampling of the rich textile resources the Peabody can offer designers who will take the trouble to explore.

CHICAGO, ILL.

The Art Institute of Chicago

Michigan Avenue at Adams Street
ZIP: 60603   TEL: (312) 443-3696

C. C. Mayer-Thurman, Textile Curator

Among the major textile collections in North America I know of none that is better organized or more efficiently administered that the Department of Textiles at The Art Institute of Chicago. Under Mildred Davison (the former curator, now retired) and Christa C. Mayer-Thurman, the present curator, the department has long been highly regarded in the museum world. More important, the collection is easily accessible to researchers, and documentary cataloging of its holdings is constantly being expanded. It is also a remarkably active department both in the publications it has issued on its holdings and in the exposure its textiles are given through frequent and important exhibits.

The Department of Textiles is housed in relatively spacious offices with excellent but limited facilities for research. Storage facilities are also excellent but filled to capacity. It is more fortunate than most textile collections in the exhibit space available to it. One major gallery—adjacent to the department and some forty yards long—is frequently devoted to changing displays of textiles. Its exhibit program is one of the most active in the field.

Among other facilities for research is a small but comprehensive library of about 400 volumes related to textile history and the different textile arts as practiced in many parts of the world. For example, I was delighted to find in this library a rare set of portfolios from Japan on the outstanding Kanebo Collection of ancient Coptic and Peruvian grave cloths.

(It should be noted that due to limited staff time and space the Department's facilities

RIGHT. Exhibit of American hooked rugs in the Textile Gallery, Art Institute of Chicago.

BELOW. The Art Institute of Chicago. Entrance facade on Michigan Avenue.

are available by appointment only from 10:30 to 4:30 Mondays through Fridays.)

In this connection I would like to call attention to a study unit of 140 color slides based on the Institute's 1969 exhibit *Masterpieces of Western Textiles*. This unit is available for rental only from the Research & Education Department of the American Crafts Council at 44 West 53 Street, NY 10019 (cat. No. C11, rental fee $14). The study unit covers western tapestries, silks, velvets, needlework, lace, and prints. The range is from ancient Peru to the 20th Century, and all pieces photographed are in the Institute Collection.

In size the Art Institute's textile holdings are in the medium range among major collections in the United States. But they are choice, international in scope, and representative of the most important areas of textile history. Especially notable are the collections of tapestries, coverlets, woven textiles from France-Italy-Peru, printed textiles and needlework from France-England, and lace from many countries.

In all, the Institute's holdings number about 8,000 pieces. Of this total some 6,500 pieces are held by the Department of Textiles, and 1,400 by the Department of Oriental Art.

To this total should be added an important group of 78 sample books containing over 26,000 swatches and covering a wide range of Western textiles. They include woven and printed fabrics as well as painted designs. It is worth noting that this is the only collection I know which can offer an exact count (26,302) of the number of fabric swatches in its possession. That is because a great many of the swatches have been carefully preserved by removing them from the original deteriorating sample books and remounting them in modern portfolios. Such a demonstration of conservation efficiency must surely be unique in the museum field.

LEFT. Another view of the coverlet exhibition, Art Institute of Chicago.

BELOW. Masterpieces of western textiles exhibit at Art Institute of Chicago.

CHICAGO ART INSTITUTE cont'd

Broken down by categories the Textile Department's holdings show the following tabulation:

Woven textiles	3,231
Printed textiles	478
Needlework & accessories	1,043
Lace & accessories	1,053
Fashion accessories	654

The Department of Textiles

I. Woven Fabrics. In this category there are over 3,200 pieces of flat fabric and some 22,000 swatches. The countries represented are: Austria, Bolivia, Canada, Czechoslovakia, Egypt, England, Flanders, France, Germany, Guatemala, Holland, Hungary, Italy, Mexico, New Zealand, Norway, Peru, Poland, Portugal, Rumania, Sardinia, Scotland, Spain, Sweden, Switzerland, the U.S., and the U.S.S.R.

For comparative purposes the Department also holds some non-Western woven fabrics from Africa, China, India, Indonesia, Japan, Syria, and Turkey.

Among the more important groups of woven textiles are the following

1. Egypt. About 30 pieces, 3rd Century B.C. to the 20th Century. Coptic fragments and pieces of burial shrouds.

2. England. About 40 pieces, chiefly 19th Century. Shawls, panels, wedding veils, bookmarks, woven pictures, handkerchiefs, and runners.

3. France. About 230 pieces, 17th to 20th Century. Panels, waistcoats, chasubles, copes, bedspreads, hangings, and shawls.

4. Guatemala. About 90 pieces, 20th Century. Belts, panels, carrying cloths, skirts, huipils, rebozos, headbands, etc.

5. Italy. About 260 pieces, 13th to 20th Century. Panels, fringes, tassels, galloons, guimpes, borders, chasubles, copes, and a number of patterned fragments.

6. Peru. About 300 pieces, 10th to 20th Century. Borders, panels, ponchos, caps, bands, and patterned fragments.

7. Spain. About 60 pieces, 13th to 19th Century. Altar panels, bed hangings, table covers, copes, chasubles, and patterned fragments.

8. United States. About 400 pieces, 18th to 20th Century. Bed covers, curtains, woven pictures, cushion covers, panels, shawls, blankets, wall hangings, bed valances, towels, commemorative ribbons, and sample lengths of apparel fabrics. There are also 103 samples of wool dyed with natural dyes indigenous to Illinois.

In addition, the U.S. holdings include one of the most important collections of coverlets in the country. It consists of 160 pieces woven during the 19th Century. They are definitively described and discussed in the 228-page paperback titled *Coverlets* by Mildred Davison & Christa C. Mayer-Thurman, published by the Institute in 1973 as a handbook and catalog for the important exhibit held July 14–October 14, 1973.

9. Rugs. About 30 pieces, 15th to 20th Century. Representative rugs from England, Finland, France, Holland, Portugal, Spain, and the United States. (Nonwoven rugs from the U.S. are listed under needlework.)

10. Tapestries. About 150 pieces, 15th to 20th Century. Representative work from England, Flanders, France, Germany, Italy, Spain, Switzerland, and the United States.

II. Printed Fabrics. The Department holds about 500 pieces of printed textile from Austria, England, Finland, France, Germany, Holland, Italy, Ireland, Portugal, the U.S., and the U.S.S.R. For comparative study there are also a few pieces from India and China and about 30 printing tools. The three largest print groups are noted below.

1. England. About 150 pieces, 18th to 20th Century. Panels, fragments, handkerchiefs, curtains, shawls, bed sets, and maps.

2. France. About 135 pieces, 18th to 20th Century. Curtain panels, wall panels, hand-

RIGHT. Exhibit of selected acquisitions since 1967, Art Institute of Chicago.

BELOW. Entrance to masterpieces of western textiles, Art Institute of Chicago.

kerchiefs, valances, bedspreads, fragments, and a number of costume pieces.

3. United States. About 80 pieces, 19th and 20th Century. Panels, aprons, handkerchiefs, covers, fragments, shawls, bedspreads, and a few costume accessories.

III. Needlework. This part of the collection has about 1,000 pieces, including 70 quilts and 40 rugs. Countries represented are: Austria, Belgium, Czechoslovakia, Denmark, Egypt, England, France, Germany, Guatemala, Holland, Hungary, Ireland, Italy, Mexico, Panama, Peru, Philippines, Portugal, Rumania, Scotland, Spain, Sweden, Switzerland, the U.S., the U.S.S.R., and Yugoslavia. For comparative study there are also a few pieces from China, India, Morocco, and Turkey.

Among the more important groups of needlework are the following.

1. England. About 160 pieces, 17th to 20th Century. Boxes, mirrors, caskets, embroidered pictures, cuffs, samplers, curtains, caps, waistcoats, coats, bags, panels, handkerchiefs, chair seats, table covers, fine screens, and bedspreads.

2. France. About 140 pieces, 17th to 19th Century. Panels, waistcoats, borders, chair seats, caps, handkerchiefs, cloth samples, dress trimmings, shawls, edges, stomachers, skirts, altar frontals, samplers, chalice covers, and embroidered book covers.

3. Greece. An important collection of Greek Island embroideries is held by the Department of Oriental Art.

4. Italy. About 70 pieces, 16th to 19th Century. Panels, borders, medallions, cuffs, pillowcases, bands, orphreys, samplers, altar frontals, apron panels, embroidered pictures, covers, and fragments.

5. Spain. About 40 pieces, 17th to 19th Century. Borders, fragments, panels, bedspreads, sleeves, purses, handkerchiefs, scarves, samplers, and altar covers.

6. United States. About 300 pieces, 17th to 20th Century. Dress accessories, samplers, panels, embroidered pictures, chair seats, covers, bedspreads, tablecloths, towels, shawls, and curtain panels. In addition there is an outstanding group of 70 quilts (19th and 20th Century) and 40 rugs of different types (18th and 19th Century).

IV. Lace. The collection of laces numbers about 900 pieces, dating from the 16th to the 20th Century. There are representative pieces from Belgium, Czechoslovakia, Egypt, England, Flanders, France, Germany, Greece, Holland, Ireland, Italy, Norway, Paraguay, South America, Spain, Switzerland, the U.S., the U.S.S.R., and the West Indies.

Among these the largest groups are from Italy (290 pieces), Flanders (130), Belgium (80), and England (50). Also included are 60 lace accessories—patterns, pillows, and bobbins.

The Department of Oriental Art

The collection of about 1,400 textiles and costumes now held by the Department of Oriental Art will probably be transferred to the Department of Textiles in due time. It is a rich collection with pieces from nine different cultures and regions.

1. China. About 320 pieces. Silk tapestries, woven hangings, embroidered panels, brocades, sleeve bands, embroidered robes, and coats.

2. Greece. An outstanding collection of embroideries from the Greek islands, formerly owned by Burton Yost Berry. It is described in *Turkish and Greek Island Embroideries* by Margaret Gentles, published by the Art Institute of Chicago in 1964.

3. India. About 125 pieces, including 18 saris and a large group of 66 shawls.

4. Japan. This is the largest category in the Department. It holds 437 pieces in all. Among these are 383 fragments, illustrating many different silk textile constructions. There are also 14 obis, some 30 different types of robes, and two 20th-Century sample books with many swatches.

5. Morocco. About 28 pieces, including borders, scarves, and embroideries.

6. Persia. About 150 pieces. Shawls, brocade, brocaded-silk borders, compound satins, and silks.

7. Philippines. About 14 pieces. Saris, scarves, kerchiefs, and mindanaos.

8. Southeast Asia. A sampling of 12 embroidered pieces.

9. Turkey. About 290 pieces. Almost half of these are towels with woven and embroidered designs. There are also 10 sashes, 15 bedspreads, 30 embroidered squares and covers, 17 bed decorations, and a number of other household furnishings.

Publications. The following publications on textiles have been issued under the imprint of the Art Institute of Chicago.

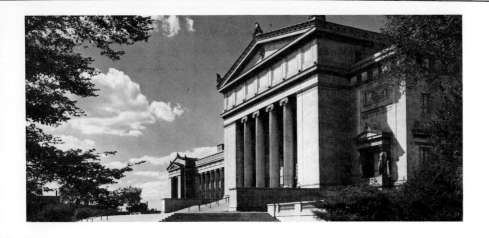

LEFT. Main entrance to the Field Museum of Natural History, Chicago.

BELOW. Descriptive exhibit of weaving techniques and designs from Indonesia at the Field Museum.

CHICAGO ART INSTITUTE cont'd

1. *Masterpieces of Western Textiles.* By Christa Charlotte Mayer. Chicago, 1969. A fine survey book with excellent historical background essays on tapestries, woven textiles, printed textiles, embroidery, and lace. Fully illustrated.

2. *Coverlets.* By Mildred Davison & Christa C. Mayer-Thurman, Chicago, 1973.

3. *American Quilts.* By Mildred Davison. Chicago, 1966 (out of print).

The following articles have also been published on the Art Institute's textile collection: since 1962.

1. *Altarpiece from Burgo de Osma.* By Mildred Davison. *Museum Studies*, No. 3, pp. 108–24. The Art Institute, Chicago, 1968.

2. *Handwoven Coverlets in the Art Institute of Chicago.* By Mildred Davison. *Antiques Magazine*, May 1970, pp. 734–40.

3. *Early German Needlework Fragment.* By Christa C. Mayer. *Museum Studies*, No. 6, 1971, pp. 66–76.

4. *Five Related Coverlets.* By Mildred Davison. *Antiques Magazine*, October, 1972, pp. 650–2.

5. *Masterpieces of Western Textiles.* By Christa C. Mayer. *Antiques Magazine*, February, 1969, pp. 265–9.

6. *Three Centuries of the Decorative Arts in Italy.* By Allen Wardwell & Mildred Davison. *Apollo Magazine*, September 1966, pp. 178–89.

7. *New Look at Textiles.* By Mildred Davison. *Art Institute Quarterly*, March 1962, pp. 6–11.

Additional articles on the collection by C. C. Mayer-Thurman and others have appeared in recent issues of the Art Institute publications *Calendar* and *Bulletin*. A full list is obtainable from the Department of Textiles at the Art Institute.

Color Slides. A group of 98 35mm color slides showing historic textiles in the Art Institute Collection are available @ $1.50 each from Rosenthal Art Slides, 5456 S. Ridgewood Court, Chicago, Ill. 60615. The slides cover 46 woven textiles, 21 pieces of needlework, 6 printed fabrics, 5 pieces of lace, and 20 representative pieces from the Oriental Department holdings.

CHICAGO, ILL.

Field Museum of Natural History
Roosevelt Road at Lake Shore Drive
ZIP: 60605   TEL: (312) 922-9410

James W. Van Stone,
Chairman, Anthropology Department

The Field Museum is reputed to own the third largest anthropological collection in the United States, following in size the American Museum of Natural History in New York and the Smithsonian in Washington. Its textile collection is also large and impressive. It owns a little over 10,000 pieces, all held by the Anthropology Department of the museum.

These textiles fall into two main categories, as they do in most natural-history museums—ethnological and archaeological. The archaeological fabrics are the early ones, chiefly from ancient Egypt and ancient Peru, some of them dating from the 4th Century. There are about 1,800 pieces. The ethnological textiles are much more recent, some of them contemporary and others dating from the late 19th and early 20th Centuries. There are over 8,000 pieces. They are mainly garments or accessories, and among them are some unusual categories seldom seen in museums of anthropology. One such is a large and representative collection from Madagascar.

Statistics aside, the Field Museum is an incredibly rich resource for all textile designers, especially so because the fabrics of so many different cultures are openly displayed in the museum's great echoing galleries. It becomes an unending feast of design ideas, and it certainly cannot be digested in one visit. For example, a major portion of the museum's large Coptic collection of 800 pieces is openly displayed in one of the galleries. This gives visitors a panoramic view of ancient Egyptian weaving which they could probably find nowhere else outside the pages of a book. And here it is all alive.

A similar exhibit approach is taken to many other cultures. Masses of material are on display, and they include a great many textiles, costumes, and fabric-making processes. This is of course not a modern approach to display and it can be a little overwhelming at times, yet I feel it has much that should recommend it to textile designers. It offers them a great many ideas and it allows them to find their own way through the artifacts of these preindustrial cultures—rather than being presented with a reduced and edited version of the materials.

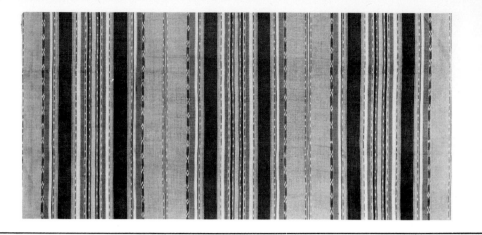

RIGHT. Sarong skirt of woven cotton for either sex from the Philippines (Lanas Moro). *Field Museum—34627 (95813).*

BELOW. Another section of the Indonesian weaving exhibit at the Field Museum.

In addition to textiles on display in the galleries, the Anthropology Department holds a large reserve store of fabrics which researchers can see by appointment. I counted 17 huge metal storage cabinets, each 8 × 4½ feet in size, and their drawers were filled to capacity with an exotic array of flat textiles and garments from some 50 regions of the world.

The strongest areas in the collection are those with textiles and/or costumes from China (1,500 pieces), New Guinea (1,065), ancient Peru (900), Central America (830), the Philippines (815), Ancient Egypt (800), North American Indians (750), South America (665), Madagascar (615), India (550), the Bismarck Archipelago (450), Southeast Asia (400), the Caribbean area (290), Mexico (255), Polynesia (225), and Tibet (125).

The following paragraphs contain more detailed listings of large holdings from these different areas, as well as smaller holdings from some 35 other regions of the world.

Archaeology

South America. The archaeological collections from South America include 100 pieces from Chile (Iquique) and a much larger group of some 900 woven and embroidered textiles from ancient Peru. There are representative pieces from the Central Coast (500) and the South Coast (300), as well as a few pieces (10) from the Highlands.

Egypt. The Egyptian collection is almost entirely Coptic and consists of about 800 pieces. A number of these are large hangings or garments—very rare. The remainder are small fragments of representative Coptic tapestry weaving. Altogether this ranks as one of the largest and most important Coptic collections in the country with good representation of different periods and styles. And, as noted, a great many of the pieces are on display in the museum galleries.

Ethnology

North American Indians. A large and very representative collection of about 750 pieces drawn from six major regions of Indian culture—Woodlands, Southeast, Plains, Southwest, California, and the Northwest Coast.

The strongest group comes from the Southwest with about 365 pieces of Navajo and Pueblo work, including 150 blankets. There is also a large group of Pueblo ceremonial kilts and sashes (175) and smaller groups of shirts and dresses.

From the Woodland regions comes another strong collection of about 275 pieces, most of them examples of the handsome appliqué work for which these people are famous. It takes the form of either bags or clothing. The collection also contains about 30 woven sashes from this culture.

From the Northwest Coast comes a smaller but very interesting group of 60 pieces, including 15 fine Chilkat blankets and a number of garments made from woven

cedar-bark cloth. Even more fascinating are several Eskimo fish-skin garments decorated with graceful and elaborate appliqué work and embroidery.

Among the smaller groups in the American Indian collection are 15 examples of Seminole appliqué work from the Southeast, an equal number of woven bags from the Plains Indians (Oklahoma Osage), and ten woven bags from California.

Central America. The chief areas represented are Mexico, Guatemala, and some Caribbean islands. From Mexico come serapes, ponchos, blankets, woven sashes, headbands, and embroidered clothing. There are 120 pieces from North Mexico and 135 pieces from the central region. Guatemala is also represented by woven sashes, shawls, and embroidered clothing— 285 pieces in all. From the Caribbean region come woven cotton belts, netted bags and a large group of some 200 molas (appliqué panels) from the Cuna Indians of San Blas (Panama).

South America. Representation is from three regions—the Andes villages, the tropical-forest area, and the marginal lands (chiefly Paraguay). In all there are 665 pieces. The largest number (425) comes from Paraguay. There are 200 examples of indigenous Andean weaving and about 40 pieces from the tropical forest region. Included are garments, belts, caps, bags, hammocks, rugs, and ponchos. Bags predominate with almost 400 examples.

Africa. The African continent is represented by textiles and costumes from six different areas—Madagascar, Guinea/ Cameroons, North Africa, the Sudan, the Congo, and Southeast Africa.

The largest and most unique group comes from Madagascar with over 600 examples of indigenous weaving in raffia, cotton, and wild silk. There are excellent displays of these textiles in the exhibit galleries. They show smocks, dresses, baby covers, belts,

Education-wing building at the Cleveland Museum of Art—a modern addition to the older structure.

FIELD MUSEUM cont'd

patterned loincloths, and some very interesting robes of wild silk with designs in black and brown.

From North Africa comes a varied collection of about 70 pieces. It includes a number of stamps used in textile printing, as well as rugs and costume.

From the Sudan there is a small group of about 30 garments and tie-dyed fabrics.

From Guinea/Cameroons comes a larger group of 125 pieces which includes excellent examples of narrow-strip weaving, tie-dyeing, and paste-resist dyeing.

The Congo contributes 40 pieces of raffia work in woven belts and knitted caps.

From Southeast Africa there is a small group of 15 netting costumes and belts.

Asia. On the Asian continent eight regions are represented in the collection—China, Japan, Formosa, India, Burma, Tibet, Bhutan/Nepal/Assam, and the Malay Peninsula.

The largest group comes from China. It is also the largest unit in the whole textile collection with about 1,500 pieces. Of these about 600 pieces are costume—court robes and everyday garments. Another 450 pieces are household furnishings. There are also 40 tapestries, 30 examples of resist dyeing, and 80 pieces of embroidery, including an especially noteworthy group in blue and white. An additional group consists of 160 borders for peasant garments. Finally there are 120 samples of woven textiles in different constructions, including brocade, satin, damask, and cut velvet.

This collection makes the Field Museum one of the country's most important resources for Chinese textiles and costume of both the court and the peasantry.

The second most important Asian group held by the Anthropology Department

comes from India. It consists chiefly of work from the textile center of Ahmedabad. Though there are 550 pieces in this unit, most of them are not textiles but woodblocks for textile printing. There are 400 such blocks in the collection—a most valuable resource for all textile print designers. The rest of the Indian group consists of woven saris (80 pieces), embroidered garments (45), and decorative borders (20).

From Tibet the museum holds a modest but most important collection of textiles and costume—important because, as far as I can determine, it is one of only two such representative holdings in North America. The other is owned by the Newark Museum.

At the Field Museum the Tibetan material is given a special exhibit area which uses modern display techniques and a dramatic setting. I was especially pleased to see examples of the distinctive striped aprons made in Tibet, as well as fine examples of the traditional Tibetan tanka (banner).

Other smaller groupings within the Asian collection include about 60 pieces of Japanese textile work and representative costume pieces from Formosa (15), Bhutan/Nepal/Assam (25), Burma (40), and the Malay Peninsula (35).

Southeast Asia. The Field Museum owns about 400 pieces of flat textiles, clothing, and textile tools from Java, Sumatra, and Borneo. The largest group comes from Java—230 pieces. Of these, 150 are not textiles but batik stamps used in waxing the design. The remainder consists of batik sarongs (60) and a small number of embroidered garments. There is also an excellent exhibit on the batik process in the public galleries.

From Sumatra there are about 135 pieces of ceremonial and everyday costume, some woven with silk and gold yarns. From

Borneo comes a small group of some 35 coats and skirts.

Philippines. A large and most comprehensive group of over 800 pieces—chiefly costume and accessories. It contains large numbers of woven belts, sarongs, and loincloths, as well as ceremonial clothing, cotton blankets, and bags. Many of the textiles are made by the ikat process, and among the gallery exhibits is an excellent diorama of ikat making with Manila hemp yarns. I also noted an interesting group of resist-dyed fabrics made by "sewing in" the design with waxed threads.

New Guinea. One of the largest units in the collection—with over 1,000 pieces. At least four different areas of the island are represented—the North, Huon Gulf, Papua, and the region under Dutch influence. The largest unit comes from the northern area and contains 535 pieces. Of these 250 are netted bags and 280 are aprons and belts, many of them of tapa cloth but some woven. Similar costume pieces come from the Huon Gulf (230), Papua (160), and the Dutch area (40). Another 100 pieces have no specified source on the island but are similar to the other types.

Bismarck Archipelago. A total of some 450 pieces from New Hebrides, New Ireland, New Britain, the Admiralty Islands, and the Solomon Islands. They consist chiefly of netted bags, loincloths and aprons of tapa cloth, woven belts, and skirts.

Polynesia. An impressive collection of 175 tapa-cloth pieces in many different patterns. Also 50 examples of Polynesian costume.

Research Facilities. The Anthropology Department at the Field Museum has an excellent library of works on the ethnology of all regions from which it holds textiles. It also has a comprehensive file of B/W photos showing artifacts and textiles in the collection—filed by regions. Prints can be ordered.

RIGHT. Silk fragment in compound-tabby weave from Iran, Seljuk period, 12th Century. Gift of Mr. & Mrs. Werner Abegg. *Cleveland Museum—66.133 (35188).*

BELOW. Silk-embroidered cotton bedspread from India, possibly Gujarat, 17th Century. The Norweb Collection. *Cleveland Museum of Art—69.295 (36924-F).*

CLEVELAND, OHIO

The Cleveland Museum of Art

11150 East Boulevard
ZIP: 44106   TEL: (216) 421-7340

Dorothy G. Shepherd, Textile Curator
Martha Thomas, Assistant

The Cleveland Museum's collection of historic textiles—under the guidance of its well-known curator, Dorothy Shepherd—has been assembled with an articulated frame of reference which has put aesthetic values above historic importance. This approach should make the collection especially rewarding to designers.

It holds approximately 3,500 pieces, and the chief area of specialization covers the textile arts of Islam as they developed both in Spain and the Near East, chiefly Iran (Persia). Beyond these major holdings the collection is well known for its early Italian silks and its medieval pieces from England, France, and Germany. The museum also owns interesting and representative textiles from India, China, ancient Egypt, Greece, and ancient Peru, as well as a fine group of medieval and Renaissance tapestries.

The Textile Department is remarkably well organized, has pleasant study facilities and an excellent picture file of its holdings, and displays many of its important pieces in the public galleries. At the time of my visit there were five exhibits of Peruvian, Coptic, and Near Eastern textiles, as well as early tapestries.

Following is a breakdown of the museum's textile holdings.

Africa. The most important African group comes from ancient Egypt—218 pieces. It includes good examples from the Roman and Byzantine periods (4th–7th Century), as well as from the early Islamic period. Most are woven fabrics and Coptic tapestry decorations, but a few are em-

CLEVELAND MUSEUM cont'd

broideries. A number of the pieces are quite well known in the field.

Africa also contributes a group of representative embroideries from Morocco (24 pieces) and from Algeria (10). The work dates from the 17th–19th Century.

Europe. The collection holds more than 800 pieces from various parts of Europe and from many different periods.

Austria is represented by four pieces, two of which are important 15th- and 16th-Century examples of ecclesiastical embroidery.

Belgium. About 25 pieces, most of them tapestries.

England. About 100 pieces, including good examples of Opus Anglicanum, stumpwork, and other early embroidery of the 14th–16th Century. Also copperplate prints, brocaded silks, samplers, and other prints dating from the 18th–20th Century.

Germany. Nineteen examples, chiefly embroidered, including an early 13th-Century Lenten cloth.

France. About 155 examples. Among them are 20 important medieval and Renaissance tapestries; 17th-Century silks; 18th-Century embroideries, woodblock prints, and brocaded silks; 19th-Century copperplates and embroideries; and a few examples of 20th-Century weaving.

Italy. About 340 pieces. The museum is justly proud of its Italian group. It owns important 14th–15th Century silks from Florence, Lucca, and other important centers of weaving in the period. It also has substantial representation of later weaving from the 16th, 17th, and 18th Centuries, particularly in brocaded silks and velvets. In addition there are good examples of Italian embroidery dating from the 16th–19th Century.

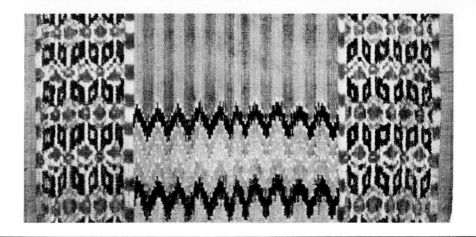

RIGHT. Persian silk velvet, 19th Century, in a design similar to warp-dyed patterning. Gift of Mr. & Mrs. J. H. Wade. *Cleveland Museum—16.1382 (31011).*

BELOW. Fragment of silk coffin cover, double-faced compound-twill weave, Persia, Buyid period, 998 A.D. J. H. Wade Fund. *Cleveland—55.52 (38088).*

Spain-Portugal. About 130 pieces. The outstanding part of this group is considered to be the 40-odd Hispano-Moresque weavings of the 13th–15th Century. They are chiefly silk fabrics, some of them woven by Mudejars—that is, people who remained Mohammedan under Christian rule. In addition, the collection also owns Spanish brocaded silks, velvets, and embroideries of the 16th–18th Century.

Near East. As previously noted, this is the area for which the Cleveland textile collection has long been best known. In all, there are about 300 pieces in the group.

Iran (Persia) is the major source, with a total of about 125 pieces. They include some 50 early examples, dating from the 9th–12th Century. There are also even earlier Sassanian fabrics of the 6th–7th Century. The later periods (16th–17th Century) are represented by brocaded silks, velvets, and other weavings in the Persian tradition.

Turkey. About 100 pieces, chiefly 16th–19th-Century weaving and embroidery.

Greece. Over 50 pieces of embroidery from the Greek Islands. There are good examples of different styles from most of the islands.

Other Near East Areas. Other smaller groups of Near Eastern fabrics come from ancient Mesopotamia and Syria (17 pieces) and a few pieces of more recent date from other regions.

Far East. Adding together the holdings from India, China, and Japan, the collection owns about 500 Far Eastern fabrics.

India. This is the largest group with about 250 pieces covering all the various Indian forms of fabric decoration from the different states and from most periods in the country's textile history. Among them are a number of very early painted-and-dyed fragments from the 12th Century. The collection includes wovens, embroideries, painted-and-dyed cottons, and other pieces dating from the 16th–20th Century. The largest group is 19th-Century work.

China. About 180 pieces. Among them is an important group of 8th-Century T'ang weaves and painted silks, as well as fine examples of 18th-Century silk tapestry weaving (k'o-ssu). Also a large number of embroidered and brocaded silks of the 18th–19th Century.

Japan. About 75 pieces. The most important are Nō robes of the Tokugawa period (1600–1850) and an album of 18th-Century silk weavings. Also fragments of silk damask—19th–20th Century.

Pacific. About 50 pieces with representative work from Cambodia, Ceylon, Indonesia, and the Philippines. Particularly interesting are the Javanese batiks and the ikats from other parts of Indonesia.

South America. About 70 pieces, chiefly from ancient Peru and including an unusual painted mantle from the early Paracas culture. There are also good examples of both weaving and embroidery from several of the different cultures and periods in Peruvian history.

United States. About 170 pieces. They include a number of 18th–19th-Century coverlets and a group of 20th-Century screen and roller prints designed by Clevelanders.

Carpets. About 30 examples, including several outstanding pieces from the Near East.

Lace. A substantial collection of 1,150 pieces awaiting curatorial attention.

Bedroom of the Secretary House at the Henry Ford Museum, one of 20-odd period buildings in Greenfield Village. It comes from Exeter, N.H., about 1750.

COOPERSTOWN, N.Y.

The Farmers' Museum & Fenimore House

ZIP: 13326   TEL: (607) 547-2533

Minor W. Thomas, Jr., Chief Curator

Between The Farmers' Museum and Fenimore House there is an extensive collection of textiles and costumes numbering about 4,000 pieces. Both museums are part of the New York State Historical Association.

The Farmers' Museum—which holds a majority of the textiles—is a complex of buildings designed to reveal the patterns of living in pioneer America. Many of these exhibit buildings are furnished with the types of textiles produced by hand in farm communities during the 18–19th Century. Beds are made up with handwoven sheets, pillow cases, bedcovers, coverlets, and embroidered blankets. There are also carpets, table linens, and window hangings of the same genre on display. And the museum conducts demonstrations to show how these American farm communities grew and processed flax and wool, as well as how they wove cotton textiles from yarns they purchased commercially.

There are also many small samples of the fabric types used in farm communities during the period covered.

Fenimore House also owns a number of textiles—those falling into the category of folk art. These are chiefly sewn and hooked rugs, and bed quilts of both the appliqué and pieced types. The museum's library also owns old weaving pattern books and weavers' account books. While most of the textiles on display are of American origin, some were imported from England—for example, quilted bedcovers made of copper-plate-printed cottons.

A brief survey of textile holdings in The Farmers' Museum shows the following estimates of pieces held:

About 150 quilts and coverlets; some 50 samplers; several hundred examples of bed clothing—sheets, pillowcases, blankets; more than 1,000 textile samples; several thousand items of clothing, dating from 1790 to 1900.

Since only a small portion of the textile holdings are on display, an appointment must be made to examine the reserve collections which are accessible to researchers.

DEARBORN, MICH.

Henry Ford Museum

Greenfield Village

ZIP: 48121   TEL: (313) 271-1620

George O. Bird, Curator

Until 9 August 70 the Henry Ford Museum owned an outstanding collection of early American textiles and costume. It included at least 250 quilts and coverlets, some 50 hooked rugs, many sets of bed hangings and bedding, over 50 shawls, 50 samplers, and more than 100 examples of printed cottons. On that day all these and more were destroyed in a disastrous fire.

What remains is a token collection of pieces which were on display in gallery exhibits at the time of the fire, as well as the furnishings in some 20 period houses spread out over the 260 acres of Greenfield Village.

The museum is now making an effort to replace some of these lost treasures. At this writing it has acquired an excellent collection of quilts and coverlets (about 80 pieces), as well as a dozen Paisley and Kashmir shawls, about 20 silk-embroidered pictures, and a number of hooked rugs.

I should also mention that the museum was able to salvage scorched fragments of the superb Greenfield Hill picture quilt which was the pride of the collection before the fire. Many of the design details are still visible in the fragments.

Some of the replacements, together with surviving pieces, were on exhibit in the museum galleries at the time of my visit. I noted the following.

Quilts & Coverlets. A representative group of about 20 quilts and coverlets—all excellent pieces. One outstanding piece is an 18th-Century Indian mordant-painted palampore which has been padded with wool and quilted.

Rugs. A notable display of different homemade rugs including examples of appliqué (1800), needlework (1820–40), embroidered wool (1840), caterpillar strips, knitted (1825), and hooked. Also a fine bed rug dated 1813.

The museum also owns a unique collection of almost 200 zinc stencils produced by Edward Sands Frost, an itinerant Maine peddler, who used the stencils to print hooked-rug patterns. The collection is described in a catalog available from the museum (see list of museum publications).

Embroidery. A dozen pieces of 17th-Century English stumpwork, beadwork, and quillwork, including one elaborate beadwork casket dated 1650. Also several good samplers.

Shawls. Three fine Paisley shawls.

Homespuns. A number of homespun and handwoven fabrics in linen and wool, dating from the 18th to the 19th Century.

Period House Furnishings. The 20-odd houses in Greenfield Village cover a period from the 17th to the end of the 19th Century and display furnishings appropriate to their times. Altogether there are more than 1,000 textiles in these settings.

Publications. 1. *Selected Treasures of Greenfield Village & Henry Ford Museum.* 1969. 80 pages, 107 illustrations. The Greenfield Hill quilt is included.

2. *Descriptive Catalogue of E. S. Frost & Co.'s Hooked Rug Patterns.* 1970. 60 pages, 204 illustrations.

RIGHT. Fragment from Greece, 18th Century. *Denver Art Museum—E-902.*

BELOW. The Denver Art Museum, west side of the building. Entrance is on right.

DEERFIELD, MASS.

Historic Deerfield, Inc.
Route 5
ZIP: 01342   TEL: (413) 772-0882
Joseph Peter Spang III, Curator

Historic Deerfield (formerly Heritage Foundation) was established in 1952 by Mr. & Mrs. Henry N. Flynt. It consists of twelve historic houses which have been restored as museums, in addition to a new museum/library which was built in 1970.

Between the museum and the historic houses Deerfield owns a textile collection of about 1,500 pieces—with the emphasis on embroidery and prints. Most of the work dates from the 18th and early 19th Centuries. It includes a considerable collection of embroidered coverlets, both English and American, as well as pieced quilts made before 1850. Other textiles in the holdings include English Spitalfields silk dresses (18th Century), English upholstered furniture, laces, velvets, painted silks, and a unique collection of local blue and white needlework.

Many of the fabrics are exhibited in the Helen G. Flynt Fabric Hall and in the Hall Tavern Fabric Display Room, as well as in each of the historic houses.

Library. The Henry N. Flynt Library is a reference resource with about 3,000 volumes, many of them dealing with American decorative arts. It also holds records from The Deerfield Society of Blue & White Needlework, which was part of the crafts-revival movement and operated from 1896 to 1926. The records include sketches, patterns, manuscripts, and printed material which complements the embroideries and color swatches in the museum collection.

Publication. *Early American Embroideries in Deerfield, Mass.* By Margery Burnham Howe. Published by the Heritage Foundation, 1963. 30 pages of B/W photographs.

DENVER, COL.

The Denver Art Museum
100 West 14th Avenue Parkway
ZIP: 80204   TEL: (303) 297-2793

Imelda G. DeGraw, Textile Curator
Richard Conn, Native Arts Curator

The Denver Art Museum has a combined collection of textiles and costume which numbers close to 6,000 pieces. The major part of it—about 5,000 pieces—is kept by the museum's Textile Department. The remainder is in the care of the Native Arts Department and includes an important group of American Indian textiles.

Textile Department

The museum has a new gallery devoted to exhibits of its textiles. This was opened in late 1974, and its first show was given over to a survey of its most important holdings. These are American, Oriental, European, pre-Columbian, and Ancient Mediterranean textiles—in a descending scale of size.

The American holdings are by far the largest—about 3,500 pieces—with more in costumes than in flat textiles. However, the museum owns a notable collection of quilts and coverlets which were the subject of a highly regarded exhibit in 1974. It is also known for its early crewelwork and samplers.

The Oriental collection of textiles numbers about 850 pieces. Among these the most outstanding are embroideries, batiks, and tie-dyes from India, as well as a number of gold saris. There are also examples of early Chinese silks recovered from tombs, and an impressive group of mandarin robes.

European textiles date back to a 13th-Century German fragment, and other European countries are well represented through the centuries, including tapestries of the 15th and 16th Centuries. There are also a number of French toiles, one designed by Huet of the Oberkampf printworks at Jouy.

The pre-Columbian group contains about 150 examples, including a number of dolls

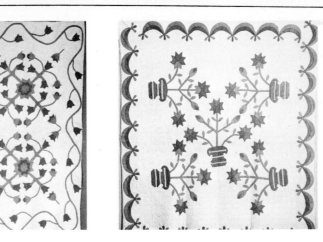

DENVER ART MUSEUM cont'd

uncovered from graves of the Chancay culture (1000–1420 A.D.).

The Ancient Mediterranean group contains about 50 pieces, most of them Coptic fragments of tapestry weaving but also several tunic sections with decorations. The material dates from the 4th to the 6th Century.

Native Arts

Textiles in this department number about 600 pieces and represent American Indian, Black Africa, and the Pacific Islands cultures. Of these, by far the largest and most important group consists of American Indian textiles and clothing. In all there were about 550 pieces in the group at this writing, broken down as follows.

Navajo. About 200 blankets and other woven fabrics such as sashes; 50 chief blankets; 50 shawls; 12 dresses.

Pueblo. Some 200 pieces, including blankets, dresses, shirts, and sashes.

Northwest Coast. About 25 varied fabrics, including Chilkat and Salish blankets.

Facilities. In addition to its new public gallery, the Textile Department also recently acquired a textile study room with space for about a dozen people to work comfortably. The room contains publications related to the collection and slides of museum textiles, together with a projector. It also has a collection of what the department calls "touchables"—examples of different textile techniques which can be examined without restrictions.

Publications. 1. *Denver Art Museum Costume Collection.* Dresses from 1800 to 1950. 98 pages, 48 illustrations.

2. *The Neusteter Institute of Fashion.* Costume and Textiles of the Denver Art Museum. 1955, 40 pages, 28 illustrations.

3. *Fibre Structures.* 1972 exhibition catalog.

4. *Quilts & Coverlets.* Handbook of 1974 exhibition. 144 pages, over 100 illustrations.

5. *Indian Leaflets.* A series of 119 short but excellent leaflets devoted to different aspects of American Indian life and customs. Of this total, 21 leaflets are on the textile crafts or the clothing of different Indian peoples—Navajo, Pueblo, Hopi, and Plains Indians. A catalog is available.

DETROIT, MICH.

The Detroit Institute of Arts
5200 Woodward Avenue
ZIP: 48202   TEL: (313) 831-0360

**Franny Golden, Textile Conservation
James Greaves, Chief Conservator**

The Detroit Institute of Arts owns a modest-sized collection of textiles and costume—under 3,000 pieces—and at this writing has no curator of textiles. Yet this is a collection of international renown, largely due to the work of its former textile curator, Adèle Coulin Weibel, who reproduced a number of Detroit's textile treasures in her notable book—*2,000 Years of Textiles.*

From the viewpoint of textile researchers it is also a very rich and representative collection, holding many fine pieces from over 50 countries or cultures and covering a time span from 2nd-Century Coptic Egypt and Peru to 20th-Century America and its contemporary art fabrics.

Among these 50-odd sources the strongest categories are those from Czechoslovakia (454 pieces), Italy (337), Spain (247), the United States (165), France (159), Peru (150), and Egypt (145). There are also smaller but representative groups of textiles from England (65), the North American Indians (60), China (52), India (48), Persia (27), Turkey (26), and Germany (25).

Other cultures from which the museum holds some textile examples include: African, Argentinian, Belgian, Bulgarian, Byzantine, Danish, Dutch, Flemish, Greek, Hispano-Moresque, Hungarian, Indonesian, Japanese, Mexican, Philippine, Polish, Polynesian, Portuguese, Russian, Scandinavian, Scottish, and Swiss.

There are also substantial groups of lace (400) pieces, rugs (100), and tapestries (75).

Exhibits. Detroit gives its textiles important display space in its handsome building,

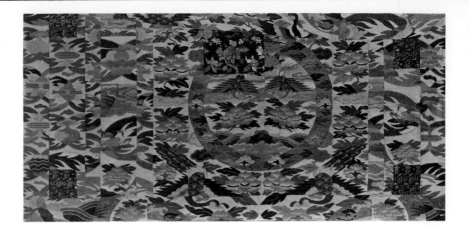

RIGHT. Japanese Zen monk's robe in woven silk and metal thread, about 1750. Gift of Peggy & Albert de Salle in memory of Adele Coulin Weibel. *Detroit Institute of Arts—63.161 (13418).*

BELOW. Embroidered panel, Netherlands, 17th Century. Gift of Mrs. Walter O. Briggs. *Detroit Inst.—49.419 (8009).*

one of whose major attractions is a large and elegant Italian Renaissance courtyard which serves as a restaurant. Among the exhibits I particularly noted good examples of English embroidery, Italian velvets and brocades, lace, samplers, and an especially fine display of ancient Peruvian fabric in the pre-Columbian gallery.

Conservation. The museum also maintains an active conservation department for its textile collection so that most of its holdings are in an excellent state of preservation.

The Major Textile Holdings

Further details of the larger textile categories follow.

Czechoslovakia. Among the 454 pieces in this category are large numbers of peasant embroideries, most often found as costume decorations.

Italy. Many fragments of early Italian silk weaving and velvet, some of them from the 15th and 16th Centuries. The major strength of this group is in 18–19th Century work.

Spain. The collection includes costume as well as lace, rugs, and numerous fragments of elaborate Spanish weaving, some from the 17th Century.

United States. Among the 165 pieces in this category are quilts, coverlets, bed curtains, table linens, embroideries, samplers, and costumes. Most of the pieces date from the middle to the end of the 19th Century, but there are also examples dating from the 18th Century.

France. A representative sampling of France's textile arts—jacquard silks from Lyon, 18th-Century toiles of the Jouy type, shawls, lace, costume, and tapestries. 159 pieces in all.

Peru. The Peruvian collection of about 150 pieces dates from the 2nd Century to the Colonial Period. Some 80 percent of the material is pre-Conquest, representing the Paracas, Nazca, and Tiahuanaco cultures. Included are four early feather capes and a particularly handsome woven hanging of large size from the Colonial period. There are also examples of stuffed knitting-crocheting techniques.

Egypt. The Egyptian collection of 145 pieces contains 105 textiles from the Islamic period and 40 "Coptic" tapestry fragments. Among the latter group is a well-known Graeco-Roman tapestry weaving of a woman's head, which is probably Syrian in origin and is dated 2–4th Century.

England. Though the number of English pieces is not large (65), it is choice. Some of the textiles date from the 17th Century, and there are good examples of Spitalfields silks, Paisley shawls, embroidered caskets, stumpwork, and tapestries.

China. A small group of 52 textiles and costume, including a number of court robes and several examples of provincial fabrics. The Chinese group also includes several appliquéd temple banners from Tibet.

India. A small but interesting collection of 48 pieces which includes Kashmir shawls, silk saris, embroideries, mordant-painted cottons, and printed chintz.

Persia. The 27 pieces in this group are chiefly rugs.

Turkey. Also chiefly rugs—26 examples.

Germany. Tapestries and costumes—25 pieces.

LEFT. Peruvian tapestry detail, silk-cotton, 800–900 A.D. Gift of Robert H. Tannahill. *Detroit Inst.—49.283 (10199).*

BELOW. Tibetan temple banner, 18th C., in a mosaic of Chinese silks. *Detroit Institute of Arts—29.241 (1894).*

DETROIT ART INSTITUTE cont'd

Research Facilities. The museum maintains a file of excellent photographs showing about 500 of its textiles. Prints of these can be ordered. It also has a library with good resources, including some 300 volumes on the textile arts which cover most of the basic needs of textile researchers.

Publication. *2,000 Years of Textiles.* By Adèle Coulin Weibel. New York, 1952. Published by Pantheon Books for The Detroit Institute of Arts. This is a comprehensive and learned treatment of figured textiles from Europe and the Near East.

DURHAM, N.C.

The Duke University Museum of Art
6877 College Station
ZIP: 27708   TEL: (919) 684-5153

Paul A. Clifford, Curator

For anyone wishing to study Peruvian textile art in all its variety I strongly recommend an extended visit to the Museum of Art at Duke University. Here, in concentrated form and under the enthusiastic guardianship of Paul Clifford, has been assembled a full range of Peruvian fabrics covering a time span from 500 B.C. to 1532 A.D.

There are over 200 pieces in the collection representing the following major periods in Peruvian art history: Paracas and Proto-Nazca (500-200 B.C.); Nazca (200–800 A.D.); Tiahuanaco-Wari (900–1100 A.D.); Chancay and Chimu (1000–1400 A.D.); and Inca (1200–1532 A.D.).

Broken down into these different categories the collection shows the following statistics: Paracas—9 pieces; Nazca—30; Tiahuanaco—12; Central Coast—6; Chancay—124; Chimu—2; Inca—8.

These 200-odd textiles are part of a much larger collection of pre-Columbian artifacts (800 pieces) collected privately by Mr. Clifford since the 1950s and taken by him to Duke, where it is known as the Paul A. Clifford Collection of pre-Columbian Art.

Mr. Clifford himself considers the textile holdings to be a teaching collection because of its completeness and because it holds textile tools such as workbaskets, looms, spindles, and needles, as well as examples of cloaks, ponchos, hats, turbans, belts, bags, breechcloths, sandals, and other pieces of costume. There is also a Nazca mummy replica dressed in textiles of the period.

Moreover, as a further aid to study the entire collection has been fully photographed in 35mm color—some 1,400 slides.

There is a good study area in the museum, and Mr. Clifford's personal library is available to researchers. It contains most of the important works on Peruvian textiles, as well as pamphlets in both English and Spanish.

To indicate the devotion and enthusiasm with which this fine collection has been assembled, it seems appropriate to quote Mr. Clifford's eloquent statement. He says:

"The studying and collecting of ancient art makes one feel a part of the continuity of human existence. It seeks to interpret man's relationship to nature, his environment, or perhaps the unknown. One becomes intrigued with man's ability to incorporate form, color, and beauty into those things which clothed, protected, and fed him here, as well as in the after-life. **What a wonderful experience it has been to find that our New World has produced some of antiquity's greatest weavers, sculptors, and metal workers who could either represent nature with camera-like perfection or who could produce abstract art as fresh and modern as today."**

GRANVILLE, OHIO

Museum of Burmese Art & Culture
Denison University
ZIP: 43023   TEL: (614) 582-9181

Jane Terry Bailey, Curator
Ann. M. Kessler, Registrar

Denison owns a small but unique collection of textiles which may well be the largest of its kind in the United States. It consists entirely of fabrics from Burma and is known as the Helen K. Hunt Burmese Textile Collection. It was collected by Baptist missionaries to Burma and is mostly 20th-Century work, though some of the court silks date back to the 19th Century. The holdings have been carefully studied,

RIGHT. Coptic fragment, 4–7th Century. *Wadsworth Atheneum—1925.119 (162C).*

BELOW. Coptic roundel, 4–7th Century. *Wadsworth Atheneum—1925.104 (162C).*

are well cared for, and are frequently exhibited in the university's Burke Hall of Fine Arts.

All the fabrics are woven, and a number of pieces are also embroidered.

At this writing the collection consists of 412 pieces and is growing through new acquisitions. It is divided into three categories:

1. Court silks worn only by royalty and the aristocracy.

2. Cottons (and occasionally silks) worn by artisans and farmers in the river valleys of Central and South Burma.

3. Ethnic textiles made and worn by the different tribal groups who constitute the Union of Burma and who live in the mountains and isolated areas of the country. The tribes represented in the collection are Akha, Chin, Kachin, Karen, Lahu, Matu, Mon, Naga, Shan, and Wa. This third category forms the largest unit of the three.

The court silks and the peasant fabrics reveal sophisticated designs in traditional national styles. The ethnic weavings of the tribal groups, by contrast, are more primitive and more varied in design. Each of the tribes has developed its own distinctive patterns.

The court silks are described in the university's Burmese Art Newsletter of June 1969. It is worth quoting:

"The Burmese court silks are called *Kyoe-gyi-Geik.* The word *Geik* refers to a particular type of design that is characteristic of one style. The word *lun-taya* is also used to describe the *Geik* patterns. It means 100 spools, referring to the number of shuttles required to weave the complex patterns. It takes an accomplished weaver eight hours to weave one inch of this material thirty-two inches wide. However all *lun-taya* are not made with 100 spools; they vary from as low as 20 spools to 125 or more. the best

examples were always expensive. For example, a first quality *lun-taya* in 1875 cost 200 rupees, which was about 20 English pounds at 1875 values."

When worn by men, these silks were called *paso.* The women's silk was called *tamein.* The *tamein* was composed of three pieces joined into an oblong (2 × 1½ yards) which was wrapped around the body somewhat like a sari. The male *paso* was woven 18 yards long and 27 inches wide, then doubled over to form a piece 9 yards long. It was also wrapped around the body to form a skirt. The woven designs of the *Kyoe-gyi-Geik* generally form seven irregular bands of horizontal stripes in varying widths and colors.

HARTFORD, CONN.

Wadsworth Atheneum
600 Main Street
ZIP: 06103   TEL: (203) 278-2670

J. Herbert Callister, Curator, Textiles & Costumes

The Wadsworth Atheneum owns a combined collection of some 5,000 pieces in its Textile/Costume Department. Of the two categories the costume holdings are stronger, with about 3,500 pieces. The flat textiles number about 1,700 pieces, with the largest units in lace and embroidery.

Considering the relatively small size of the flat textile holdings, the collection is quite varied. Following is a breakdown of the chief classifications:

Egypt. About 50 fragments of Coptic tapestry weaving.

England. Some 50 examples of English printing, including early copperplate work of the 18th Century.

France. About 100 examples of French silk weaving and 40 pieces of French printing, mostly 18th–19th-Century work.

Italy. About 30 pieces of Italian silk—17th–18th Century.

Japan. A small group of Japanese silks dating from the 18th–20th Century.

Persia. About 25 examples of Persian silk weaving of the 16th–17th Century.

Peru. Ancient Peruvian weaving is represented by a substantial group of about 100 pieces.

Spain. Ten pieces of Spanish weaving.

United States. Over 300 pieces. The collection includes 19th-Century cotton prints (50); Shaker fabrics from Enfield, Connecticut (10); quilts and coverlets, some from the 18th Century (30); two embroidered bed rugs from New England; a large group of 19th-Century towels, blankets, and other household linens (125); a representative group of 19th-Century dress fabrics, many of them silk (100).

Silks. In addition to the silks already listed there is another group of about 125 pieces, some of them from China.

Velvets. A group of 25 European vel-

WADSWORTH ATHENEUM cont'd

vets—chiefly Italian and French—dating from the 17th–19th Century.

Lace. A study collection mounted on large display boards. They hold about 500 pieces and illustrate the most important types of lace from many different regions.

Embroidery. Several hundred pieces, including samplers and a representative group from the Greek Islands.

Costume. The collection of costume and accessories holds about 3,500 pieces, of which 1,000 are dresses dating from the 18th Century to the present. Also about 300 outer garments and smaller groups of men's and children's dress. The accessories, including undergarments, number over 2,000 pieces and date fom the 18th Century forward. The collection is primarily devoted to western urban dress.

Publication. *Bed Ruggs, 1722–1833.* Catalog of the 1972 exhibit organized by J. Herbert Callister, Curator of Textiles & Costumes.

Library. The Avery Memorial Reference Library, which is part of the Wadsworth Atheneum, has a modest but interesting collection of books on textiles. There are about 80 volumes, in addition to exhibition catalogs, dealing with the textile arts.

INDIANAPOLIS, IND.

Indianapolis Museum of Art
1200 West 38 Street
ZIP: 46208   TEL: (317) 923-1331

Peggy S. Gilfoy, Curator, Decorative Arts

The size and range of the textile collection at the Indianapolis Museum of Art comes as a surprise, even to many curators in the field. Until 1972 it was given little attention, and much of it is only now in the process of being accessioned and researched. But it is an important collection, international in scope and occasionally deep in its coverage of specific cultures.

It holds over 7,000 pieces, and its range is very wide both in time and in countries of origin. It is strongest in Oriental and European fabrics, but it owns representative pieces from more than 60 other cultures and regions. Its earliest pieces were woven in ancient Peru and Coptic Egypt. Its latest holdings include contemporary women's haute-couture costumes by name designers.

Apart from size and scope the Indianapolis collection has one of the handsomest homes of any collection in North America. A visit to the museum quite literally becomes a pleasure outing. The buildings form a large complex set in 54 acres of elegant parkland on the outskirts of Indianapolis. Long vistas, landscaped grounds, immaculate rolling lawns, ponds, spurting fountains, and impressive architecture—all this is reminiscent of the superbly groomed parks which surround some of the great manor houses in England.

Much of this park was the former estate of the J. K. Lilly family (of pharmaceutical fame), and perhaps the most pleasant of all the amenities in this pleasant complex is a quiet and gracious restaurant in a building that was formerly the Lilly "playhouse." It serves excellent meals Tuesday through Sunday.

RIGHT. One of the textile rooms in the Lilly Pavilion of Decorative Arts.

BELOW. Another of the textile display rooms in the Lilly Pavilion.

The main museum buildings are handsome modern structures known as the Krannert and Clowes Pavilions, and they display textiles prominently with other art treasures. The buildings also contain one of the most elegant and comfortable reference libraries I have seen in any museum. The collection of books on textiles is small but quite adequate for general research. The catalog shows about 100 volumes on the textile arts.

The bulk of the textile collection is separately housed in the Lilly Pavilion of Decorative Arts. This was the former mansion on the Lilly estate. It is set in its own handsome grounds a short distance from the main museum building and is maintained as a living museum of the interior furnishing arts. One of its upstairs wings was established as a Textile Study in October 1973. This large suite of five rooms is now given over to the textile collection for display, storage, and work areas.

Altogether, the Indianapolis complex is a delightful and surprising facility to find on the Indiana prairie.

The Textile Study is arranged in a series of five connecting rooms, and its textile treasures are easily explored in seven large art files (70 drawers) as well as in closets and other storage facilities. Additional storage and work rooms are in the large third floor ballroom. Displays—which are changed about four times a year—are informal and informative. They are accompanied by well-researched mimeographed information sheets and every effort is made to interest the general public in the collection. For example, I noted with pleasure that magnifying glasses had been attached to each of the large storage files, inviting visitors to examine the inner intricacies of complicated textile constructions.

Highlights of the Collection

A sampling of the museum's textile hold-ings is listed in the following paragraphs. It should be noted, however, that this does not completely represent the collection since approximately one-third of the holdings have not yet been accessioned or cataloged.

Africa. A small group of Berber weavings from North Africa and four examples of Kuba cut-pile cloth from the Belgian Congo. Also examples of contemporary traditional weaving.

America (U.S.). Varied pieces which include fine quilts, wool coverlets, and embroidered samplers—all 19th-Century work. There are also many fragments of woven fabrics from the late 19th and early 20th Centuries. Altogether about 300 pieces.

Armenia-Balkans. About 100 examples of peasant embroidery of the 19th and 20th Centuries from the Armenian-Balkan region. They are chiefly towel and scarf embroideries.

Asia Minor. Several pieces of embroidery from the 16–17th Century.

China. This is a major group in the collection with well over 500 pieces. The Chinese holdings include several large and outstanding silk tapestries and temple hangings of the 17th and 18th Centuries. Also a number of robes and mandarin squares of the 19th Century. One of the most impressive pieces is a superb silk tapestry of the K'ang Hsi period (1654–1722). It is 160 × 92 inches in size and is titled *Reunion of Poets in the Garden of the West*. There are also two fine earlier tapestries from the Ming Dynasty (1368–1644).

In addition there are examples of Chinese textile art in fragments of brocade, cut velvet, damask, appliqué, embroidery, and silk tapestry. The largest number of pieces dates from the 19th Century, but the earlier centuries are also well represented.

Dutch East Indies. The collection of batiks and ikats from this part of the world is outstanding. Some of them date from the 17th and 18th Centuries. In all there are more than 100 pieces, and they represent work from Java, Bali, Borneo, Sumba, Sumatra, and other parts of the region.

Egypt. A large group of some 200 pieces, chiefly Coptic tapestry fragments, dating mainly from the 3rd to the 7th Century.

England. Textiles from England number over 100 pieces. The largest group is composed of woven and printed fabrics from the 18th and 19th Centuries, including half a dozen prints by William Morris. There are also about a dozen 19th-Century English shawls.

Flanders. Nine important Flemish tapestries—all from the 16th Century. Six of the pieces are devoted to the story of Anthony and Cleopatra and are attributed to Karel Van Mander II (1579–1623).

France. A representative group of over 350 woven, printed, and embroidered textiles. There are 18th-Century designs by Pillement and Huet, some 17th-Century fragments of woven silks of the Lyon type,

LEFT. Flouncing of point d'Angleterre lace, Flemish, 18th Century. *Indianapolis Museum of Art—13.13 (2337).*

BELOW. Italian madonna robe, late 17th Century. *Indianapolis—43.59 (7932).*

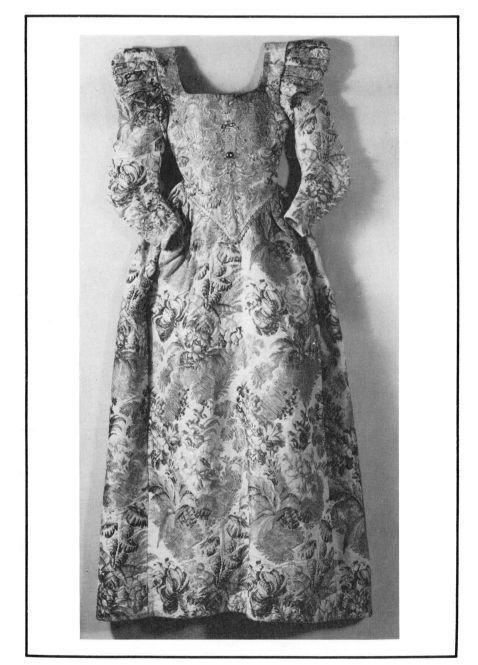

INDIANAPOLIS MUSEUM cont'd

and a large number of 18th- and 19th-Century pieces, including some excellent toiles de Jouy.

Germany. A few pieces dating from the 16th to the 20th Century. They include some early damasks and some recent printed fragments.

Greece. About 30 pieces, chiefly 19th-Century embroidery but also including examples of earlier work from the 16th, 17th, and 18th Centuries.

Guatemala. A very good representation of modern Guatemalan peasant weaving. About 30 pieces.

Hungary. Eight pieces of 19–20th-Century peasant embroidery.

India. About 200 pieces, including woven, printed, and embroidered work from the 17th to the 20th Century. One piece is much older—a patterned wool shawl of the 3–7th Century. In the group are many examples of Indian textile art made for export to the European markets in the 17th and 18th Centuries.

Italy. A substantial and representative group of about 300 pieces dating from the 16th to the 20th Century. They include many examples of early Italian silk and velvet weaving and are equally strong in 16th-, 17th-, and 18th-Century work.

Japan. Over 400 examples of Japanese art fabrics. The largest group is made up of 19th-Century pieces and includes good fragments of brocade, tapestry, and embroidery. There are some examples of 18th-Century silk weaving and 66 20th-Century pieces. Also several important early Japanese kimonos from the late 17th and 18th Centuries. The museum owns one most unusual Japanese piece of more recent date—a large tapestry panel woven for the St. Louis World's Fair in 1903.

Morocco. Over 200 pieces originating in

RIGHT. Section of French needlepoint panel, 16th C. *Indianapolis Museum.*

BELOW. Chinese k'o-ssu panel woven in silk and linen, 34" square, 19th Century. Gift of J. Otis Adams Estate. *Indianapolis Museum of Art—55.56.*

ten regions of Morocco. The majority are embroideries, but some of the pieces are either large hangings or handsome robes, and the whole group is an impressive demonstration of Moroccan weaving skill.

Persia. This is another large and important category in the collection with over 350 pieces dating from the 15th to the 20th Century. From Isfahan alone (and it was the most important weaving center of the Safavid Dynasty in the 17th Century) there are over 40 examples of elaborate silk weaving spanning four centuries. There are also embroideries, printed textiles, tapestries, carpets, shawls, robes, and many fragments of wool, cotton, and silk from other important Persian textile centers. The whole collection is a varied and representative sampling from one of civilization's greatest textile cultures.

Peru. The group of ancient Peruvian weavings is small (about 35 pieces), but it has good representation from the important weaving periods in Peru's long history. It includes the earliest pieces owned by the museum, dating from the 2nd Century. It also has fine examples of patterned weavings from Paracas, Nazca, Tiahuanaco, as well as the Chimu, Ica, Inca, and Mala cultures.

Portugal. About 35 pieces dating from the 17th through the 20th Century. Most are woven fragments of silk, linen, and cotton. A few are 19th-Century printed cottons.

Samoa. A dozen good examples of painted tapa cloth probably from Samoa and made during the late 19th Century.

Scotland. Two dozen examples of 19th-Century Paisley shawls.

Spain. A large group of over 250 pieces— 15th to 20th Century. There are silk brocades, velvets, damask, and embroideries. Among the older pieces are about 25 fabrics from the 16th Century, 75 from the 17th, and 100 from the 18th. Also four 15th-Century fragments of silk brocade.

Turkey. A group of about 75 pieces— 18th to 20th Century. Of these some 50 are undated fragments of towel and scarf embroidery.

Other Countries. In addition to the countries listed above there are smaller groups of representative textiles (sometimes only single pieces) from the following sources: Afghanistan, Algeria, American Indian, Arabia, Argentina, Austria, Belgium, Bolivia, Bulgaria, Ceylon, Colombia, Crete, Hawaii, Mexico, Norway, Palestine, Paraguay, the Philippines, Rhodes, Rumania, Russia, Sweden, Switzerland, Syria, Thailand, Tibet, and Yugoslavia.

Lace. The lace collection consists of more than 500 pieces with excellent examples of needle and bobbin lace, drawn chiefly from the great lace-making centers in Europe and covering a time span of 500 years.

Costume. This is a small but growing collection of about 200 pieces from various cultures and mostly fairly recent in origin. It is expanding through the acquisition of work by contemporary fashion designers. For example, one of its recent acquisitions was a group of five models by Norman Norell.

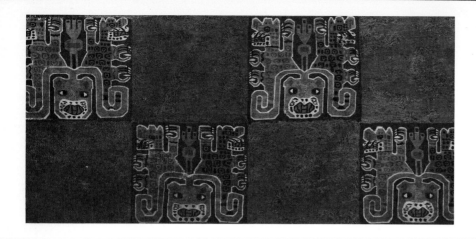

KANSAS CITY, MO.

Nelson Gallery-Atkins Museum
4525 Oak Street
ZIP: 64111   TEL: (816) 561-4000

Ross El Taggart, Senior Curator
Mrs. Lindsay H. Cooper, Assistant

The Nelson-Atkins Gallery owns an important collection of Chinese textiles. Among its most ancient holdings are pattern-weave gauze fabrics of the early T'ang Dynasty (618–907). From the Ming Dynasty (1368–1644) come a number of Imperial costumes. Particularly notable, also, are pieces from the tomb of Kuo Ch'in Wang, seventeenth son of the K'ang Hsi emperor (1654–1722). From later periods the collection owns a number of 18th- and 19th-Century Imperial robes.

In all, the Chinese collection numbers about 400 pieces. In addition to those mentioned there are 22 rugs, 63 robes and skirts, 52 mandarin squares, and 29 sutra covers. Also a number of hangings, streamers, and chair and table covers.

The museum's Japanese collection is also substantial—96 robes and kimonos.

From the Occident the Nelson-Atkins Gallery holds a modest group of about 600 textiles. They include some 70 American Indian blankets, Flemish and French tapestries, and several Italian ecclesiastical vestments in brocaded velvet.

LAWRENCE, KANSAS

University of Kansas Museum of Art
University of Kansas
ZIP: 66044   TEL: (913) UN 4-3616

Lea Rosson, Assistant Curator

This university museum owns a small textile collection of perhaps 500 pieces, but among them is a collection of American quilts which is one of the most outstanding in the country. It covers the full range of American quilt making from the last quarter of the 18th Century through the first half of the 20th Century. All the different construction techniques and fabrics, as well as the quilt patterns themselves, are represented in the museum holdings. In all there are about 150 pieces, divided between patchwork, appliqué, and stuffed techniques.

The quilt collection was launched in 1928 with a bequest of 53 quilts from Mrs. William B. Thayer. This was considerably expanded through gifts from Carrie A. Hall and Rose G. Kretsinger, authors of *The Romance of the Patchwork Quilt in America* (1935). Included in Miss Hall's gift are more than 1,000 pattern blocks, which she made to illustrate every type of quilt pattern she had been able to discover.

In addition to its quilt collection the museum also owns the following textiles:

About 50 19th-Century American woven coverlets, plus a number of handwoven fabrics.

Ten Navajo blankets—19th–20th-Century work.

More than 15 pieces of Coptic tapestry weaving dating from the 4th–6th Century.

A group of Persian textiles including 20 19th–20th-Century rugs and ten pieces of brocade dating from the 16th–18th Century.

Also small groups of representative fabrics and costumes from India, 18th-Century England (prints), China, and Japan.

Publication. *150 Years of American Quilts.* A catalog of the museum's 1973 exhibition.

Persian hanging (detail), interlocking twill tapestry in silk and metallic threads, 83" wide. Costume Council Fund. *L.A. County Museum—M.71.52.*

LOS ANGELES, CAL.

Los Angeles County Museum of Art
5905 Wilshire Boulevard
ZIP: 90038   TEL: (213) 937-4250

Mary Hunt Kahlenberg, Curator, Textiles & Costumes

The museum's Department of Textiles & Costumes has been a separate entity only since 1952 when it was launched with gifts from the Fashion Group. In the short period since then it has grown into one of the country's leading collections with total holdings of about 9,000 pieces. As might be expected from its fashion origins, the strongest part of the holdings is the section on costume and accessories—at least 8,000 pieces. The collection of flat textiles is much smaller—about 1,000 pieces.

Though its size is modest, the textile collection is an important one with good representation and some outstanding pieces from 14 different regions of the world. The most important categories are those from the Islamic cultures of Persia/India/Turkey and from pre-Columbian Peru. It also owns representative groups of fabrics from Japan, China, Southeast Asia, England, France, Italy, and Coptic Egypt. A more detailed listing follows.

China. About 100 pieces, including a number of priest's robes, mandarin squares, k'o-ssu silks and velvets.

Coptic Egypt. About 30 examples of tapestry weaving, including a few outstanding pieces and one complete tunic with tapestry decorations.

England. About 50 pieces with some fine examples of British silk and crewel embroidery as well as printed cottons.

Europe (North). About 50 examples of representative laces, embroidery, ecclesiastical vestments, and damasks.

France. A substantial group of 70 pieces with strength in silk brocades and printed cottons.

India. Approximately 100 pieces. There are printed cottons and silks, embroideries, and other examples of Indian textile art, including some fine pieces of 17th-Century Mughal work.

Italy. About 50 examples of cut velvet, brocades, patterned silks, lace, and embroidery.

Japan. An interesting collection of about 100 fragments from the Momyana and Edo periods. Also folk ikats (kasuri) and resist-dyed textiles. Also one superb appliquéd Ainu robe of the 19th Century.

Persia. A group of 30 Islamic fabrics which, together with Islamic pieces from India and Turkey, represent the outstanding category in the collection. Designs are both floral and figurative. They include early costume pieces, some from the 16th Century.

Peru. A group of about 130 pieces representative of the major periods in ancient Peruvian textile history—from Paracas to the Colonial period. Among them are two large Paracas mantles.

Southeast Asia. A good diversity of batik and ikat work from Indonesia and other Southeast Asian areas. Also an interesting group of Sumatran ceremonial fabrics known as "Ship Cloths." Altogether about 100 pieces.

Spain. About 15 examples of intricate early Spanish silk weaving and ecclesiastical embroidery.

Turkey. Another facet of the Islamic collection. About 20 examples of brocading, embroidery, and velvet, some from the great velvet-producing center at Brusa.

United States. About 50 quilts, coverlets, and embroideries, together with a few early printed fabrics. The major part of the United States collection consists of costume and accessories.

Costume. Chiefly western dress, with strength in 18th-Century French and English work. Also a smaller group of American costumes of the 18th–19th Century and a large collection of couture garments by 20th-Century American name designers, particularly from California.

Research Facilities. The Department of Textiles & Costumes has an exhibit gallery with changing displays, as well as material on permanent display throughout the museum. It also has a research room with facilities for study of the holdings by appointment. The library owns about 1,700 volumes, in addition to periodicals, and has an extensive clipping file on 20th-Century designers and on ethnic costume.

Publications. The following publications have been issued by the Department of Textiles & Costumes.

2000 Years of Silk Weaving. By Gabrille Loewi. 1944. A catalog for 1944 exhibition.

Art of the Weaver. By S. & E. I. Holt. 1955. A catalog for 1954–1955 exhibition.

Woven Treasures of Persian Art. By S. & E. I. Holt. 1959. A catalog for 1959 exhibition.

Painted & Printed Textiles. By S. & E. I. Holt. 1961. A catalog for 1961 exhibition.

Velvets East & West. By S. & E. I. Holt. 1966. A catalog for 1966 exhibition.

A Remembrance of Mariano Fortuny. By Dorothy Jenkins. 1968. A brochure for 1968 exhibition with catalog listing (out of print).

The Smart Set. By M. H. Kahlenberg. 1969. Brochure for 1969 exhibition with brief essay.

Patterns in Fashion. By M. H. Kahlenberg. 1970. Brochure for 1970 exhibition with brief essay.

Huene and the Fashionable Image. By Wallace Nethery, Oreste F. Pucciani, H. P. Horst, Main R. Bocher, Leo Lerman, Katharine Hepburn, Charles E. Israel, Lesley Blanch, and Alson Clark. 1970 exhibition.

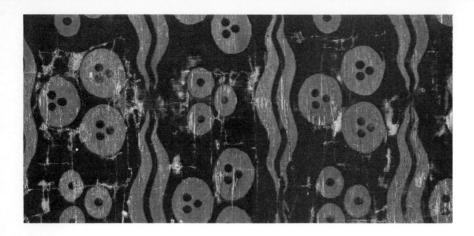

LEFT. Voided cut velvet with gold threads from Brusa, Turkey, 16th or 17th Century. 13½" × 20". Gift of Mr. & Mrs. Allan C. Balch Fund. *Los Angeles County Museum of Art—M.55.12.78.*

BELOW. A section of the Newark Museum as seen from Washington Street.

LOS ANGELES MUSEUM cont'd

Japanese Textiles of the Edo Period. By M. H. Kahlenberg. Brochure for a 1970 exhibit with brief essay on Japanese textile art during 1615–1867.

Tapestry—Tradition and Technique. By M. H. Kahlenberg. 1971. A brochure for 1971 exhibition with brief essay.

Ornamental Costumes from the John Wise Collection of Ancient Peruvian Textiles. By M. H. **Kahlenberg.** 1971. Brochure for 1971–1972 exhibition with an excellent essay on the different Peruvian styles and periods.

Body Shells and Shadows. By M. H. Kahlenberg, Jan Kowalek, and Doris Shadbolt. 1972. A catalog for 1972 exhibition and show of wearable sculpture by Heidi Bucher and Carl Lander (out of print).

The Navajo Blanket. By M. H. Kahlenberg & **Anthony Berlant.** 1972. Catalog for 1972 exhibition.

Ten Designers of the 20th Century. By M. H. Kahlenberg and Maggie Murray. 1972. Brochure for 1972 exhibition.

Block, Brush and Stencil. By C. Dimmick. 1972. Brochure for 1972–1973 exhibition with brief essay (out of print).

L. A. Flash. By Beth Ann Krier. 1973. Brochure for 1973 exhibition.

Anatomy in Fabric. By M. H. Kahlenberg. 1973. Brochure for 1973 exhibition with brief essay.

If the Crinoline Comes Back. By M. H. Kahlenberg. 1973. Brochure for 1973–1974 exhibition with brief essay.

Fabric & Fashion. By M. H. Kahlenberg. 1974. Handbook of museum exhibit. Contains a history of the collection.

Tapestries of Helena Hernmarck. By M. H. **Kahlenberg. 1974.** Brochure for 1974–1975 exhibition with brief essay.

Textile and Costume material is included in the following catalogs. *Islamic Art.* By Dr. Pal. *A Decade of Collecting 1965–1975.*

MINNEAPOLIS, MINN.

The Minneapolis Institute of Arts
201 East 24 Street
ZIP: 55404   TEL: (612) 339-7661

Merribell Parsons, Curator

In terms of textile holdings the Minneapolis Institute of Arts is best known for two major collections.

1. Possibly the country's largest collection of Chinese robes—about 350 examples from the early and later Ch'ing Dynasty (1644–1912). Among them are a number of Imperial robes.

2. A fine collection of about 40 European tapestries. They are chiefly Flemish and French, dating from the 15th through the 18th Century. Several of them are considered to be of major importance in the history of tapestry weaving.

NEWARK, N.J.

The Newark Museum
43-49 Washington Street
ZIP: 07101   TEL: (201) 733-6600

CURATORS:
Valrae Reynolds, Oriental Collections
Phillip Curtis, Decorative Arts
Susan Auth, Classical Collections

The Newark Museum has no textile department as such, but it does own a varied collection of textiles and costume distributed among several departments. The combined holdings number about 4,000 pieces with strength in four areas: Tibet, China, India, and American quilts.

In addition, the museum holds smaller but representative groups of fabrics from many cultures and periods going back to Coptic Egypt and extending into 20th-Century America. These different ranges of fabrics are distributed between four departments of the museum: (1) Decorative Arts; (2) Oriental; (3) Classical; and (4) Ethnology.

The four major groupings are outlined below.

Tibet. Newark's collection of Tibetan textiles and costumes is one of the two most representative in the country, the other being owned by the Field Museum in Chicago.

The Newark holdings were given to the museum in 1910 by Dr. Shelton, a medical missionary who collected the material in Tibet during the early years of the century. They reveal a full range of Tibet's distinctive textile art and offer a fresh source of contemporary textile design. Included are woven and tie-dyed designs, unusual striped silk aprons, quite marvelous headdresses, felt rugs, painted banners (tankas), remarkable appliqué work, and many pieces of decorative apparel designed for a very cold climate. Many of the pieces are woven from the hair of the yak, as well as from

RIGHT. Peruvian embroidery, South Coast, Paracas Necropolis culture, possibly 400–100 B.C. Section shown is 14" wide. Sophronia Anderson Bequest. *Newark Museum—45.118 (12465W).*

BELOW. Costume of a Tibetan priest dancer. The fabric is 17th Century Chinese silk; 20th Century mask. Gift of Alice Boney. *Newark Museum—48.19 (8096).*

sheep and goat's wool. Typical are narrow-strip weavings sewn together into larger pieces.

Perhaps the most unique piece in the collection is a large ceremonial tent almost completely covered with intricate appliqué designs which are native to the region. Similar appliquéd decorations are seen on temple hangings and huge outdoor ceremonial banners which are used in Tibet's religious rituals.

The woven silks in the collecton are not native to Tibet but were imported from China to be used by Tibetan craftsmen.

In all, the Tibetan group consists of 151 pieces, dating from the 18th to the 20th Century.

China. Fabrics and costumes from China make up the largest single geographical unit in the collection—434 pieces. They include cut velvets, resist dyes, silk brocades, and tapestry weaves. These add up to a fourth of the group. In addition, there are about 100 examples of Chinese embroidery art, 15 rugs, and 192 pieces of costume, including a number of court robes. They cover a period from the 15th to the 20th Century.

There is also a small group of textiles and costumes from Manchuria and Mongolia.

India. The Oriental Department owns about 200 fabrics from India, some of them very early pieces, dating from the 17th Century. They run the gamut of India's textile arts—mordant-painted and printed cottons, silk sari weaves, embroideries, and elegant costume pieces, as well as about 20 Kashmir shawls.

Quilts & Coverlets. The Newark museum is well known for its strong collection of quilts and coverlets in the care of the Decorative Arts Department. The quilts form the larger group with 126 examples from the United States, England, and Ireland. They date from 1710 to 1949 and in-

clude pieced, appliquéd, and solid color pieces. The coverlet collection is smaller—59 pieces, all from the United States. The work dates from the late 18th to the mid-19th Century and includes examples of double-woven, overshot, and Jacquard weaves.

Beyond these four major groups the Newark textile collection is wide-ranging. Brief descriptions of the different categories follow, listed by departments.

Decorative Arts Department

Flat Textiles. A group of some 600 woven, printed, and embroidered fabrics covering a full range of techniques and extending from the 16th Century to the 1950s. Countries represented are: Albania, Austria, the Balkans, Czechoslovakia, Denmark, England, Finland, France, Germany, Greece, Holland, Hungary, Italy, Labrador, Norway, Poland, Portugal, Rumania, Russia, Scotland (24 tartans), Spain, Sweden, Switzerland, United States, Yugoslavia.
In addition, there is a study collection of about 100 sample cards. Also a group of home furnishings—table and bed linens, curtains, draperies, and upholstery.

Lace. The museum accession cards show 428 examples of lace in a variety of techniques. The major sources are: Belgium, England, France, Germany, Holland, Ireland, Italy, Portugal, Spain, and the United States. In addition, there are several hundred lace accessory pieces such as handkerchiefs. The collection also owns a large number of lace-making tools and patterns, as well as examples of tatting and knitting.

Samplers & Embroidery. The sampler collection consists of 65 pieces made in England and the United States from the 17th Century up to 1938. Also 15 needlework pictures and a large number of other embroidered pieces such as purses, boxes, and shawls.

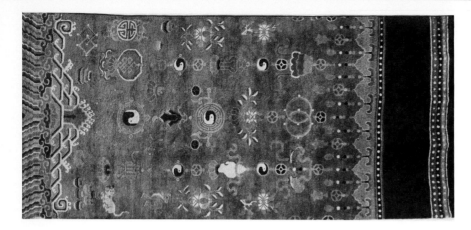

NEWARK MUSEUM cont'd

Rugs. A group of 46 American hooked rugs—made in the latter half of the 19th Century.

Tapestries. 11 pieces ranging from a 16th-Century Flemish panel to a contemporary American work. Most of the other examples are French in origin.

Costume. A group of 520 ensembles ranging in date from 1680 to 1973. The emphasis is on costumes made or owned by residents of New Jersey, but the sources are American, European, and Russian. In addition to these full costumes there are a large number of related accessories and minor articles of clothing, as well as a smaller group of ecclesiastical vestments.

Oriental Department

In addition to the collections from China, India, and Tibet, this department owns smaller groups of textiles, as follows.

Japan. Just under 100 pieces. They include cotton resist dyes, silk brocades, embroideries, and robes—dating from the 18th to the 20th Century.

Western Asia. About 200 pieces of textiles, rugs, and costumes. They cover a long period from the 15th to the 20th Century and include work from Afghanistan, Arabia, the Caucasus, Mesopotamia, Persia, and Turkey.

Southeast Asia. About 100 pieces, chiefly 19th- and 20th-Century work. Countries represented are: Bali, Burma, Cambodia, Java, Korea, the Philippines, and Sumatra.

North Africa. Accession cards show 138 pieces of textiles, rugs, and costumes, mostly of the 19th and 20th Century. Examples are from Algeria, Egypt, Morocco, and Tunisia.

Classical Department

A small group of ancient Coptic textiles from Egypt. There are nine examples in all, including two large tunic sections with tapestry decorations.

Ethnology Department

About 165 pieces in all, chiefly 19th- and 20th-Century work. There are representative textiles from West Africa, Central and South America, Mexico, and the North American Indians. The largest single unit is from Peru and includes examples of ancient Peruvian weaving.

Publications. 1. *Handwoven Coverlets in the Newark Museum.* 1947. 83 pages, with 33 illustrations.

2. *Quilts & Counterpanes in the Newark Museum.* 1948. 90 pages, 40 illustrations.

3. *Tibetan Collection & Other Lamaist Articles in the Newark Museum.* Volume IV (1961) in this five-volume series of catalogs deals with textiles, rugs, needlework, costumes, and jewelry. 112 pages, 47 illustrations.

4. *Printed Textiles of Europe & America.* By Margaret E. White. 1960. 24 pages, 31 illustrations.

5. *Primitive Design.* By Edward H. Ross. 1964. 27 pages, 31 illustrations.

6. *The Textiles & Costumes of India.* By Eleanor Olson. 1965. 39 pages, with 33 illustrations.

NEW HAVEN, CONN.

Yale University Art Gallery

1111 Chapel Street
Box 2006 Yale Station
ZIP: 06532   TEL: (203) 436-2490

Alan Shestack, Director
Sarah Buie Pauly, Gallery Lecturer

The Yale University Art Gallery owns an extensive and important textile collection of more than 3,000 pieces. Unfortunately, however, it is not an active collection at this writing. Most of the fabrics are in storage, and there has been no textile curator attached to the gallery for over 20 years. As a result, study facilities are not readily available.

The textile holdings are known as The Hobart & Edward Small Moore Memorial Collection. This was established by Mrs. William H. Moore in 1937 with pieces acquired during her travels. It was later supplemented by her acquisition of the Ackerman-Pope Collection of Coptic and Persian textiles. Subsequent gifts to the Gallery, including the Harriet Engelhardt Memorial Collection, have given additional range and depth to the textile holdings.

The chief strength lies in Islamic material, but the Egyptian (Coptic) and South American holdings, as well as those from India, are also quite extensive. Among other cultures represented are those of Persia, China, Japan, Southeast Asia, North Africa, Greece, and Turkey. Some European and American pieces are also included, as well as a number from ancient Peru and modern Guatemala.

NEW YORK CITY

American Museum of Natural History
Central Park West at 79th Street
ZIP: 10024   TEL: (212) 873-1300

For Textiles: Milica Skinner;

Lisa Whittall; Philip Gifford

The American Museum of Natural History owns one of the world's richest and most exciting collections of ethnographic textiles. They are not easy to examine since few are on public display and most are locked away in remote storage cabinets in the nonpublic areas of the museum. However, a little patience will gain access to them, and the rewards will more than justify the effort.

I recommend that any such exploration begin in the museum's Division of Photography. It owns a vast file of excellent photographs which provide a general survey of the whole textile collection. Textile pictures are cataloged by the cultures which produced them but are usually segregated from other artifacts and easy to find. Prints of most pieces can be ordered.

How large is the textile collection? And what does it contain?

Size is almost impossible to determine with any exactness. I estimate at least 10,000 pieces, probably more. Most are kept by the Department of Anthropology and came to the museum with ethnographic and archaeological collections gathered by people with no special expertise in textiles. No textile inventory has ever been made, and no member of the staff has been specifically concerned with textiles as such, though the staff people listed above are the ones most familiar with the textile holdings.

Having said this, I must call special attention to the pioneer work of anthropologist Junius Bird, who is an authority on early Peruvian textiles. Dr. Bird has long been associated with the Museum's Department of Anthropology. It was he who uncovered and dated fabrics from 2500 B.C. in a dig at Huaca Prieta on the Northern Coast of Peru—among the most ancient textiles discovered anywhere. With his help the museum has assembled one of the world's outstanding collections of ancient Peruvian fabrics. He has written extensively on the subject, particularly in the book *Paracas Fabrics & Nazca Needlework* (1954).

Content of the textile collection is wide-ranging. It has coverage of depth in at least four areas.

1. Peru. A major collection of ancient Peruvian fabrics dating from 2500 B.C. forward. Milica Skinner, assistant to Dr. Bird, has charge of this collection.

2. Guatemala. Another major collection—of modern textiles from Guatemala, mainly late 19th- and early 20th-Century work.

3. India. Third in size among the museum's textile holdings. Lisa Whittall of the Asia Section has charge of this group.

4. American Indian. The fourth major

category which—among many other Indian textiles—owns about 400 Navajo rugs.

Beyond these four main areas there are lesser holdings from preindustrial societies in many parts of the world. These are briefly noted in the regional listings which follow.

South & Central America. The collection of textiles from ancient Peru, as already noted, is outstanding. Two huge steel cabinets, near Dr. Bird's workrooms, are crammed to capacity with smaller pieces from the collection. To open them and explore the contents is an adventure in aesthetics.

I particularly noted a large and varied collection of small patterned bags, most in a fine state of preservation.

It was also a privilege to be shown one of the 4,500-year-old Huaca Prieta fabrics, a reproduction of which has been woven by Milica Skinner. Under Dr. Bird's direction she has graphed the courses of the woven yarns, and—sheer magic—a spread-eagled design appears on the reproduction where no design whatsoever is visible on the dessicated original. This is typical of the creative work performed by Dr. Bird in this field.

Nor are the pieces in the ancient Peruvian collection only small ones. The museum owns several large Peruvian mantles, superb in design and preservation. At least two of these (woven and embroidered) are from the Paracas Necropolis and are dated 3rd Century B.C. to 3rd Century A.D.

There are also many other Peruvian fabrics, covering the full time span of Peruvian textile skill up to the Colonial period of the 16th Century.

In addition to fabrics from Peru, there is a notable collection of Guatemalan fabrics, predominantly woven pieces of the subtle and softer-colored types, which it seems no longer possible to find in contemporary Guatemalan weaving.

AMERICAN MUSEUM cont'd

Also a fine collection of Mexican blankets, particularly those of the Chimayo style.

Several other areas of preindustrial South and Central America are represented by smaller holdings.

North America. American Indian textiles represent another major category in the museum's holdings. In addition to Navajo rugs, there are representative fabrics from most of the Indian tribes who inhabited North America. Particularly notable are a substantial number of Chilkat and Salish blankets—some of which are on display in the public galleries.

Also—though not a fabric—the museum owns a superb painted buffalo robe (Sioux) with an exquisite design of running horses.

Asia. The Asian section of the museum owns a tremendous range of textiles—not so much in numbers as in variety and geographic spread. It extends from Balkan peasant embroidery to Tibetan banners. Here is a partial list.

Embroidered costumes and towels from the Balkans and Turkey. Palestinian embroidery. Costumes from Iran (Persia). A full-sized yurt (tent) with elaborate woven designs, from Afghanistan. Exotic pieces from Bokhara. Saris, shawls, and hangings from India—particularly from Rajistan and Gujurat. Pakistani head shawls. Batiks from Java. Ikats from Sumba and other parts of Indonesia. Costume pieces from Burma, Laos, and Thailand. Chinese dragon robes of the 19th Century. Costumes from Tibet, as well as a major collection of some 300 Tibetan banners and hangings. Early Ainu robes from Japan, woven with elm bark fiber. A superb example of dyed deerskin appliqué on a fishskin garment from Siberia (Amin River).

Quite obviously, a large and exciting representation of Asiatic textile arts, though no count is available.

Pacific. The most important groups of textiles from the Pacific area are one from the Philippines and another of tapa cloth, particularly from Samoa. The Philippine material includes a large number of pieces from Mindanao (Bagobo tribe) and is notable for the intricate lacy quality of the designs. There are also ikats and batiks from the Philippines. The Samoan tapa cloths should be equally interesting to contemporary print designers because of the great variety in their patternings.

Africa. A modest collection of textiles with particular representation from North Africa but also from other regions on the continent. Some of these are exhibited in the museum's Hall of Man in Africa.

NEW YORK CITY

Artweave Textile Gallery
924 Madison Avenue (73 Street)
ZIP: 10021   TEL: (212) 794-0384

Vladimir Haustov, Gail Martin, Ocsi Ullman

Many of the fabrics are the dowries of peasant girls, the portable wealth they made with their hands and carried with them to their marriages. Most are large needlework hangings, stitched in the village homes of Central Asia during the 19th Century. They were years in the making,

often begun when a girl was five or six years old. They show great skill and are quite beautiful, truly art fabrics.

They can be seen any day hanging on the walls of this New York gallery—a gallery that sells no painting or sculpture but collects, shows, and sells fabrics as art.

At the time of my visit Central Asiatic embroideries were on exhibit in the gallery. but exhibits are not limited to the work of one region or one technique. There have been woven ikats on display—silk ikats from both Indonesia and Central Asia. One of the gallery's early shows was of pre-Columbian fabrics from the Andes. Kilim hangings and rugs are a permanent part of the collection, together with about 100 ikats, 40 Coptic fragments, and some 500 woven or embroidered hangings from Bokhara, Samarkand, Iran, and the Caucasus.

Each month the gallery tries to mount a new exhibit. From time to time it also shows contemporary art fabrics, and the emphasis here is on pieces that match the level of skill and dedication seen in its historic collection. The aim is to demonstrate a continuity between work of the past and the present.

The three gallery owners have a point of view which rises above the level of merchandising. Fabrics chosen for display reveal a sophistication of taste which is both educated and sure. Each piece is choice, and they know its history and provenance. In many cases the pieces have been acquired from the original owners or their descendants, since most of the collection is 19th-Century work.

To contemporary designers the Artweave Gallery can thus be more inspirational in its field than many museum collections of textiles. The pieces are on open display and can be examined easily. The same, unfortunately, cannot be said of many museum collections.

RIGHT. Imposing structure of the Brooklyn Museum on Eastern Parkway.

BELOW. Coptic tapestry roundel, 6–7th Century. Charles Edwin Wilbour Fund. *Brooklyn Museum—05.305.*

NEW YORK CITY

The Brooklyn Museum

Eastern Parkway, Brooklyn
ZIP: 11238   TEL: (212) 638-5000

Elizabeth Ann Coleman, Curator, Department of Costumes & Textiles
Dorothy Tricarico, Director, Edward C. Blum Design Laboratory
Arno Jakobson, Photo Service

The Brooklyn Museum has always impressed me as the friendliest of public institutions. It projects the image of a place established to serve and to educate its community rather than to be merely a hallowed repository for works of art. Though it occupies a huge and impressive structure, there is a quality of intimacy about its galleries. Children are encouraged to wander and the sound of human voices is seldom restrained.

This quality of informal cooperation with its public is important to designers working in a museum. Even more important is the fact that the Brooklyn Museum has long been accustomed to forging links between its collections and the commercial community in New York. As early as 1915 it mounted a textile exhibition of museum holdings for the National Association of Silk Manufacturers, under the direction of its staff anthropologist, Stewart Culin. This type of association has continued through the years, culminating in the establishment of its Design Laboratory in 1948. More on that later.

As for the museum's curatorial collection of flat textiles (as distinct from the study collections in the Design Lab), it is wide in range and often superb in quality, though modest in size—under 3,000 pieces. Yet this figure must be qualified since it does not include a vast collection of some 3,000,000 swatches. At this writing the swatch collection is "in limbo." The material is accessible at the museum, but it is not clear whether

it will eventually be held by the Design Lab or the Department of Costumes & Textiles.

Design Lab Facilities

The Edward C. Blum Industrial Design Laboratory (to give its full title) was named for a man who was President of the Abraham & Straus department store as well as President of the Brooklyn Institute of Arts & Sciences, the museum's parent organization. Mr. Blum was himself an important link between the worlds of art and commerce. From its beginnings the Lab also had the enthusiastic and knowledgeable guidance of M. D. C. Crawford, Research Editor of the Fairchild textile/apparel trade publications. It was he who conceived and implemented the now-famous 1946 exhibition *5,000 Years of Fibers & Fabrics*, which opened at the Brooklyn Museum, toured the country, and had the active support of New York's leading textile houses (see the list of publications).

The Design Lab's first head was Michelle Murphy. Under her direction and that of her successor Robert Riley (now Director of

the F.I.T. Lab), it has served the fashion, textile, and home-furnishings industries of New York with great distinction and has been an invaluable research facility for several generations of New York designers and students of design.

Before they were placed "in limbo" the Design Lab collections, as noted, were vast and held separately from those of other curatorial departments in the museum. They included the 3,000,000 fabric swatches, many of them in sample books which date back to 1780. There are literally several thousand old sample books in the collection, in addition to thousands of individual swatches filed on cards. I have personally worked with these files over a number of years and can testify to their value. The collection is enormous and wide-ranging.

In addition, the Design Lab has large holdings of costume, accessories, and other flat textiles as part of a study collection which can be used and handled by designers. Moreover, it has at its disposal additional fine materials (including paintings and prints) from five other departments in the museum—Oriental, Middle East, Primitive, Egyptian, and Costume/Textiles. These have long been drawn on to supply particular needs of designers.

A substantial portion of these large holdings is being transferred to the new Design Lab at F.I.T. in Manhattan on long-term loan. The F.I.T. facility is the joint project of F.I.T. and the Brooklyn Museum, which was planned as long ago as 1965. Designers will thus have access to both facilities and the same museum staff will operate at both.

Textiles in Five Departments

Aside from its holdings in the Design Lab, the Brooklyn Museum owns both textiles and costumes distributed among the five departments previously listed. Following is a rough breakdown of the holdings in each

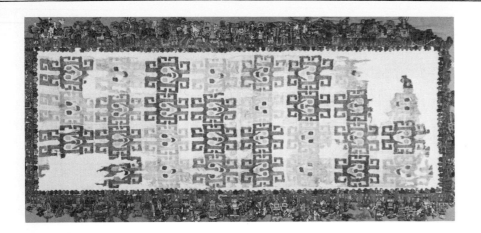

LEFT. Peruvian shawl, 65" × 20", from the Paracas Necropolis—1st Century B.C. to 1st Century A.D. The center is loosely woven cotton, double-faced; the border, also double-faced, is made of intricate needlework in wool yarns. The border figures are three-dimensional. John T. Underwood Memorial Fund. *Brooklyn Museum—38.121.*

BELOW. Fragment of Peruvian mantle, Paracas. Alfred W. Jenkins Fund. *Brooklyn Museum—34.1549.*

BROOKLYN MUSEUM cont'd

of these departments. The numbers given are approximations.

Department of Costumes & Textiles

This is one of the largest museum departments of its kind in the country. Its costume collection alone is generally considered to be one of the largest in the United States. It may possibly be even larger than the costume collection at the Met, since it is reputed to own some 25,000 pieces. The museum describes these costume holdings modestly as "an extensive collection of West European and American high fashion dating from approximately the mid-18th Century to the present and particularly strong in mid-20th Century designer garments."

Aside from the huge costume collection, this department has charge of some 1,200 pieces covering many different periods and regions. Among its most interesting holdings are the following.

About 200 American quilts dating from the 18th to the 20th Century.

About 20 19th-Century American woven coverlets, several of the candlewick type.

A substantial collection of lace dating from the 17th Century to the present.

A fine group of embroidered bed coverings with both silk and crewelwork—18th–19th Century.

About 75 sets of window hangings—18th–19th Century.

Russian folk textiles. This is one of the world's outstanding collections of such fabrics. There are several hundred pieces in the group—most with embroidery.

A large group of sheet edgings.

A small group of French toiles—18th–19th Century.

A sampling of 18th-Century brocades from France, Italy, and Spain.

An interesting collection of printed commemorative handkerchiefs.

Early German blue-and-white prints.

About 200 samplers from various regions and periods.

Egyptian Department.

About 300 pieces. This is one of the country's outstanding collections of Coptic textiles. Most of the pieces date from the late Roman to the Islamic periods—chiefly 4th to 7th Century. The museum owns several complete tunics with decorative panels (claves), as well as numerous fragments in a fine state of preservation. This collection is the subject of a now classic work by Deborah Thompson: *Coptic Textiles in the Brooklyn Museum.*

Middle Eastern Department.

About 200 pieces, including house adornments, religious articles, and costumes. They date from the 9th Century to modern times. There are embroidered, printed, and woven pieces from Algeria, Morocco, Turkey, Asia Minor, Bokhara, Uzbekistan, Greece, Persia, and Egypt under Arab influence.

Primitive Department.

About 600 pieces. This department holds examples of textile art from ancient Peru, Africa, Indonesia, Panama, and the American Indians. The Peruvian collection of 414 pieces contains some of the finest examples of Paracas weaving and embroidery. The African and Oceanic group (50) includes tapa cloth and raffia work, as well as woven fabrics and costumes from Ghana and Dahomey. The Indonesian collection (30) has woven and embroidered pieces as well as batiks. From Panama there is a small but choice group of Cuna molas (10). And the American Indian holdings (100) include a fine group of Navajo blankets, in addition to the well-known Jarvis Collection of beadwork and other fabrics of the Eastern Plains Indians.

Oriental Department.

About 300 pieces. Among them are representative examples of work from Japan, China, India, and Indonesia. The Japanese group is the largest with about 135 pieces. They include court costumes, kimonos, livery coats, and early textile fragments. Some of the latter are on exhibit in the Oriental gallery. From China the museum owns 20 mandarin robes and 25 hats. Indonesia is represented by some 40 pieces of batik work. And from India comes a group of 25 saris and some 50 pieces of painted and printed cottons. Among the latter is the famous painted-cotton curtain from the Golconda region of India, dating from the mid-17th Century. Though it was originally a single piece—23 × 8 feet—it has been preserved by cutting it into seven panels which are mounted on canvas and displayed in the Oriental gallery. The work reveals a fascinating mixture of Rajput and Mughal styles.

Textiles on Exhibit

As to the museum's international collection of historic textiles with which I am most concerned in this review, it is a notable one. Moreover, it is given extensive display in the museum's public galleries as an

RIGHT. Detail of needlework similar to the border on the left. Peruvian Chimu culture, 1000–1500 A.D. A. Augustus Healy Fund. *Brooklyn Museum—42.334.*

BELOW. Peruvian tapestry-weave mantle, probably Ica culture. A. Augustus Healy and Carll H. De Silver Funds. *Brooklyn Museum—46.46.1.*

integral part of the cultures represented in different areas of the museum.

For example, the ground floor has a major exhibit of ancient Peruvian textiles which includes some of the finest Paracas fabrics held by any museum. Adjacent areas exhibit fine examples of African tapa cloth, Chilkat blankets, and decorative beadwork of the Plains Indians. Similarly, Persian textiles are exhibited in conjunction with Persian miniature painting, since the same artists were often responsible for both. The Middle Eastern gallery shows robes, rugs, and textiles from the region. In the Oriental galleries there is a superb example of a painted-cotton curtain from India (Golconda), and in the gallery adjacent to the Wilbour Library of Egyptology are displayed remarkably fine examples of Coptic tapestry weaving.

These and other gallery exhibits demonstrate the importance assigned to textiles by the museum's management—more than can be said for many other major museums.

Research Facilities

The Brooklyn Museum offers excellent research facilities to designers and students through its Art Reference Library and its specialized Wilbour Library of Egyptology.

The Art Reference Library owns about 60,000 volumes dealing with art, anthropology, and social history—all related to the museum collections. Of this total some 5,000 works deal specifically with textiles, costume, and design. The library also owns several thousand original fashion sketches from the period 1900–1950.

The Wilbour Library is devoted entirely to Egyptology and owns about 300 works on textiles, including the most important works on Coptic textiles.

Photographs. The museum maintains an excellent file of B/W negatives and color transparencies. Prints can be ordered from the Photo Service Department.

Publications. Five publications specifically related to textiles and costume have been issued by the museum.

1. *Coptic Textiles in the Brooklyn Museum.* By Deborah Thompson. 1971. 124 pages, 33 B/W illustrations, 16 color plates. This work contains clear drawings showing the different ornamentation schemes used by the Copts in decorating their garments.

2. *Changing Fashions: 1800–1970.* By Elizabeth Ann Coleman. 1972. 70 pages, 34 B/W illustrations, 8 color plates.

3. *The Lace with the Delicate Air.* Introduction by Dassah Saulpaugh. 1965. A 14-page brochure with 21 illustrations.

4. *Introduction to Peruvian Costume.* By Natalie H. Zimmern. 1949. 60 pages.

5. *5,000 Years of Fibers & Fabrics.* By M.D.C. Crawford. Out of print but available in some libraries. This is a 34-page handbook of a famous exhibition held at the Brooklyn Museum in 1946. In it Mr. Crawford has written a condensed but most perceptive history of textile evolution in an effort "to relate the vast, modern, mechanized textile industry to the artistic and technological history of cloth as produced by many peoples over a wide area of time."

NEW YORK CITY

Cooper-Hewitt Museum of Design

Smithsonian Institution
Fifth Avenue at 91st Street
ZIP: 10028   TEL: (212) 860-2011

Milton Sonday, Textile Curator
Lisa M. Taylor, Director
Christian Rohlfing, Administrator

At this writing (mid-1975) Cooper-Hewitt is a museum in transition. Whatever is written about it now must be read in terms of its eventual emergence as perhaps the leading facility in the U.S. for the study of applied design—and especially of textile design.

This will not be a new role for Cooper-Hewitt. Until 1963 it was known as the Cooper Union Museum, handsomely and comfortably housed in a brown sandstone building on Third Avenue at 7th Street in New York City. There it served several generations of designers as well as students of the Cooper Union Art School, which was in the same building. Alice Baldwin Beer was its Curator of Textiles and trained many of the younger poeple now heading textile departments in other U.S. museums.

The Cooper Union Museum was founded in 1897 by Sarah, Eleanor, and Amy Hewitt, granddaughters of Peter Cooper. Its aim was to provide New York City—and America—with the kind of resources offered by the Victoria & Albert Museum in London and the Musée des Arts Décoratifs in Paris.

It succeeded admirably, and many U.S. designers have been deeply indebted to its splendid resources and library, known for their accessibility.

But in 1963 financial support from the Cooper Union Foundation ended, and the museum was closed to the public. A skeleton staff remained in operation, and the collections were partially accessible to researchers. In 1967 the Smithsonian Institution assumed responsibility for the collections (though the museum remained self-supporting), and in 1972 the Carnegie Mansion at 91st Street & Fifth Avenue was given to the museum as its new home. During renovation of the mansion the collections were available by appointment, and the museum was opened again for public use in 1975.

Cooper-Hewitt is now designated as a national museum of design in the decorative arts. In addition to its major textile holdings it owns the largest collection of prints and drawings in the U.S. (30,000 pieces), as well as smaller holdings of ceramics, metalwork, woodwork, glass, enamel, packaging, and furniture.

Pattern Archive. Plans have been formulated to establish a Pattern Archive at Cooper-Hewitt. This will include photographs and other illustrations of flat design adaptable to textiles as well as to other end uses such as wallpaper, ceramics, decorative papers, woodwork, and architecture. Such an archive will obviously become an

important asset to all designers and students working in applied design.

Library. Owning some 25,000 volumes, the Cooper-Hewitt library may well be the largest in America on the decorative arts. It has the most complete textile reference library in the country. For example, among its treasures on the textile arts is a very rare 15-volume work by John Forbes Watson titled: *Collection of Specimens of the Textile Manufactures of India—1872-77.* It is illustrated with actual swatches of fabric.

The library also owns a collection of some 9,000 hand-colored fashion plates illustrating 19th-Century costume. It was assembled by Vyvyan Holland, son of Oscar Wilde.

For designers an even more important resource is an encyclopedic picture collection of over 500,000 classified items, chiefly in the decorative arts.

Textile Slide Catalog. This will unquestionably become the most meaningful resource of the textile collection as far as working designers and students are concerned. It is now in process, and when completed it will provide a comprehensive pictorial catalog of the museum's textile holdings on 2 × 2 color slides—in duplicate. Many of the pieces will be photographed in full as well as in closeup detail. Thus researchers will be able to obtain a quick visual inspection of the whole collection or any of its parts. Not only will this save wear and tear on rare textiles, but it will make possible the comparison of different textiles by using two projectors at the same time. The slide catalog is also planned as a teaching tool. Additionally, it will be used for continuous slide projections to accompany exhibits in the public galleries.

Card Catalog. Arranged in file drawers as in a library, the museum's card catalog lists art objects instead of books. Textiles are cataloged by region, period, and type. This catalog is available for public use.

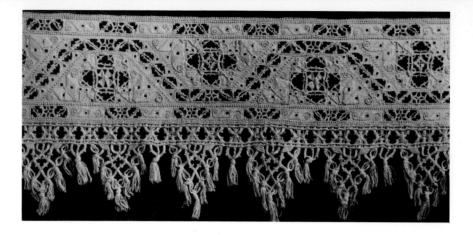

RIGHT. From Italy, late 16th Century. An embroidered-linen border, macramé fringe. *Cooper-Hewitt—1951-11-67 (11848).*

BELOW. From India, mid-18th Century. A lacelike print for the Dutch market. *Cooper-Hewitt—1961-19-1 (6675).*

Photo File. An excellent resource for designers seeking general pattern inspiration, photos are arranged by accession number and not by period or culture so that it is not possible to see all the photos of pieces in one culture sequentially. However, this is one of the best collections of B/W textile photographs in any museum and well worth the effort. In many cases there are several copies of each print already in the file, and this avoids the delay of waiting for a print to be ordered.

Range of the Textile Collection

Cooper-Hewitt owns one of the largest international textile collections in the United States. It runs to about 18,000 pieces—not counting many thousands of individual swatches in some 500 sample books, but counting each book as one piece.

In addition, about 3,000 drawings of fabric and embroidery designs on paper bring the textile total to about 21,000 pieces. Also one of the country's major collections of wallpaper—about 5,000 pieces, dating from the 17th Century forwards.

In terms of construction techniques, the following are well represented.

Nonwoven. Felt, barkcloth, looping, knitting, crochet, macramé, needle lace, bobbin lace.

Woven. Backstrap loom, inkle loom, draw loom, jacquard, card weaving, etc.

Applied Decoration. Embroidery, prints (woodblock, copperplate, roller, screen), resist dyes (batik, starch paste, tie-dye, ikat, mordant dyeing), painted designs.

Trimmings. Tassels, fringes, etc.

Each of these techniques is broken down by geographic source and period. The following regions and countries are represented.

Asia. China, Japan, India, Persia.

Southeast Asia. Burma, Thailand, Indonesia, etc.

Central Asia. Bhutan, Tibet, Turkestan, etc.

Ancient Near East. Coptic, early Islamic to the 15th Century.

Modern Near East. Syria, Turkey, etc.

Eastern Europe. Greece, Yugoslavia, etc.

Western Europe. England, France, Germany, Italy, Spain, Islamic Spain.

Northern Europe. Denmark, Sweden, etc.

Africa. North Africa, Central Africa.

North America. American Indian, Colonial.

Central America. Guatemala, Mexico.

South America. Pre-Columbian, post-Conquest.

Oceania. Pacific Islands, etc.

The museum card catalog also has alphabetical listings of manufacturers, craftsmen, and designers.

In terms of the time span covered, this is one of the world's most representative collections. It ranges from the 3rd Century B.C. (China and Peru) to contemporary art

fabrics and notable commercial textiles of the seventies.

High Points of the Collection

Following are some of the strongest sections of the Cooper-Hewitt holdings.

Islamic Textiles. One of the world's most important and representative collections of woven fabrics from the Mediterranean and Middle East, dating from the 8th to the 13th Century.

Egypt. A major group including Coptic and Egypto-Arabic fabrics from the 4th to the 12th Century.

Europe. The whole range of European textile history, with emphasis on the 14th to the 18th Century. Among the strongest groups are those from 14th-Century Italy, English and French silk weaving, Spanish and Italian silks, and 18th-Century woodblock prints.

England/France. This is the largest single category in the collection. The English fabrics—both wovens and prints—cover a period from the 18th to the 20th Century. The French fabric group is larger than the English and extends from the 17th to the 19th Century. It holds many silks, brocades, and prints, as well as 19th-Century ribbons.

India. An important collection of 18th-Century painted palampores.

United States. The collection provides excellent coverage of American textiles from the 18th Century to the present.

Peru. A small but representative collection covering a wide time span from the 3rd Century B.C. to post-Conquest.

Resist Dyes. An excellent representation of many techniques from all parts of the world. Batik, ikat, tie-dye, starch paste, and mordant dyeing from India are all represented.

Embroidery. A vast range of over 2,000 pieces, not including close to 1,000 em-

COOPER-HEWITT cont'd

broidery designs on paper. Coverage extends from 5th-Century Egypt to 20th-Century Europe and the United States. Among these are over 450 samplers and a unique group of waistcoat embroideries of the 18th to the 19th Century (the Greenleaf Collection).

Lace. Over 2,000 pieces of all types and from most lace-producing regions.

Designs on Paper. There are over 2,000 drawings of textile designs, many from the 18th Century. Also close to 1,000 embroidery designs.

Trimmings. Tassels, fringes, beadwork, and other trimmings. Over 1,000 pieces.

Sample Books. An impressive group of close to 500 volumes covering a period from the 18th to the 20th Century.

Publications. Thirteen publications relating to different aspects of the textile collection are available from the museum (list on request). Several are monographs dealing with the lace and embroidery collections. The most extensive is Alice Beer's excellent illustrated paperback on the story of Indian chintz (*Trade Goods*, 1970).

NEW YORK CITY

F.I.T.—Design Laboratory
27th Street & Seventh Avenue
ZIP: 10001   TEL: (212) 760-7700

Robert Riley, Director
Dorothy Tricarico, Textile Curator

By the time this review is published, the Design Lab at New York's Fashion Institute of Technology (F.I.T.) will be operating in its imposing new home as probably the largest (and certainly the most luxuriously equipped) working facility in the world for the study of costume and textiles. It will also hold what may well be the largest combined collection of costumes and flat textiles in the country. The Lab will serve students of design, as well as designers in New York's fashion and textile industries, which are adjacent to its block-long building. It should provide these major industries with a long-needed institution which can match their large stature on the world scene.

The new facility is a joint project of F.I.T. and the Brooklyn Museum. Here, as in Brooklyn, services are available on a membership basis. Schools, fashion and fabric producers, and independent designers can join the Lab for an annual fee. They are then in a position to take advantage of its outstanding facilities on a year-round basis.

How the Lab will operate is best explained through a typical case history.

Let us say a member designer has an idea for a fashion collection based on the traditional court costumes and fabrics of Thailand. The designer telephones the Lab, describes the project, and makes an appointment for, say, a week ahead. During that week the staff of the Lab will be assembling garments, textiles, photographs, slides, and printed material on Thai costume from its collections and its library. These materials will be assembled in one of the designer workrooms, which has now

been assigned to this specific project. There are 16 such workrooms in the new building, two large enough for staff conferences.

When the designer appears on the appointed day, he or she will find a well-equipped workroom with table, pinup board, slide projector, and other working tools—plus the materials assembled for the project. The workroom will be available as long as it is needed, and knowledgeable staff members will be on hand to answer questions or provide further information.

The workrooms are large, private, comfortable, and well-lit. Backing them up are four major resources within the F.I.T. Lab.

The Costume Collection. With the exception of one or two vast ethnographic holdings, this is probably the largest collection of costumes and accessories in the country. It is estimated at about 50,000 pieces. A large number of them come from the Brooklyn Museum. Many others were acquired over the years by F.I.T.

The unique aspect of this whole collection is that—unlike traditional museum holdings—everything is meant to be used and worked with rather than kept inviolate as a record of the past. That means member designers can handle and study the garments at close range, borrow them, even take some of them apart if necessary. In every sense of the word, this is a study collection.

Among its strongest sections are 19th- and 20th-Century work from Western Europe and America. In this area it owns important collections of haute couture from many of the leading fashion names of this century—Balenciaga, Dior, Chanel, Schiaparelli, Norell, Adrian, McCardell, Worth—to name only a few. For example, the Balenciaga collection alone numbers about 200 pieces. The aim throughout has been to provide a "dictionary" of the work created by these world-famous designers. And the holdings in this area are constantly expanding through new acquisitions.

In addition, the Lab owns smaller groups of costumes from 18th-Century Europe and from the Far East, as well as a large number of paper garment patterns.

This impressive range of costumes and accessories is kept on double racks and cases in a huge storeroom which is approximately 135 by 50 feet in size. This vast repository—mirabile dictu—is entirely accessible to members. They can browse at will or consult a reference file which indexes fashion designers by name.

The Textile Collection. No count is yet available for the flat textile holdings in the new Design Lab. However, some indication of their eventual size can be gained from the dimensions of the storage area assigned to them. It is even larger than the costume area. When fully organized, this vast space will be filled with files—many of which are expected to contain some of the three million or more fabric samples owned by the Brooklyn Design Lab, as well as weaving diagrams, jacquard cards, and swatches already in use at F.I.T.

Eventually this astronomical store of textile samples will be arranged, not by period or source, but by type of construction or design motif. For example, a designer will be able to search through fabric drawers marked "Jacquards—Small," or "Jacquards—Large," or "Dobbies—Small"—and so on. Similarly, prints will be arranged by type of motif—say, dot patterns of different sizes. In short, the storage arrangements will be geared to the designer's needs.

The largest portion of this material is of European and American origin. However, the collection also includes many examples of work from the Near and Far East.

In addition to these extensive holdings, the **Design Lab** at this writing is in the process of acquiring the large textile collection of **Galey & Lord,** one of the oldest and most important names in U.S. textiles. The collection contains many sample books of the

company's earliest production runs, as well as examples of fabric from many foreign sources originally acquired as research material for the firm's own designers.

Other textile holdings in the Design Lab include several albums of work from the German Wiener Werkstätte and about 120 American patchwork quilts collected chiefly as a source of print designs.

The Lab also owns substantial collections of related materials such as straw mats, basketry, African raffia work, screening, and other objects which are helpful as sources for contemporary textile design.

The Library. The F.I.T. library is housed on three floors of the new structure, immediately above the Design Lab. Here the member designer has access to a collection of some 50,000 books and periodicals almost entirely devoted to fashion, fabric, and design. Among some 8,000 bound volumes of periodicals are extensive files of magazines such as Godey's, Harper's, and Vogue. Many of these date from the late 19th Century or earlier.

The Photograph/Slide Collection. This is a substantial design resource with the emphasis on women's fashions. It includes some 6,000 color slides of both fabrics and fashions, many of them showing important pieces in foreign collections. For example, one series of slides is devoted to jacquard silks from the Musée Historique des Tissus at Lyon, France. Other slides illustrate changing fashion trends through the pages of periodicals. And there are at least 500 daguerrotypes and photographs of fashions from the 19th Century up to the present.

* * *

If and when any of these four major resources are inadequate to supply a particular need, arrangements will be made to draw on the historic resources of the Brooklyn Museum.

Exhibits & Other Facilities. In addition to the extraordinary facilities already described, the new Design Lab is well equipped with exhibit galleries, a restoration department, and an experimental workroom. There are four large exhibition areas in the building, and they will be the scene of changing fabric, fashion, and design exhibits on a year-round basis. The building is also equipped with a large restoration department and an experimental workshop. The latter is available to designers and students who wish to experiment with different techniques—say, batik, ikat, or even new types of dress forms.

When all these factors are taken into consideration, it is no exaggeration to say that the F.I.T. Design Laboratory should eventually become the most important design research center for textiles and fashion in the country—if not in the world.

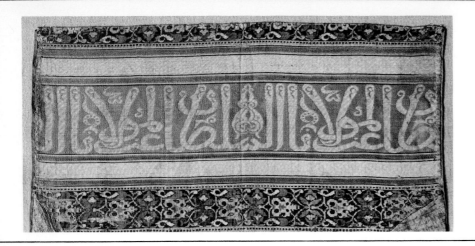

NEW YORK CITY

The Hispanic Society of America
613 West 155 Street (Broadway)
ZIP: 10032 TEL: (212) 926-2234

Florence L. May, Curator of Textiles

The museum and library of the Hispanic Society form an important center for research into the cultures of Spain and Portugal. As such, the Society's chief appeal will be to scholars, since the library holds 100,000 volumes and thousands of manuscripts, as well as an impressive photo reference file with some 200,000 pictures of Hispanic art.

The photo reference file can also be a rich resource for designers who have a special interest in the textile arts of Spain. I counted 17 file drawers containing over 3,000 photographs of Hispanic textiles, predominantly ecclesiastical and with many fine examples of Hispano-Moresque work.

The museum's actual collection of textiles is small but quite important since a number of its pieces are very old and quite rare. The majority are displayed under glass on hinged panels behind locked cabinet doors. They are opened by attendants on request.

Among the rare pieces in these and other storage areas of the museum the following are notable.

Gold and silver brocades in the Hispano-Moresque style, dating from the 13th to the 17th Century.

Mudejar silks of the 15th Century.

Early ecclesiastical vestments with heavy raised embroidery.

A number of luxurious patterned velvets.

About 20 rugs dating from the 16th and the 17th Century.

An important collection of Spanish laces dating from the 15th to the 18th Century. Among them are exquisite pieces from Andalusia, as well as silk laces from Catalonia, Castile, and Galicia. There are also several hundred examples of French, Flemish, and Italian laces.

Research Facilities. The library and reading room is open from 1–4:30 Tuesday through Friday. On Saturday it is open 10–4:30.

Publications. *Handbook* of the museum and library collections. 1938. It contains an informative essay by Florence L. May on the history of Spanish textile art.

Spanish Costume: Extremadura. By Ruth M. Anderson. 1951.

Catalogue of Laces & Embroideries in the Collection. By Florence L. May. 1936.

Hispanic Lace & Lace Making. By Florence L. May. 1939.

Modern Bobbin Lace in the Collection. By Florence L. May.

Silk Textiles of Spain. By Florence L. May. 1957. It covers a period from the 8th to the 15th Century.

NEW YORK CITY

The Metropolitan Museum of Art
Fifth Avenue at 82nd Street
ZIP: 10028 TEL: (212) TR 9-5500

Jean E. Mailey, Associate Curator
In Charge of Textile Study Room
Barbara Teague, Assistant

Few people realize that the Met owns the largest international collection of historic textiles in the United States—over 30,000 pieces.

Since other museums count textiles and costumes as one unit, I now add to this figure the 20,000 or more pieces owned by the Met's Costume Institute.

Plus several thousand textile designs on paper held by the museum's Print Department.

Plus the collection of medieval tapestries and textiles at the Cloisters—a part of the Met.

Plus the small but very choice collection of ethnographic textiles and costumes owned by The Museum of Primitive Art which will soon be housed in a new wing at the Met.

Putting these holdings together I arrive at a total of about 55,000 pieces. Thus the Met may possibly own the largest textile/costume collection in the world.

Yet—I repeat—few people realize this. Even curators in other museums are surprised to learn it. I was not aware of it myself until I began to explore the Met holdings. Nor did my discussion with other curators prepare me for the vast range and diversity of textile art I found in the remote corner of the museum where the Textile Study Room is housed.

The Met has many demands on its exhibit space, and most areas of art traditionally take priority over textiles. I understand that, though I cannot condone it. What I

The Metropolitan Museum of Art, which houses the most important collection of textiles in the United States and possibly the largest in the world.

cannot understand is why this superb collection—one of the world's most important in quality as well as in size—is given so little public exposure through exhibits. I should add that this is not true of Islamic textiles, which are separately held and exhibited in the galleries of the Islamic Department.

Nor do I wish to strike a negative note, for though the Textile Department has no assigned gallery space at the Met and though it operates from cramped quarters with a minimal staff, it has nevertheless managed to offer designers and researchers a service as fine as I have yet encountered anywhere.

This is unquestionably due to Jean Mailey, who is in charge of the Textile Study Room, and to her assistant, Barbara Teague. Under Miss Mailey's friendly and knowledgeable guidance a visitor is made to feel completely at home in the Textile Study Room. The vast resources of civilization's textile art are opened up for inspection—helpfully and without stint.

One caution—it is a busy department. Study space and staff time are limited, so an appointment must be made.

Research Facilities

Within the Textile Study Room the facilities for research are remarkably good and well organized. Cataloging is complete and exhaustive. Best of all, each catalog entry shows a small B/W photograph of the piece described. Once the card index has been consulted, the actual textile is quickly and easily found. From that point of view the cramped storage area becomes almost a virtue.

The storage system makes it easy to examine much of the collection. Several thousand smaller pieces—covering a selective range from the whole collection—are mounted on framed linen panels without glass. The frames are stored vertically in cabinets and labeled by period and by country of origin. This system is similar to the one used by the Victoria & Albert Museum in London and makes it possible to examine thousands of textiles with relative ease, since they do not need to be removed from drawers and unwrapped.

Another notable service to researchers is photographic. Since most pieces in the collection have been photographed for the card-index record, it is possible to order B/W prints of virtually everything in the collection.

In addition, the museum maintains a large photograph and slide library on its lower level. Here the researcher will find an art reference file which holds some 5,000 B/W photographs of textiles owned by other museums both in the U.S. and in foreign countries. These photographs must be studied in the museum. They are not for sale or duplication.

The slide collection, however, is available for rental. The Met now owns close to 250,000 photographic slides of art objects in its own and other collections. They illustrate the history of art from prehistoric times to the present. Among them are more than 1,000 slides of textiles, showing important pieces from the Met and comparable pieces from other collections. It is thus a remarkable international resource for designers, students, and teachers. The slides cover tapestries, woven and printed fabrics, carpets, needlework, embroidery, and lace from many of the significant periods in textile history. Enlarging screens are provided for viewing the slides, and the staff is most helpful. For those designers who have not yet discovered the slide collection it will be a revelation.

Finally, among these various research facilities at the Met there is a modest library of about 1,500 bound volumes dealing with textile design and history. It is conveniently kept in the Textile Study Room, and I have found it more than adequate for all areas of general textile research. In addition to bound volumes, it contains numerous monographs, current periodicals in the field, and bound issues of the museum Bulletin, which has published many articles on the textile arts. It also contains a unique record in six portfolios of 8 × 10 B/W photographs. They provide a survey of the Victoria & Albert Museum's outstanding collection of English printed cottons and linens, 1760–1800.

Scope of the Textile Collection

The Textile Study Room holds most of the Met's textile collection and is thus a repository for several departments within the museum. An approximate breakdown of these holdings by region is shown below:

Western Europe	20,000
Far East	7,000
(China, Japan, Southeast Asia)	
Americas	850
(Chiefly U.S. & Mexico)	
Pre-Columbian	150
(Chiefly Peru)	
Near East	3,500
(Includes India &	
Coptic Egypt)	
Medieval	200
	31,800

The following paragraphs provide more detailed information on these categories:

Western European Collections

Lace. The Met holds one of the largest and most important collections of lace in the world—about 5,000 pieces.

It covers all types of lacework from the 16th through the 20th Century. In effect it provides a complete history of lace making with examples from all periods and not only from the countries of Western Europe but also from Africa, Greece, Scandinavia, and czarist Russia.

METROPOLITAN MUSEUM cont'd

It carries the lace art from its earliest beginnings as a handcraft to the development of machine-made lace. In addition to all types of needle and bobbin lace, it owns examples of such variations as applied work, cutwork, drawnwork, crochet, knitting, macramé, network, tatting, sprang, raised work, and bebilla.

(A brief and illuminating history of lace, based on the Met collection, was written by Ruth P. Hellmann to accompany her exhibit of historic laces from the Met. It was shown at Adelphi University, Garden City, N.Y. from April 1 to June 1, 1973. A copy of the essay can be consulted in the Textile Study Room.)

Embroidery. The Met's embroidery collection contains some 2,500 pieces and covers six centuries—from 14th-Century Italian work to 20th-Century examples from England, France, Germany, Hungary, Italy, Portugal, Switzerland, and the U.S.S.R. In between there are fine examples of embroidery made in all the countries of Western Europe, in the Greek Islands, in Scandinavia, and in czarist Russia, as well as in China and India for European export. (It should be noted that this range does not include the Met's important collections of embroidery from the Far East, Near East, and ancient Peru—all cataloged under those regional headings.)

One of the strongest sections of the embroidery division is a large number of English domestic embroideries which came to the museum in the Irwin Untermyer Collection. Other strong groups are those from the Greek Islands, from 18th-Century France, and from the East India trade during the 17th through the 19th Centuries. Embroidered coverlets, quilting, and canvas work from many sources are also especially well represented.

Samplers. The collection of samplers is large and exceptionally fine. There are some 900 pieces covering a period from the early 17th through the 19th Century and representing 16 different countries. These are: Austria, England, France, Germany, Greece, Holland, Hungary, Ireland, Italy, Roumania, Scandinavia, Scotland, Spain, Sweden, Switzerland, and Wales.

Wovens. Western European woven fabrics make up the largest single category in the collection—about 6,000 pieces. They date from the 15th Century to the present and cover virtually all important historic constructions in the weaving lexicon, as well as all key sources on the European continent.

(Not included in this unit are woven fabrics from Coptic Egypt, Ancient Peru, or the Near East, which add up to at least 2,500 additional pieces.)

Within the Western European unit one of the strongest groups is made up of about 1,000 velvets dating from the 15th Century forward and covering most of the major velvet-producing centers in Italy, Spain, France, England, and the Low Countries.

Another strong group is French in origin, with special emphasis on drawloom and jacquard silks of the 17th, 18th, and 19th Centuries. Many of the most famous French designers and producers of silk textiles are identified by name in the collection.

A smaller but very choice group contains examples of English silk weaving made in Spitalfields during the 18th Century.

In sum, the Met's collection of woven textiles is one of the most outstanding in the world and offers researchers a comprehensive picture of the weaving craft throughout its long history.

Tapestries. As everyone knows, the Met owns the world-renowned Unicorn tapestries which are permanently exhibited in The Cloisters—a branch of the Met at Fort Tryon Park, N.Y.C. But these are far from the only important tapestries in the Met holdings.

The museum owns about 200 tapestry works dating from 14th-Century Franco-Flemish pieces to a 20th-Century Aubusson work designed by Lurçat and one of William Morris' later panels.

In between these two poles most major centers and periods of tapestry weaving are covered, including those of France, Switzerland, Flanders, Germany, Belgium, Holland, Italy, Portugal, Norway, Sweden, and czarist Russia.

Painted Fabrics. A small group of about 75 painted textiles from Austria, China (export), France, India (export—painted/dyed), Spain, and Sweden. Most of the pieces date from the 18th through the 19th Century.

Prints. The Met owns some 2,000 printed fabrics made in Western European countries. There is representative work from more than a dozen nationalities, a few dating from the 16th Century. The strongest part of the collection, however, covers

RIGHT. French or Spanish velvet (*velours miniature*), 18th Century. Rogers Fund. *Metropolitan—61.205 (173298 tf).*

BELOW. French beaded bag, 19th Century. Bequest of Catherine D. Wentworth, 1948. *Metropolitan—48.187.653 (144556B).*

English and French printing during the "great" period of the 18th and 19th Centuries—woodblock and copperplate.

In this area there are English prints from such important sources as Old Ford, Bromley Hall, Crayford, Nixon & Co., Bannister Hall, Woolmers, Shepley Hall, John Burg (Lancashire), Wandsworth, and the William Morris Co.

Among the French prints are pieces designed by Huet, Pillement, Vernet, and many other well-known artists working for the country's leading printworks. The collection owns representative work from factories in Alsace, Munster, Beautiran, Bordeaux, Jouy, Marseilles, Melun, Montpellier, Nantes, Rouen, Orleans, and Orange.

Rugs. The Department of Western European Art owns about 100 rugs dating from the 16th Century. The most recent are 20th-Century rugs from Austria, Bulgaria, and France. There are also examples of rugs made in England (18–19th Century), France (17–20th Century), Roumania (18th Century) and Spain (17–19th Century).

(In addition to rugs from Western European countries the museum also owns a large collection of rugs from the Near East and smaller groups from the Far East and America.)

Knits. The Textile Study Room and the Islamic Department between them hold perhaps 75 knitted pieces—from the Near East, Kashmir, Germany, and a larger number from the U.S. The latter are chiefly Vogue Award knits of the recent past.

Trimmings. A large collection of at least 1,500 pieces dating from the 16th to the 20th Century. They consist of such decorations as cords, fringes, galloons, gimps, passementerie, ribbons, and tassels. There are examples of work from each century since the 16th, and the largest number of pieces are of French, Italian, English,

and Spanish origin.

Fans. This is a major collection of fans numbering about 800 pieces—an interesting source of textile design ideas. The earliest pieces come from 17th Century Italy, and the largest number are from 18–19th-Century France. Other examples were made in China and Japan for European export, Belgium, Holland, England, Germany, Spain, and czarist Russia.

Costume. In addition to very choice pieces in the Untermyer Collection the Textile Study Room has a small group of Western European costumes and accessories which are not part of the collection at the Met's Costume Institute. They are kept in the Textile Department to demonstrate different textile techniques. Of such, there are about 50 peasant costumes and some 500 accessories. Among them are aprons, bags, bodices, boxes, kerchiefs, shawls, waistcoats, and other pieces which are rich in textile design motifs.

Vestments. This group consists of about 100 ecclesiastical vestments dating from the 15th through the 19th Century. Countries represented are Austria, Belgium, France, Germany, Greece, Italy, the Netherlands, Portugal, czarist Russia, and Spain.

Sample Books. This is a most important collection of sample books containing many thousands of swatches and therefore a rich resource for designers. In all there are almost 150 such volumes—English, French, German, Austrian, and American. Some date from the latter part of the 18th Century and into the first third of the 19th Century. Others are of more recent date, but all reveal a fascinating record of public taste in textiles as shown in the production runs of commercial houses over a period of more than 200 years. A number of these large volumes are salesmen's sample books. An especially interesting one of this type is French and dates from the 1770s. It shows a wide range of woolens, linens, and corduroys, many in striped patternings.

Far Eastern Collection

The Far Eastern textile holdings contain large collections from Japan and China, as well as small groups from several regions in Southeast Asia. In all there are over 7,000 pieces in this category, broken down into the following approximate numbers:

Japan	5,000
China	2,000
Southeast Asia	230
	7,230

A more detailed description of these holdings follows.

Japanese Textiles. This is the largest group in the Far Eastern category, holding some 5,000 pieces of Japanese textile and costume art. There is a wide range of materials, strongest in work of the 17th

METROPOLITAN MUSEUM cont'd

to the 19th Century but including a number of earlier silk weavings from the 15th Century.

Woven fabrics in this group number about 300 pieces, including early silks used as tribute, hangings, curtains, panels, woven pictures, brocades, velvets, compound weaves, and damasks. Some of the more elaborate weavings have been made into sword guard cases. There are also several good examples of Japanese tapestry work (tsuzure) and a few rugs.

The embroidered group is smaller, with about 75 pieces, including fragments of robes and hanging temple scrolls.

Printed fabrics number about 150 pieces, originating in a dozen different regions of Japan. There are many resist-dyed fabrics (kasuri), as well as a number of folk textiles printed by stencil.

The actual stencils used to make these cotton fabrics are one of the most interesting groups in the collection. There are more than 450 of them stored in the Textile Study Room, and they are a delight to examine. Many of them are early work in which the unconnected sections of the stencil are held together by a fine web of human hair. Others have patterns so finely cut or pricked that they would produce fabrics with the most intricate and subtle overall textures. The skill which went into such stencil making is an ancient folk craft in Japan and is still practiced today. For myself—and I suspect for many designers—these stencils are among the richest treasures in the whole collection.

Japanese Costume. An interesting and varied group with about 400 pieces of flat-fold costume and different types of accessories. There are folk kiminos, obis, uchikake, hats, wrestlers' costumes, a large number of priests' robes, and a notable small collection of Nō costumes, which is

considered by many to be the finest group held anywhere outside of Japan.

Japanese Connoisseur Collections. Though these textiles consist almost entirely of woven fabrics, they are separately stored and cataloged in the Textile Study Room, and they deserve special attention. The Met has designated them as Connoisseur Collections since they were assembled by connoisseurs of Japanese textiles rather than as records of industry. The largest are the Havemeyer Collection, the Hattori Collection, and the Frank Edward Sherman Collection.

What are they? A vast study collection of some 3,500 choice fabric swatches, large and small, all handsomely mounted on decorative panels and each piece separately numbered. The pieces themselves are elaborately patterned brocades and other complicated weaves dating from the 17th through the 19th Century. There are floral and geometric designs of infinite variety, mostly in subtle colorings, and predominantly small in scale. In addition there are books of miniature stencil designs, printed cottons, and other decorated fabrics.

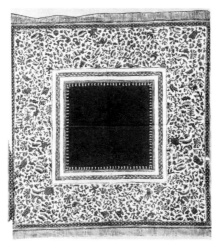

These "connoisseur" textiles reveal a degree of weaving skill which is a high point of the weaver's craft. Among the many woven-fabric collections I have examined, this group stands out in my mind as one which will probably be among the most useful I have seen for the practical day-to-day work of designing commercal textiles. And not only for woven design: the motifs and the small-scale geometrics would make excellent print designs.

Chinese Textiles. The collection of fabrics from China, though not as large as the Japanese group, is a most important one with many fine examples of weaving and embroidery art going back to the T'ang Dynasty (618–907 A.D.). In all there are approximately 2,100 pieces in this group, broken down into the following categories.

Embroideries. About 500 pieces including banners, hangings, valances, covers, curtains, scrolls, screen panels, appliqué, sutra covers, and other decorative work. They cover a period from the 9th to the 19th Century.

Wovens. More than 700 pieces, covering a time span from the T'ang to the Ch'ing Dynasty (1644–1912). There are export and tribute silks, early fragments of intricate weaves, temple hangings, damasks, double cloths, gauze, and an important group of about 75 velvets, some of them early pieces.

In addition there is an interesting group of about 100 silk tapestries (k'o-ssu), one of them from the 14th Century.

Also 45 rugs, 9 screens, and 16 elbow pillows in a variety of techniques.

Costume. This is a large and quite spectacular group of more than 700 costumes and at least 100 accessories, which reveals Chinese weaving and embroidery skills in their most elaborate forms.

Among the costumes are a large number of Imperial court robes which represent one of

RIGHT. Woven cloth, Egypto-Arabic, 11th Century. Rogers Fund, 1929. *Metropolitan—29.136.1 (77003B).*

BELOW. Chinese Lamaist dancer's robe of satin brocade, early 19th Century. Gift of Mrs. Edward A. Nis, 1934. *Metropolitan—34.80.1 (97127B).*

the outstanding collections of this kind in the Western Hemisphere. In addition to robes which once belonged to members of the Imperial families, there are many other garments indicating the ranks of different court officials. There are also a number of more informal decorated garments, as well as the robes of priests and resplendent theatrical costumes.

Among the accessories are many rank badges showing positions at the Imperial Court. Also embroidered sleeve bands, cap finials, circular mirror cases, fans, shawls, and many other intricately decorated pieces.

In many cases the pieces in the Chinese collection can be so magnificent that a researcher may conceivably be dazzled into seeing them as treasures rather than as sources of textile design. This would be a mistake, for this is rich and rewarding source material, full of ideas for the contemporary designer.

Other Asian Textiles. Compared to the Chinese and Japanese collections the group from Southeast Asia and Indonesia is relatively small—about 230 pieces in all. However, it is choice and quite representative of the different cultures included. As might be expected, this whole category contains many fine examples of batik and ikat work. There are also Tibetan, Mongolian, and Korean examples—each with about 10 or so pieces.

American Wing Fabrics. The Met's American Wing holds art objects not only from the United States but also from Central America and the Caribbean, as well as from pre-Columbian South America, chiefly ancient Peru. It is not a large collection—about 1,000 pieces in all—but it has many fine pieces and it should grow rapidly in the future since it is being given increasing attention. Its main holdings are listed below:

Needlework—Prints—Wovens. In the needlework category the collection owns about 300 pieces dating from the 17th to the 20th Century and including a fine collection of early American patchwork quilts, which was the subject of a special museum exhibit and brochure in 1974. In addition to quilts there are bed hangings, a variety of decorated furnishings, a group of some 75 samplers, and 35 rugs, including several rare bed ruggs.

Printed and painted fabrics number about 300 and date from the 18th to the 20th Century. The later pieces include contemporary tie-dye and batik work which received a Vogue award.

Woven fabrics number about 200 pieces, date from the 17th Century forward, and include a good collection of U.S. coverlets, weavings of the Navajo Indians, and work from both Mexico and Guatemala. There is also a small group of about 35 laces, some of which were made in Cuba, Jamaica, Mexico, and the Barbados.

Ancient Peru. The collection of pre-Columbian fabrics from Peru is outstanding. There are perhaps 150 pieces in the

group and many are in a fine state of preservation. They cover the major periods of Peruvian textile art—from at least 1000 B.C. to the post-Conquest period in the 16th Century. There are examples of weaving, embroidery, lace, textile painting, and feather work. The periods and cultures covered include: Pre-Nazca, Early Nazca and Paracas, Tiahuanaco, Late Chimu, Coast Transitional, Highlands, Inca and the post-Conquest Colonial period.

Medieval Textiles—The Cloisters. Between the Medieval Department, the Textile Study Room, and The Cloisters (a separate branch of the Met devoted to medieval art) the museum owns more than 200 medieval textiles—not including tapestries. Most of them date from the 10th to the 16th Century, though a few embroideries in the Byzantine tradition extend into the 17th Century.

Of the total, over 100 are woven fabrics, about 75 are embroidered pieces, and at least 25 are ecclesiastical garments. Among the countries represented by this work are Austria, Bohemia, England, Flanders, France, Germany, Italy, Russia (Eastern Catholic), and Spain.

Near Eastern (Islamic) Fabrics. The Islamic Department, as already noted, is the only department at the Met which currently provides major exhibit space for its textiles. For this it can draw upon a rich and extremely varied collection which numbers over 3,500 pieces and includes one of the world's largest holdings of Coptic tapestry fragments.

A brief breakdown of the Islamic collections follows.

Islamic Rugs. A notable collection of over 300 pieces from many sources including the Near East, Central Asia, Egypt, India, Persia, and Turkey.

Islamic Printed & Painted. There are more than 200 pieces in this category.

METROPOLITAN MUSEUM cont'd

Among them is the Met's outstanding collection of painted-and-dyed cottons from India, those exotic and colorful designs which created a great fashion vogue in Europe during the 17th–18th Century. The group also holds a fine collection of batiks made in the Dutch East Indies from the 19th to the 20th Century, as well as Persian, Mesopotamian, and Yemenite prints of the 14th to the 19th Century.

Islamic Woven Textiles. The department owns more than 500 woven textiles dating from the 5th to the 19th Century. The Persian group is particularly strong with fine examples of Sassanian and Seljuk weavings. Another strong group is Ottoman Turkish dating from the 16th to the 19th Century. There is work from Armenia, Egypt, India, North Africa, Morocco, Spain (Hispano-Moresque), Syria, Sumatra, and Turkestan. Examples of early velvet weaving are well represented from many of the countries already mentioned but particularly from Turkey (Brusa).

Coptic Fabrics. The Met owns one of the world's largest and most varied collections of Coptic tapestry fragments—over 1,500 pieces, many of them mounted on panels and easily examined in the Textile Study Room. They date from the 3rd to the 9th Century. In addition to this group there are 300–400 examples of other Coptic and Egypto-Arabic weavings dating from the 8th to the 14th Century, as well as a number of very early printed and painted fabrics from Egypt.

Islamic Embroideries. This is another large group of about 500 pieces—some of them dated as early as the 9th Century, others near-contemporary. Among the strongest groups are those from Persia, India, Morocco, Bokhara, and Turkey.

Islamic Costume & Accessories. This final group in the Near Eastern collections hold about 250 pieces, including both religious and secular costumes from more than 20 regions which at one time or another came under the control and influence of Islam. Among the costumes are also a number of accessories such as laces, fans, trimmings, tunics, caps, shawls, saris, bags, and handkerchiefs—all interesting sources for contemporary textile design.

Department of Prints & Photographs. This department of the Met deserves mention here as a source of textile design ideas. Among its holdings are several thousand textile designs on paper, but only a small proportion of these will be of interest to most designers. I noted the following.

1. A textile design idea book maintained by an English silk house—F. W. Grafton & Co., Ltd.—during the 18th and 19th Centuries. It contains about 1,800 print designs, either on paper or cloth, measuring anywhere from one inch square to 20 × 15 inches. Many of the designs are French; some are excellent.

2. A swatch book containing several hundred early 19th-Century Paisley designs. The book was assembled in France, but the designs come both from India and Europe. The volume came to the museum from the Everfast Collection.

3. Nine hand-bound scrapbooks and sketchbooks from the Collection of Benjamin E. Marks. They contain hundreds of rough sketches for textile and wallpaper designs.

4. A large French sample book containing 262 colored woodblock impressions of designs for shawls. Dated Paris, 1870–1880.

5. Eight superb hand-painted design motifs for Kashmir shawls. They were brought to England from India in 1823 by William Moorcroft.

6. Some 200 early printed pattern books for lace and embroidery, most of them printed in France, Italy, and England.

7. Several portfolios of stencil designs for furniture.

8. A number of paper patterns for lace making—with the pin holes punched through.

9. Bound volumes of French and English floral designs for textiles.

10. A number of woven designs graphed on point paper.

NOTE: The facilities of the Print Department are available to researchers by appointment only.

The Cloisters. For those who do not know this branch of the Met it should be said that the museum building itself is the reconstruction of a medieval complex formed of several authentic cloisters and other European structures. It is set on a hill overlooking a magnificent sweep of the Hudson River. Its collection of textiles is small, but it is exactly the right place in which to examine medieval fabrics—especially the Unicorn tapestries for which the museum is world renowned.

In addition to the Unicorn tapestries the Cloisters holds about 25 other tapestries dating from the 14th to the early 16th Century. It also owns a number of 14th- and 15th-Century ecclesiastical embroideries,

including two of the rare St. Martin embroideries, four Franco-Flemish roundels, and seven Florentine pieces.

Among its other holdings are a 15th-Century woven hanging from Burgundy and about a dozen vestments—Italian, Spanish, and English—of the 13th to 15th Century. Also two large 15th-Century Hispano-Moresque rugs.

The Costume Institute. The Met's Costume Institute is not properly a subject for this volume since, unlike other costume collections, it is entirely separate from the museum's textile department. However, since costume holdings in other major museums have been listed, this most important collection cannot be left unrecorded in this review.

It is one of the largest international costume collections in the United States with some 20,000 pieces, including accessories. It covers a period from 1690 to the present, and its strongest representation is in fashionable women's clothes from Europe of the 19–20th Century. However, it has substantial holdings from the 18th Century and representative pieces from the cultures of the Near and Far East, as well as ethnological costumes from countries in Asia, Africa, and the Americas.

Its facilities for study are among the finest in the world. It has climate-controlled storage—and plenty of it, so that individual garments are easy to examine. It has a comprehensive catalog system and it has study rooms for designers. It is frequently used by textile designers who want to know how a design might look after cutting and sewing the cloth.

The Costume Institute maintains its own library with some 22,000 bound volumes and periodicals covering the history of costume art throughout the world. It also owns thousands of individual fashion plates, chiefly of the 19th Century.

Publications. Following is a list of Met publications related to textiles.

1. The museum's *Bulletin*, now a quarterly publication, has published many articles on textiles. They are too numerous to list here, but an index of articles can be consulted in the museum library and bound issues of the publication are available in the Textile Study Room.

2. *English Domestic Needlework of the 16th, 17th, and 18th Centuries.* By Preston Remington. 1945. Paper. 80 pages, 70 illustrations.

3. *The St. Martin Embroideries.* By Margaret B. Freeman. 1968. 132 pages, with 120 illustrations.

4. *Islamic Carpets.* By Joseph V. McMullan. 1965. 387 pages, 152 illustrations (123 in color). Many of the rugs described are in the Met collection.

5. *Oriental Rugs in the MMA.* By M. S. Dimand & Jean Mailey. 1973. 356 pages, 141 illustrations (19 in color).

6. *Chinese Textiles.* By Alan Priest & Pauline Simmons. 1934. New edition of a 1931 exhibition handbook.

7. *Chinese Patterned Silks.* By Pauline Simmons. 1948.

8. *The Unicorn Tapestries.* By James J. Rorimer. 1938.

9. *The Nine Heroes Tapestries.* By James J. Rorimer & Margaret B. Freeman. 1953. These tapestries are at The Cloisters.

10. *The Textile Collection & Its Use.* May, 1915. A *Bulletin* supplement.

11. *Painted & Printed Fabrics.* By Henri Clouzot & Frances Morris. 1927. Translated from the French. This is the definitive story of the famous printworks at Jouy and other parts of France from 1760 to 1815. (Recent scholarship indicates that some of the plate prints are English, not French.)

12. *The Irwin Untermyer Collection—Catalogue, Volume IV.* By Yvonne Hackenbroch. 1960.

This volume deals with the needlework, tapestries, and textiles in the Untermyer Collection.

13. *Coptic Tunics in the MMA.* By Maurice S. Dimand. 1928.

14. *Dated Egypto-Arabic Textiles in the MMA.* By Joseph M. Upton. 1928.

15. *An Early Cut-Pile Rug from Egypt.* By Maurice S. Dimand. 1928.

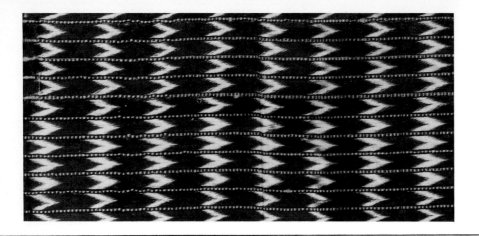

A piece of woven silk-cotton from India, 18–19th Century. Gift of Cranbrook Academy of Art/Museum, 1946. *Metropolitan—46.37.1 (136313 LS).*

NEW YORK CITY

Museum of the American Indian

Broadway at 155th Street
ZIP: 10032   TEL: (212) AU 3-2420

Frederick J. Dockstader, Director
G. Lynette Miller, Registrar

The Museum of the American Indian (Heye Foundation) is one of the most attractive facilities of its kind that I know. Ethnographic museums are often so large as to be overwhelming. This one is small enough to be coped with in a single visit. It is filled to capacity with exciting and well-lit exhibits.

Even so, the exhibits reveal only one-tenth of what the museum owns. The rest is stored in the Research Annex at a different location (see Research Facilities).

In the museum itself, permanent exhibits are arranged on three floors by specific regions and cultures. Most of these exhibits contain examples of different fabric techniques as an integral part of the cultures which used them. They are rich in exciting designs for wovens, prints, knits, embroideries, and appliqué.

The museum holdings of all types are vast. They comprise perhaps the largest and most comprehensive collection of North American Indian artifacts in the world. And since textiles played a major role in these cultures, that role is reflected in great detail.

It is a major collection of textiles and costume, representing not only North America but also Middle and South America, as well as pre-Columbian Peru.

The statistics are impressive. Woven fabrics alone number about 8,500 pieces. They are the smallest part of the collection—though often the largest in dimensions. In addition, the museum estimates that it owns about 100,000 pieces of decorative beadwork and some 15,000 examples of Indian quillwork. In all, close to 125,000 pieces of woven and applied design in textiles and costumes.

Below is a detailed list of these holdings, broken down into four major categories: pre-Columbian, North American, Middle American, and South American.

Pre-Columbian

North America. 900–1600 A.D. About 25 pieces. Fragments of textiles from the eastern and southwestern United States.

Peru. 1–1600 A.D. About 1,250 pieces. A wide range of fabrics from several areas and cultural periods—Paracas to Inca.

North America

Eskimo. 1850–1925. About 300 pieces. Garments and other objects of fur and woven grass. Among these are furs and skins with appliqué and patchwork designs.

Northwest Coast. 1825–1925. About 75 pieces. Garments and ceremonial textiles, including button blankets, Chilkat blankets, and woven cedarbark.

Northern Canada. 1775–1925. About 150 pieces. Chiefly garments, including examples of woven quillwork and moose-hair embroidery.

Great Lakes. 1825–1960. About 2,500 pieces. Garments and other textile work, including silk ribbon appliqué, beaded and quilled decorations, twined bags, sashes, and early printed fabrics of European origin.

Eastern Woodlands. 1825–1970. About 1,000 pieces. Garments and other textiles, including braided corn husk, sashes, beadwork, and early printed fabrics of European origin.

Southeast. 1825–1960. About 600 pieces. Garments and other materials, including Seminole patchwork, silk-ribbon appliqué, beadwork, and early printed fabrics of European origin.

Southwest—Navajo. 1850–1950. About 250 pieces. Garments, blankets, rugs, and belting.

Southwest—Other. 1850–1972. About 600 pieces. Garments and other materials, including Pueblo embroidery and brocades as well as Chimayo blankets.

Middle America

Mexico. 1800–1970. About 100 pieces. Saltillo blankets, ponchos, and serapes. Garments, huipiles, belting, and headwear. 1890–1965. About 250 pieces.

Guatemala. 1875–1970. About 300 pieces. Garments, huipiles, skirts, belting, headwear, and yardage.

Panama. 1875–1970. Cuna molas. About 100 pieces.

South America

Lowland Brazil, Peru, & Ecuador. 1890–1970. About 350 pieces. Bark cloth, woven cloth, and belting.

Venezuela & the Guianas. 1900–1970. About 100 pieces. Bark cloth, belting, yardage, and hammocks.

Argentina & Chile. 1850–1950. About 100 pieces. Saddle bags, blankets, ponchos, and belts.

Peru & Bolivia. 1850–1970. About 250 pieces. Ponchos, belts, hats, blankets, and weaving kits.

Equipment. The holdings from many of the above areas include equipment used to produce textiles—backstrap looms, spindles, templates, stencils, and stamps used in fabric printing.

Research Facilities

Slide Collection. The slide collection on the first floor of the museum is large and well organized. I would recommend that it be explored after the exhibits have been seen. It contains a total of some 2,500 color

RIGHT. Half of a cotton poncho with woven and painted decoration, 45" long. Barbados Indians of Rio Marahon, Peru. *Museum of the American Indian—14/6353 (33923).*

BELOW. Appliqué mola, Cuna Indians, San Blas Islands, Panama. It measures 16" × 20". *Museum of the American Indian—23/861 (31973).*

slides, a large number of them on textiles. They are easily viewed on sliding vertical panels against a light box. All of them can be purchased from the museum at 75 cents each. To me this is the most helpful working tool a designer could find in any museum.

Negative File. In addition to color slides, the museum maintains a large B/W negative file in the photographic department on the fourth floor. There are thousands of negatives, arranged by numbers which correspond to listings in an adjacent card index, cataloged by subject and region. B/W prints of these negatives can be ordered from the museum.

Research Annex. Since the museum holdings are so vast and no more than one-tenth of the collection can be exhibited in the present building, the remaining nine-tenths is kept in storage at the Research Annex. This is located at 3401 Bruckner Boulevard, Bronx, N.Y. 10461. TEL: TA 8-6969. However, the whole collection is accessible to qualified researchers by appointment. This should be made with the Research Annex curator, Vincent Wilcox.

Library. Since space is at a premium in the Broadway building, the museum's extensive library is also housed in a separate facility. The address is 9 Westchester Square, Bronx, N.Y. 10461. TEL: TA9-7770. Here are kept some 40,000 volumes dealing with all aspects of Indian life in the Americas. The library is accessible to researchers but here, too, an appointment must be made in advance with the librarian, Ruth Wilcox.

Publications. Some 400 titles have been published by the museum on various aspects of Indian life, past and present. Among them are a number on Indian textile crafts. A full catalog of these titles is available from the museum.

NEW YORK CITY

Museum of the City of New York
Fifth Avenue at 103rd Street
ZIP: 10029   TEL: (212) 534-1672

Joanne Olian, Costume Curator

The handsome Georgian mansion which houses the New York City Museum holds no textile collection as such, but it is nevertheless an interesting resource for textile designers. It documents the decor of New York homes and the dress of New Yorkers from the period of early Dutch settlement to modern times.

From the viewpoint of textile designers at least four areas of the museum should be rewarding:

1. The Costume Gallery—second floor. Here are installed six alcoves revealing New York interiors over the past three centuries, together with mannikins dressed in costumes worn from 1690 to 1906.

2. The fifth-floor installation of two rooms from the late-19th-Century home of John D. Rockefeller. The furnishing textiles in these rooms are all interesting.

3. The third-floor toy gallery, which displays a fine collection of dollhouses in the prevailing styles of 18th- and 19th-Century New York homes.

4. The reserve storage areas of the museum, which are accessible by appointment. They hold a large collection of costumes, many in 18th-Century French and English silks. Also stored here are 19th-Century Kashmir and silk shawls as well as good collections of lace and embroidered men's waistcoats.

LEFT. *Orange Garden*, an appliquéd wall hanging by Shirley Kallus (U.S.), 1924. 25½" wide. Purchase prize, Michigan Artist Craftsmen Exhibit, 1963. *Detroit Institute of Arts*—63.44 (12729).

BELOW. *Gris, Noir, Rouge*—a wool Aubusson tapestry designed by Jean Arp and woven at Atelier Tabard Frères et Soeurs (France) in 1958. 60" × 52". Gift of Mrs. Suzette Morton Zurcher. *Art Institute of Chicago*—1958.527 (A19134).

NEW YORK CITY

Museum of Contemporary Crafts
29 West 53rd Street
ZIP: 10019   TEL: (212) 977-8989

Paul J. Smith, Director

The Museum of Contemporary Crafts is a very special kind of resource for designers since it owns representative works from many of the leading figures in the art-fabric movement. These are in its permanent collection. In addition, it owns a fully representative collection of work by the late Dorothy Liebes. And—perhaps even more important—its affiliation with the American Crafts Council extends its resources with dossiers and color slides on the work of some 500 artists in thread.

Among the artists represented in its permanent collection are the following: Lili Blumenau, Rubin Eshkanian, Mildred Fischer, Trude Guermonprez, Ted Hallman, Sheila Hicks, Mariska Karasz, Glen Kaufman, Jack Lenor Larsen, Dorothy Liebes, Alice Parrott, Mary Walker Phillips, Lenore Tawney, Claire Zeisler, and Nell Znamerowski.

The Dorothy Liebes bequest includes 13 of her major pieces (both hand- and power-loomed), as well as 65 large samples of the trend-setting color work and craftlike constructions which she designed for machine-made textiles.

Craft Library. The museum's facilities are vastly extended through the neighboring library of the Research & Education Department, American Crafts Council, at 44 West 53rd Street (TEL: 977-8976). Here the researcher will find over 2,000 volumes on contemporary crafts, the largest section of which is devoted to the textile crafts. The library also maintains a complete file of contemporary crafts magazines.

Beyond this the library files comprehensive dossiers on many of the leading workers in the crafts movement. At least 500 such dossiers are devoted to artists in the textile crafts. It provides resumes of their careers and photographs of their works. Also on file are hundreds of color slides showing major pieces by many of these artists.

Portable Museum. The Research & Education Department also offers for rental or sale a large selection of 35mm slide kits on all aspects of the crafts movement. Among them at this writing are 22 kits on textiles. Of special interest from my point of view is a kit titled *Masterpieces of Western Textiles* (Number C11). It contains 140 slides of pieces in the Chicago Art Institute collection. A descriptive catalog of these kits is available from the department by writing to the address noted earlier.

Publications. The American Crafts Council also issues a catalog of its publications which includes eight handbooks of museum exhibits devoted to the textile arts. Most of these have become collector's pieces, and each of them contains provocative ideas for contemporary textile design.

NEW YORK CITY

The Musem of Modern Art
11 West 53rd Street
ZIP: 10019   TEL: (212) 956-6100

Arthur Drexler, Director
Architecture & Design

The MOMA collection of textiles is small but unique since it holds examples of work from the Bauhaus period and the Wiener Werkstaetten, as well as trend-setting wall hangings by contemporary American artists in thread.

Among the 250-odd pieces in the collection the following should be important to designers and students of textiles.

Anni Albers. A former teacher at the Bauhaus, Anni Albers has long been one of the seminal influences on modern art fabrics. MOMA owns about 60 of her pieces. They are chiefly from the period 1925–1933, but a few extend to 1949. Some are part of the industrial-design collection she made at her studio in Dessau.

Gunta Stölzl. Another important designer-weaver whose work is identified with the Bauhaus. The museum owns about 50 examples of her work, covering a period from 1923 to 1966. Many are woven drapery designs.

Wiener Werkstaetten. A group of 18 textile print designs by Richard Riemerschmid of the Wiener Werkstaetten group. Also from the same group are a number of designs for drapery, upholstery, and table covers.

Other Designers. Among other modern art fabrics represented in the collection are works by the following: Lenore Tawney, Sheila Hicks, Mary Walker Phillips (knitted hangings), Thelma Becherer, Warren Platner, Lily Hoffmann, Dora Jung, and Claire Kosterlitz.

William Morris. Half a dozen examples of printed textiles designed by William

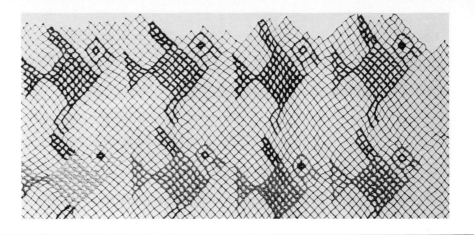

RIGHT. Peruvian gauze fragment, Chancay culture. Cotton and wool, 25" wide. *Museum of Primitive Art—61.182.*

BELOW. Fragment of tapestry-woven sash from Peru, Central Coast. *Museum of Primitive Art—57.2186.*

Morris toward the close of the 19th Century.

Contemporary Prints. A diversified group of about 100 textile prints on linen and cotton. They represent leading "good design" fabrics of the 1940s and 1950s produced by key New York houses serving the uptown decorating trade.

Study Center. Textiles in the MOMA collection can be examined in the Study Center, which is open to researchers one day a week (generally Wednesday) by appointment.

NEW YORK CITY

The Museum of Primitive Art
15 West 54th Street
ZIP: 10019   TEL: (212) CI 6-9493

Douglas Newton, Director

(Note. In early 1975 the museum galleries and library were closed, preparatory to moving the collections into a new home being built for them at The Metropolitan Museum of Art. This is expected to take place in 1976.)

This museum owns one of the world's great collections of indigenous art from Africa, North and South America, and the Pacific Islands. Among these larger holdings is a small but very choice collection of about 100 fabrics from the same regions.

One of the outstanding groups consists of extraordinarily fine pieces from ancient Peru, particularly from Tiahuanaco.

Other notable pieces include 15 large feather hangings (chiefly from Hawaii), a superb Ainu robe from Japan, excellent examples of tapa and Kente cloth from Africa, pile weaves from Zaire, Navajo blankets, and tapa from the Fiji Islands.

Research Facilities. The reasearch facilities at the museum are quite remarkable. The library holds some 14,000 volumes on indigenous art, all made easily accessible

through a geographical index file. It also includes an index of museums and private collectors in many parts of the world who own materials comparable to those in the Museum. Artifacts are also indexed by culture.

In addition, the library owns a vast photo archive of about 80,000 B/W photographs of indigenous art held in both public and private collections around the world. Again, these are classified by culture. For example, I noted at least 300 photos of Polynesian tapa cloth, an equal number on textiles from pre-Columbian South America, and large groups illustrating the textile arts of West Africa and Hawaii.

These research facilities are expected to be moved intact to the Museum's new home at the Met.

NORTH ANDOVER, MASS.

Merrimack Valley Textile Museum
Massachusetts Avenue. Box 266
ZIP: 01845   TEL: (617) 686-0191

Joyce P. Messer, Assistant Curator

The 200-year history of New England textile manufacturing is concentrated in this well-organized museum. It is a unique resource for designers and students, holding thousands of fabric samples which record the trends in commercial textile design from the middle of the 18th Century through the first half of the 20th Century.

Its chief interest is the archive of woven and printed textiles contained within some 2,300 swatch books and storage files. The following indicate the range of materials assembled here.

1. Arnold Print Works, North Adams, Mass. 60 volumes of painted cottons dating from 1890 to 1902.

2. Cocheco Print Works, Dover, N.H. 79 folders and 62 document cases of printed cottons—1881–1890.

3. Farnsworth Mfg. Co., Lisbon Center, Maine. 81 document cases of woolen suitings and coatings—1962–64.

4. Merrimack Mfg. Co., Lowell, Mass. 164 volumes of cotton shirtings and dress goods—1874–1902.

5. J. P. Stevens & Co., Inc. 1,173 volumes and 12 file cabinets of woolen samples made in the company's New England mills.

6. Strong, Hewat & Co., North Adams, Mass. 334 volumes, 208 document cases, and 11 storage boxes of woolen suitings and coatings—1899–1961.

In addition to these invaluable records the museum owns several hundred examples of 19th-Century coverlets, blankets, household linens, rugs, shawls, and woven pictures. Further details of this group follow.

Coverlets. 76 examples in all, including 32

MERRIMACK VALLEY cont'd

overshot weaves, 34 double Jacquards, and six summer/winter designs.

Blankets. 57 pieces, of which 22 are four-harness twills, 17 are embroidered "rose" blankets, and 18 are industrially made pieces in a variety of weaves.

Household Linens & Rugs. About 75 pieces in all. They include sheets, pillow cases, towels, napkins, tablecloths, and rugs. Many of the linens are in traditional damask patterns.

Shawls. 107 examples. They include Indian Kashmir shawls, Scottish Paisleys, and a number of silk pieces probably from France. There are also some knitted and lace shawls.

Pictorial Textiles. 35 examples of woven pictures made between 1840 and 1920.

Exhibits. The museum's permanent exhibits are chiefly devoted to textile machinery and the effects of the Industrial Revolution on woolen manufacturing in the United States.

Research Facilities. The museum has a library with some 25,000 books and periodicals, mainly in the field of textile technology. Included among these is a comprehensive file of U.S. Patent Office Reports covering the years 1838–1949.

There is also a large collection of manuscripts containing the records of fifteen leading textile companies in New England and the South.

The museum provides a textile study area equipped with an analytical balance and a microscope. Designer research is encouraged, and the facility is open by appointment from 9 to 5 Mondays through Fridays. Demonstrations of handspinning and weaving are held in the museum on Sundays.

Publications. Merrimack has published two lists of its textile holdings—one on its *Finished Textiles* and the other on its *Swatchbooks & Samples.* It has also issued a well-designed and well-written handbook of 108 pages (1965) which describes and illustrates the various processes used in making wool textiles. It has an excellent short review of the shift from domestic cloth making to industrial production in New England.

PALM BEACH, FLA.

Henry Morrison Flagler Museum
Whitehall Way
ZIP: 33480   TEL: (305) 655-2833

Cathryn J. McElroy, Curator

From the textile viewpoint this distinguished Palm Beach mansion is interesting for its collection of lace. There are about 280 pieces in the holdings, most of them on loan from Mrs. Flagler Matthews, President of the museum. The majority of the examples are 18th- and 19th-Century work—both bobbin and needle lace.

In addition, the museum owns about 50 costumes of the period 1900–1914; a small group of late-19th-Century ecclesiastical vestments; bed and table linens of the early 20th Century; and a dozen embroidered pictures.

The mansion which houses the museum was completed in 1902. Photographs and descriptions of the furnishing fabrics then in use are available.

PHILADELPHIA, PA.

Philadelphia Museum of Art
Parkway at 26th Street. Box 7646
ZIP: 19101   TEL: (215) PO 3-8100

Elsie McGarvey, Curator of Textiles
Christine Jackson, Assistant

Philadelphia was formerly an important production center for textiles, and its present collections of historic fabrics echo its past. At least two such collections in the city are notable, and the most important is owned by the Philadelphia Museum of Art. It ranks high in size among U.S. international collections of textiles and costume, holding a total of more than 15,000 pieces. Of these, some 6,500 are flat fabrics and 8,000 to 10,000 are costumes and accessories.

The flat fabrics in the museum are regarded as a study collection. That is, few pieces are on display in the public galleries, but all can be examined in the department's Study Room which is open to visitors by appointment. The costume holdings, however, are well displayed in a series of elegant exhibits which are changed from time to time in order to feature different facets of the holdings.

The Study Room is somewhat cramped in its facilities, but this is more than compensated for by the helpfulness of the small staff and the well-organized storage system. The department also has about 40 loose-leaf volumes of B/W photographs showing the more important pieces in the collection, and this makes it possible to survey the whole range.

Among the 6,500 pieces in the textile holdings at least eight groups are outstanding from a designer's point of view.

1. French prints of the 18th Century.

2. Italian velvets—15th to 18th Century.

3. Embroideries, Western—18th to 19th Century.

RIGHT. The Philadelphia Museum of Art seen from the Parkway, with Washington Circle in the foreground.

BELOW. French satin and brocaded silk of the early 18th Century. Gift of Mrs. George W. Childs Drexel. *Philadelphia Museum of Art—'39-1-1.*

4. Chinese sutra covers—17th to 18th Century.

5. American prints—18th to 19th Century.

6. American quilts and coverlets—18th to 19th Century.

7. Rare pattern books for woven coverlets—18th and 19th Century.

8. Samplers—over 600 pieces dating from 1662 to the end of the 19th Century. This is the famous Whitman Collection, assembled by the well-known chocolate firm which used reproductions of the samplers it its packaging. The collection contains representative pieces from America, England, Spain, Germany, Holland, France, Italy, Mexico, and several other regions. It is probably the largest collection of its kind in the world. (Most of the samplers listed later by country of origin belong to this collection.)

Further details on these and other groups follow, listed by country of origin.

America (U.S.). About 1,200 pieces in all. Printed and woven fabrics are strongest, with about 600 examples dating from the 18th Century to the present. They include printed cottons and quilt centerpieces by John Hewson, one of America's first commercial printers, who came from England in the late 18th Century and settled in the Kensington section of Philadelphia.

Equally interesting are a number of woven coverlets from Pennsylvania Dutch settlements. The American collection also includes a wide range of silks, satins, velvets, and other woven cloths, as well as a few early blue resist cottons.

Embroideries and samplers form still another large group with about 300 pieces—18th Century to the present, but strongest in 19th-Century work.

The American section also owns an important collection of sample books from The Simpson Co., predecessors to Joseph Ban-

croft & Sons and a leading textile printer in the Philadelphia area. There are some 300 of these volumes with thousands of samples, which provide a running record of commercial print-patterning trends from 1836 to 1926.

China. This is the largest single category in the collection. It holds over 1,500 examples of Chinese textile art, beginning with archaeological fragments from the Han Dynasty (206 B.C. to 220 A.D.) and ending with early 20th-Century work. The Han fragments were uncovered from graves in the Noin-Ula mountains of Northern Mongolia.

The main strength of the Chinese collection lies in 18th- and 19th-Century silks, satins, velvets, tapestry weaves, and embroideries. Also an outstanding group of sutra covers from the 17th and 18th Centuries.

Egypt. The Egyptian collection holds about 200 pieces covering a time span from the 3rd Century to the last quarter of the 19th Century. The earliest pieces are Coptic tapestry fragments from the 3rd to the

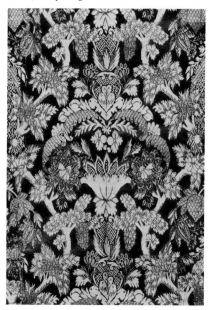

8th Century, many of them made under Graeco-Roman influence. There is also one exceptionally well-preserved complete tunic with Coptic tapestry claves and roundels. It is dated 5th to 8th Century.

About half of the collection falls into the earlier Coptic period. The other half is predominantly Islamic, chiefly 19th-Century work. Some of the pieces were acquired at the time of the 1876 Centennial.

England. About 300 examples in all. Over 200 of these are embroideries and samplers dating from the 17th to the 20th Century. The remainder—about 100 pieces—consist of printed and woven fabrics, chiefly of the 18th and 19th Centuries. They include two examples of work by William Morris.

France. This is an outstanding collection of more than 750 pieces dating from the 16th to the 20th Century. It includes a number of early woven patterned silks, satins, and velvets, but its major strength lies in 18th-Century printed toiles. There are examples of printed cottons from most of the chief production centers in 18th-Century France and from several of the famous designers associated with such printworks as those of Oberkampf at Jouy. In addition to toiles there are many smaller figured patterns and a large number of block-printed borders of the Indiennes type.

The French group also contains about 40 examples of embroidery work and samplers dating from the 17th to the 19th Century.

Germany. A small but varied group of about 90 pieces. Half of these are samplers and embroideries dating from the 17th through the 19th Century. The rest are examples of prints and woven silks from the 18th and 19th Centuries.

Greece. About 30 pieces of Greek Island embroidery—18th- and 19th-Century work.

India. About 250 examples, chiefly printed

Fragment of Turkish Karaman embroidery in wool on linen, made in the early 19th Century. Offertory Fund. *Philadelphia Museum of Art—'27-7-3.*

PHILADELPHIA MUSEUM cont'd

and woven silks, satins, and brocades dating from the 17th through the 19th Century. It also includes some 50 examples of Indian and Pakistani embroidery and needlework dating from the 17th through the 19th Century. Among them are several very unusual pieces.

Italy. Over 450 pieces. An outstanding collection with representation from the 14th to the 20th Century. Its greatest strength lies in an important group of Italian velvets dating from the 15th to the 18th Century.

Japan. About 350 pieces of printed, woven, and embroidered fabric with good representation of Japanese textile art from the 16th to the 20th Century. In addition to elaborately woven and embroidered silks, there are a number of blue resist peasant fabrics.

Persia. About 240 pieces dating from the 16th through the 19th Century. Included are printed and woven silks, satins, brocades, and velvets, as well as 40 examples of 18th- and 19th-Century Persian embroidery.

Spain. Over 250 pieces including rare examples of 14th-Century Spanish weaving art. The main strength of this collection is in velvets and satins of the 16th and 17th Centuries. It also includes some 50 examples of embroidery and sampler work dating from the 16th to the 19th Century.

Turkey. About 150 examples—satins, silks, velvets from the 16th–19th Century and embroideries of the 18th–19th Century.

Lace. Well over 600 examples of needle and bobbin lace from most of the important lace-making regions of Europe. Also a number of American and South American pieces. They date from the late 15th and early 16th Centuries up to the recent past.

Coverlet Patterns. This is a rare collection of early pattern books for coverlet designs—graphed for weaving. It contains hundreds of original designs from the 18th Century, and most are of German origin, though one volume is Pennsylvania German. Each shows a varied range of construction patterns for the then-popular woven coverlet, which was generally produced by professional handweavers. For many of these patterns the museum can provide B/W photographs, and these can be examined in the Textile Study Room.

Costume Collection. The museum's collection of costumes and accessories is one of the largest in the country. It holds between 8,000 and 10,000 pieces dating from 1720 to contemporary times. Among them are a large number of embroidered vests and many modern fashions by 20th-Century name designers, as well as a good representation of Oriental robes. Different sections of the collection are always on exhibit in a series of handsome displays where the costumes are shown on mannikins in environments suitable to the period. These are usually changed twice a year.

Publications. *Persian Textiles & their Techniques from the 6th to the 18th Centuries.* By Nancy Andrews Reath & Eleanor B. Sachs. Yale University Press. 1937.

The Story of Samplers. By Marianna Merritt Horner. Philadelphia Museum of Art. 1971.

Photographs. As already noted, many of the most important pieces in the textile collection have been photographed, and B/W prints are available from the museum's Photography Department. The same Department also carries some color slides of the same textiles. A catalog of these is available.

PHILADELPHIA, PA.

The University Museum
33rd & Spruce Streets
ZIP: 19174   TEL: (215) EV 6-7400

Claudia N. Medoff, American Section
Ellen Kohler, Registrar
Caroline Dosker, Asst. Registrar

The University Museum in Philadelphia has long been one of the most attractive museums in the country—even more so now that it has acquired a new wing with handsome exhibition galleries and a restaurant. Its collections are chiefly archaeological and ethnographic, many of them the fruit of expeditions sponsored by the University of Pennsylvania in Africa, the Americas, Asia, Egypt, Europe, the Mediterranean, the Near East, Palestine, and Oceania.

The textile/costume holdings are substantial—about 5,000 pieces. The largest group comes from the Americas—North, Central, and South—with close to 3,000 pieces. Other areas well represented are Africa, Egypt, Persia, the South Pacific, and the Far East.

A more detailed listing follows.

The Americas. Textiles from North, Central, and South America number over 2,700 pieces and are divided into five separate categories: (1) Iroquois, (2) Pacific Northwest, (3) Southwestern Indian, (4) Guatemalan, and (5) South American, chiefly from Peru. A breakdown of these categories shows the following holdings.

1. *Iroquois Sashes.* There are nine pieces from the historic period made by the finger-weaving technique. One sash is beaded.

2. *Pacific Northwest.* Eleven Chilkat blankets. Most of them were collected by Louis Shotridge, a Tlingit Indian who worked for the museum in the 1920s and 1930s. Also five bark capes from tribes other than the Chilkat.

3. *Southwestern Indian.* This group includes

RIGHT. Example of Maori finger weaving with flax yarns. *University Museum, Philadelphia—(140).*

BELOW. African tapa cloth and carved beater. *University Museum, Philadelphia.*

Pueblo, Navajo, and Chimayo weaving. The largest unit of 125 pieces is Navajo work. It includes an excellent collection of rugs, blankets, ponchos, and saddle blankets. The examples range in date from the mid-19th Century to the early 20th Century and represent varied styles such as chief's blankets, women's blankets, wedge weaves, twill weaves, etc. One of the outstanding pieces is a tapestry derived from a sand painting, known as the Clah Family Tapestry.

Pueblo weaving is represented by 22 pieces, chiefly kilts, sashes, and leggings. Most of them are either Hopi or Zuni work.

Chimayo weaving is represented by 30 pieces. These are serapes and blankets of the peoples living in the Rio Grande area which extends into Mexico. They date from the late 19th and early 20th Centuries.

4. *Guatemalan Textiles.* This is a major grouping of about 700 pieces. It contains examples of costume from 18 different departments of Guatemala, dating from both the historic and modern periods. About 400 of these textiles were collected by Lilly deJongh Osbourne. Others were assembled by Dr. Ruben Reina (Chairman of the Anthropology Department at the University of Pennsylvania) and Mrs. Josiah Marvel Greenville.

5. *South American.* This grouping includes 17 pieces of Casinua textiles from the Amazon region of Peru and one of the country's outstanding collections of ancient Peruvian fabrics. The Peruvian holdings number about 1,800 pieces in all and include tapestries, gauzes, brocades, embroidery, pouches, and a large number of fragments.

One of the highlights of this group is a blue and yellow feather skirt dating from about 1000 A.D. The oldest examples are three pieces from the Early Agricultural Period (2250–1250 B.C.). These early pieces were made either by netting, twining, or looping—rather than by true weaving. The major part of this important collection dates from the period 200 A.D. to the Conquest in 1532 A.D. Most of the pieces were collected by Dr. Max Uhle at the pioneer Pachacamac site in 1896.

The main cultures and regions represented in the Peruvian holdings are:

Pachacamac—about 1,225 pieces.

Proto-Nazca and *Nazca*—about 130 pieces. These were found in the Nazca district of southern coastal Peru.

Huaca Paraiso and *La Centinela*—110 and 93 pieces, respectively. These textiles were also collected by Uhle in 1896 at sites near Pachacamac.

Puntello Pisco—80 pieces. They come from the Pisco valley in southern coastal Peru.

Ica Valley—50 pieces. This region is also in southern coastal Peru.

Other Regions—70 pieces. These were uncovered in different sites and regions of Peru, including Caudivilla, Chira Valley, and several coastal areas.

Africa. The museum owns about 400

examples of African pile cloth—a major collection. Also a number of blue/white woven textiles from Sierra Leone.

Egypt. Another large collection, chiefly Coptic pieces. Very little information is available on this holding, but it is known to contain between 500 and 1,000 examples, including some extremely fine tapestry fragments.

Near East. A total collection of perhaps 100 pieces. The largest group of about 30 pieces comes from Persia and includes cut velvets and silk panels of the 16th–18th Century, as well as floral silk-taffeta panels and cotton prints of the 18th–19th Century. The museum also owns a large collection of fragments from Rayy (Rai, Rhagai) in ancient Persia, dating from the 1st Century A.D. Another small group of eight examples comes from Turkey and consists of pillow covers and panels dating from the 17th Century.

South Pacific. This group includes several hundred examples of tapa cloth from Hawaii and Samoa, as well as some fine pieces of featherwork from Hawaii and New Zealand (Maori).

Far East. The Far Eastern holdings are notable for a major group of over 100 Chinese mandarin squares which form the well-known Letcher Collection. They date from the 16th to the 20th Century and provide a documented source of Chinese military rank and status symbols. The Far Eastern department also owns a number of 20th-Century Chinese sashes.

Also from the Far East come small collections of East Indian textiles, Japanese Ainu robes, and Tibetan banners (tankas).

Publications. The University Museum has published a number of short articles on its textile collections in various issues of its several journals and bulletins. A complete catalog listing these shorter articles is available on request. In addition there are

UNIVERSITY MUSEUM CENTER con't

three larger works which provide valuable
research material on textiles.

*Textiles from Beneath the Temple of Pachacamac,
Peru.* By Ina VanStan. 1967. 98 pages and
83 illustrations.

Chinese Mandarin Squares. By S. Cammann.
1953. 73 pages and 35 illustrations. A brief
catalog of the Letcher Collection.

A Book of Tapa. By H. U. Hall. 1921. Volume
XII, No. 1 of *The Museum Journal*. 20 pages
and 4 illustrations.

The University Museum also publishes a
catalog of its color slides which lists 35
slides on textiles in the collection.

PROVIDENCE, R.I.

Museum of Art/R.I. School of Design
224 Benefit Street
ZIP: 02903   TEL: (401) 331-3510

Eleanor Fayerweather, Textile
Curator
Dr. Stephen Ostrow, Director

This is not a large museum, but its textile
collection compares favorably—both in size
and scope—with some held by much larger
and more publicized museums. That is because it is associated with the R.I. School of
Design where textile design studies have
always held an important position. And, of
course, it should be remembered that when
the museum was founded in 1877, Providence was central to a large and important
U.S. textile-producing area which still has
substantial facilities for the dyeing, printing, and finishing of textiles.

The textile collection at the Museum of Art
now numbers about 5,000 pieces and is remarkably varied for its size. It includes
representative pieces from most of the
important textile cultures and is outstanding in several specific areas.

The collection is also easily accessible to the
researcher and this, from my point of view,
is a paramount virtue. Many fabrics are
stored individually on rolls which are
clearly visible in flat drawers. Many
others—perhaps 2,000 or more smaller
pieces—are mounted on study cards which
are segregated by type, period, and fiber.

The Museum of Art has been very fortunate in its textile donors. Their generous
gifts have made the textile collection international in scope and very wide in range.
Among the larger gifts have been the
following.

The Lucy Truman Aldrich Collection of Far
Eastern fabrics and costume—over 300
pieces.

The Coptic Collections of Mrs. Jesse
Metcalf and Dr. Denman Ross—223 and 34
pieces, respectively.

The Marshall Gould and Bates Collections
of Chinese and Japanese fabric sample
books—12 large volumes.

The Dean Collection of trimmings and
fringes—616 pieces.

The souvenir handkerchief and print collection of Constance Wharton Smith—143
pieces.

The Francis Crosby Whitehead Collection
of 20th-Century prints, 17–19th Century
wovens, and 18th-Century toiles—400
pieces.

The Alphonse Haus Collection of printed
and woven silks from 1895–1930—369
pieces.

The large Jacob B. Ziskind Collection of
mounted 20th-Century samples (1452
pieces) and croquis (546 textile designs).
This same collection also includes 400-500
pieces of patterned woolens from the
famous Claude Frères firm, beginning in
1850.

Among the larger categories in the collection the following are outstanding.

Far East. The Aldrich Collection of Far
Eastern art is a separate unit within the
museum and has its own curator, Elizabeth
T. Casey. It holds a large and varied
collection of Oriental art, including about
300 superb examples of textile art, chiefly
from China, Japan, and India. The robes
represent many different types, and the
saris are among the most exotic I have ever
seen. Many of these pieces are on public
display behind glass, and exhibits are
changed several times a year.

Japanese Stencils. One of the largest collections of its kind. These are early textile-
printing stencils in which the open design
structure is held together by human hairs.
There are exactly 199 pieces in the group.

Japanese Prints. This is a smaller group of
43 printed cottons, some of them possibly
printed with stencils.

Oriental Sample Books. The 12 large
volumes in this collection include hundreds
of Chinese and Japanese fabric swatches,
many from the 19th Century and others
from earlier periods.

Peru. This is a large group of over 150

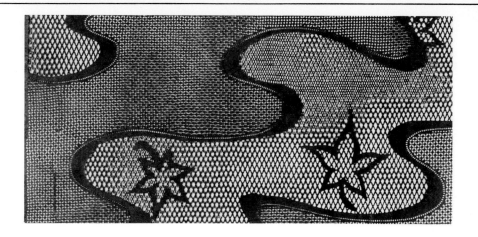

RIGHT. Japanese handcut stencil for fabric printing, about 16" wide. Bequest of Isaac C. Bates. *Museum of Art/Rhode Island School of Design—13.779.*

BELOW. Greek brocaded priest's stole, 12" wide, dated 1650–1700. *Museum of Art/ R.I. School of Design—28.011.*

pieces, chiefly representing the cultures of Chimu, Nazca, and Tiahuanaco. They cover a time span from the 5th to the 14th Century. Especially notable is a remarkably well-preserved embroidered mantle of about 500 A.D. from the Paracas region.

Batik-Ikat. Another large group of close to 150 pieces in the batik and ikat techniques from Java, Burma, and Sumatra. The Java group of batiks is especially strong with 116 pieces of early 20th-Century work.

Egypt. Over 250 fragments of Coptic tapestry weaving. The museum also holds 29 examples of Arabic textile printing from Egypt.

Persia. About 40 pieces of woven and embroidered textiles from 18th-Century Persia. Also 10 examples of painted and printed cottons.

Vestments. A substantial group of some 25 ecclesiastical vestments of the 16th to the 18th Century from France, Italy, and England.

Toiles. About 140 copperplate-printed toiles of the Jouy type. They represent French and English work of the 18th and 19th Centuries.

Arnold Print Works. This local firm played a most important role in textile printing during the 19th Century. The museum holds more than 100 of the company's sample books, showing examples of prints from 1880 forward.

Paper Designs. The collection owns 546 textile designs on paper (croquis) which, as noted, were part of the Ziskind Bequest.

Silk Brocades. A large group of about 340 pieces. Countries represented include Italy (113), Japan (77), France (71), Persia (40), Spain (17), China (10), Turkey (7), and India (6).

Silk Crepe. About 75 pieces, chiefly French and American, of the 1930s and 1940s.

Linen Damask. Just under 120 pieces, from Italy (77), France (18), Spain (10), Japan (8), and China (3).

20th-Century Prints. About 400 pieces, chiefly screen-printed silks and cottons of the recent past from France and the United States.

Lace. This is not a large group as lace collections go, but it has about 250 pieces of representative lace types from Europe.

Trimmings. Over 600 pieces, chiefly fashion trimmings and fringes, in the Dean Bequest.

Other smaller groupings in the collection include the following:

Turkey. A group of embroidered towels.

Philippines. A group of appliqué designs which are traditional to the Philippine culture.

Velvets. A small but remarkably rich group of 16th-Century velvets from Italy and other European velvet-weaving centers.

Embroidery. A modest but representative group of peasant embroideries from Eastern Europe and the Greek Islands.

Samplers. An interesting group made by students of the Balch Academy in Providence. They date from 1785 forward.

Middle East. A number of caftans and decorated textiles from the Arab countries of the Middle East.

American Indian. A small number of Indian blankets from the Hopi, Navajo, and Chilkat cultures.

Tapa Cloth. A dozen examples of decorated tapa cloth from Tonga, Hawaii, and Samoa.

Ribbons. A large sample book containing hundreds of 19th-Century French ribbons.

East India. Ten examples of the traditional painted-and-dyed cotton textiles from India.

Research Facilities. The Textile and Costume Department has a small library of specialized books in these two fields, and the museum's main reference library has over 30,000 volumes on art history.

Note. Availability of the textile collection may be limited until late 1976 due to modernization work in process.

RICHMOND, VA.

Valentine Museum—Textile Center

1015 East Clay Street
ZIP: 23219   TEL: (703) 649-0711

Mildred J. Davis, Consulting Curator
Linda Baumgarten, Associate Curator

The Valentine Museum is a private institution devoted to local history and customs, yet its combined costume-textile collection ranks among the largest of such holdings in the United States. That is because its costume division is so extensive—over 12,000 pieces.

The collection of flat textiles is more modest. It numbers about 3,000 pieces, and these, together with the costumes, are held in the museum's Textile Resource & Research Center, which was founded in 1970. One of its objectives is to cooperate with commercial houses in making textile and wallpaper reproductions of documented pieces in the collection.

The emphasis throughout the collection is on textiles and costumes either made or used in America from the 18th Century forward—particularly in the South. The large lace collection, however, is primarily European in origin. It is especially strong in lace and domestic furnishings.

The lace holdings—well over 1,000 pieces, including related needlework—are known as the Bainbridge Lace Collection. It was given to the museum by the heirs of Mabel Foster Bainbridge, a founder of the Needle & Bobbin Club. Other laces came from a study collection donated by Rollins College. The Bainbridge Collection was also conceived as a teaching tool so that it contains examples of lace-making equipment as well as an excellent library on the subject.

Another major category in the textile holdings is a large group of bed covers and decorations. There are almost 350 such pieces in all, including 139 coverlets and counterpanes, plus 124 pieced and appliquéd quilts. There are also a number of bed curtains, blankets, and lap robes. Most of these pieces are 19th- and 20th-Century work and reflect the styles of a Southern plantation culture. Altogether these bed textiles represent one of the largest holdings of its kind in the country.

Other categories in the collection: draperies and curtains (62); pillowcases and bolsters (72); tablecloths and napkins (49 sets); table covers (46); rugs (30); towels (41); centerpieces—mats and doilies (90 sets); antimacassars (11); runners for furniture (19); sheets (16); flags and banners (27); ecclesiastical textiles (20); samplers (44); other types of needlework (135).

Add to this a group of about 300 textile fragments, chiefly of domestic furnishings and apparel but also including several Coptic tapestry weavings and work by William Morris.

One unique piece among these various holdings is a textile pattern and design book which was part of the Bainbridge Collection. It dates from the late 18th Century and probably originated in Alsace. It should also be noted that the museum owns more than 400 pieces of textile and sewing equipment, including some 80 patterns for needlework and clothing.

Costumes. This major collection of costumes and accessories covers a period from the late 18th Century up to the 20th Century, including contemporary fashions by name designers. The emphasis is on clothes worn in the South.

Of the 12,300 pieces in the holdings, over 9,200 are apparel and accessories for women and girls; 1780 are for men and boys; and 820 are for infants. There are also about 500 uniforms and accompanying accessories.

Research Facilities. The Textile Center, as noted, owns an excellent library on lace. It has also become a focal point for contemporary craft needleworkers and conducts an annual Assembly for Embroiderers which attracts attendance from many parts of the country.

ST. LOUIS, MO.

The St. Louis Art Museum

Forest Park
ZIP: 63110   TEL: (314) 721-0067

Lynn E. Springer, Asst. Curator

The St. Louis Art Museum owns a modest collection of textiles and costumes—some 900 pieces divided into Western and Eastern categories. They are stored in different parts of the museum but can be seen by prior appointment. A brief listing follows.

Western Group

This group holds close to 600 pieces in eight different categories.

Lace. This is the largest single category—about 180 pieces covering a period from the 15th to the 20th Century. The chief representation is from Belgium (65 pieces), Italy (50), France (30), and England (18). There is also token representation from Spain, Ireland, Greece, the Philippines, and the United States.

RIGHT. Detail of a cotton warp ikat from Sumba, 20th Century. *M. H. de Young Memorial Museum, San Francisco.*

BELOW. Entrance to the M. H. de Young Memorial Museum, San Francisco.

Embroidery. A total of about 175 pieces—15th to 20th Century. The larger groups are from the Greek Islands (60), United States (45), England (30), and Italy (13). Also token representation from France, Ireland, Germany, Spain, Holland, Switzerland, Scandinavia, Poland, and Portugal.

Costumes & Vestments. About 65 pieces—15th to 20th Century. Representative work from Russia (28) and the United States (15). Also token examples from Armenia, Spain, Greece, France, the Philippines, Hungary, England, and Germany.

Woven Fabrics. About 60 pieces—13th to 20th Century—with representation from Italy, Spain, France, Greece, Portugal, Germany, Scotland, Sweden, and the United States. The earliest examples of weaving are from 13th-Century Italy.

Printed Fabrics. About 35 pieces—17th to 20th Century—with representation from France, England, Finland, and the United States.

Coverlets. Over 35 pieces—17th to 19th Century. Work is American, Italian, French, and Greek.

American Indian. About 15 examples of 19th-Century weaving.

Tapestries. Over 20 pieces—15th to 19th Century. The work is Flemish, Belgian, French, English, and American. The earliest work is 15th-Century Flemish.

Rugs. Sixteen pieces—15th to 20th Century. Examples are American, French, and Hispano-Moresque, the latter a 15th-Century rug.

Eastern Group

China. About 50 pieces of art fabrics and costumes dating from the 17th to the 19th Century.

Egypt. A total of 55 pieces. Of these, about 35 are Egypto-Roman, 11 are Coptic (1st to 5th Century), and the remainder are Saracenic.

Eastern Weaving. A varied group of about 125 pieces. The largest unit is Turkish—about 50 pieces dating from the 17th to the 19th Century. Persian weaving from the 16th to the 18th Century is represented by 35 pieces; India, with about 25 pieces, dating from the 17th to the 19th Century. There is also token representation from the Caucasus, Morocco, and Algeria.

Batik. A group of 15 Javanese batiks dating from the 18th to the 20th Century.

Near Eastern Rugs. The Ballard Collection of about 65 rugs from the Near East.

SAN FRANCISCO, CAL.

M. H. de Young Memorial Museum
Golden Gate Park
ZIP: 94118   TEL: (415) 558-2887

D. Graeme Keith, Curator,
Decorative Arts

The M. H. de Young Museum owns a study collection of about 1,000 pieces. Many of them are small matted swatches, but they provide researchers with an excellent representation of the textile arts throughout history. Perhaps best known is the Museum's important collection of about 90 European tapestries. It also owns excellent groups of embroidery and lace, as well as fine examples of batik, ikat, and woven work from Southeast Asia.

The bulk of the collection is kept in storage but can be examined by appointment. A more detailed listing follows, with the approximate number of pieces in each category.

Pre-Columbian Peru (50); Coptic (50); Javanese batiks (40); Sumba ikats (10); Kashmir and Paisley shawls (25); American Southwest Indian weavings (10); American patchwork quilts (30); American woven coverlets (15); American 19th-Century

damasks (20); European velvets and damasks of the 15th to the 18th Century (180); European embroideries of the 16th to the 18th Century (70); European laces (100); Oriental art fabrics from China and Japan (100); European and American printed fabrics (90); European tapestries dating from the 14th to the 18th Century, with major strength in Flemish work (90).

The costume collection, chiefly dresses, covers a period from the 18th to the 20th Century and consists of about 150 pieces.

FAR LEFT. Textile storage cabinet at the Costume & Textile Study Center, U. of Washington. The cabinet contains 6 vertical storage files, each 7' high.

LEFT. The files pull forward to expose fabrics hung on cardboard rolls and wrapped in clear plastic film.

SANTA FE, N.M.

Museum of Navajo Ceremonial Art
704 Camino Lejo
P.O. Box 5153
ZIP: 87501   TEL: (505) 983-8321

Bertha P. Dutton, Director

The collection is small but interestingly and appropriately housed in a building patterned on the hogan, or circular Navajo house. It was founded in 1937 by Mary Cabot Wheelright in order to preserve for prosperity "the full range and meaning of Navajo ceremonialism."

The textile collection, though not large, is exceptionally fine. There are some 510 pieces in all, and none are less than superior. Of these, 175 are rugs and blankets, chiefly of Navajo origin and originally in the Fred Harvey Collection. They cover the full range of Navajo rug-weaving art. In addition, there are about 100 examples of Navajo costume—kilts, skirts, dresses, sashes, ponchos, and other smaller pieces. The remainder of the textile collection consists of fragments and wool samples.

Most of the textile pieces have been photographed in color, and slides can be purchased from the museum. The collection is accessible only by appointment.

SANTA FE, N.M.

Museum of New Mexico
P.O. Box 2087
ZIP: 87501   TEL: (505) 827-2834

George H. Ewing, Director
Division of Anthropology:
Nancy Fox, Curator
Stewart Peckham, Curator-in-Charge

Museum of International Folk Art:
Nora Fisher, Curator of Textiles
Yvonne Lange, Curator-in-Charge

The Museum of New Mexico has two separate divisions which own collections of textiles and costume. One is the Division of Anthropology, which houses one of the country's most important collections of Navajo and Pueblo textiles. The second is the Museum of International Folk Art, which owns textiles and costumes from many parts of the world. Between them the two divisions hold close to 3,000 pieces.

Division of Anthropology

The collection of ethnological textiles and costumes numbers about 1,500 pieces with primary emphasis on the U.S. Southwest. It is viewed as a study collection with very little on public exhibit but with storage areas which are accessible to qualified researchers by appointment.

Navajo Weaving. The lagest single category in the holdings comprises about 900 examples of Navajo weaving in a wide and representative range of styles and materials. It includes shoulder and saddle blankets as well as dresses from the Classic to the Transition Periods. It has many and notable examples of rugs woven from handspun wools colored with vegetal dyes, in addition to others made with bayeta and commercial yarns. Most of the pieces are in tapestry or twill weaves, but there are also examples of wedge weaves, as well as "slave" blankets revealing a Mexican influence adapted to Navajo looms.

From the Transition Period come aniline-dyed blankets in handspun yarns and raveled flannel, as well as in Germantown yarns—with the typical cotton string warp. Patterning illustrates the proliferation of new design themes which typified the Transition Period.

Navajo rugs range from early bordered examples to current work. The regional pieces include styles popularized by Lorenzo Hubbell at Gandao and J. B. Moore at Crystal, as well as Two Gray Hills rugs and revivals of vegetal dyeing from Chinle and Wide Ruin. There are outline rugs, two-faced weaves, and pictorials, in addition to the so-called Yei and sand-painting rugs.

Rounding out the Navajo collection are cinches, garters, belts, throws, and pillow covers, as well as looms and weaving tools.

Clearly, this is an outstanding Navajo collection, providing the researcher with complete coverage of the textile arts for which this culture has become world-renowned.

Pueblo Textiles. This category is smaller —about 300 examples of weaving in both cotton and wool. There are plain and bordered mantas, embroidered pieces, and two examples of Hopi plaids. Also men's shoulder blankets, shirts, kilts, belts, sashes, and hair ties. In addition there are also a few examples of knitted and crocheted leggings.

Other Areas. In addition to the two major groupings, the Anthropology Division also owns smaller collections of fabrics and costumes from other cultures, among them the Huichol of Mexico. There s also a substantial collection (about 100 pieces) of Spanish-American weaving from the northern Rio Grande area of New Mexico.

Museum of International Folk Art

Among an impressive range of folk art from many parts of the world the museum owns about 1,750 examples of folk textiles and costume. It covers many periods and most textile techniques.

Very little of the collection is on permanent display, but the storage areas are well lit and easily accessible to researchers by appointment. The museum is also well known for its handsomely designed special exhibits which change three times a year. And each summer the museum sponsors a fine contemporary craft show for New Mexico's craftworkers.

Among highlights of the collection the following are notable:

RIGHT. Closeup of a fabric file. Rolls are easily removed and replaced. They hang on wooden dowels.

FAR RIGHT. Catalog cards are 5″ × 8″, with careful descriptions and a 4″-×-5″ identification photograph.

American Colonial. About 135 pieces, including examples of quilts and costumes.

American Southwest. Some 85 examples of Indian textile work.

New Mexico. Tapestries and needlework from Spanish Colonial New Mexico.

South America. About 120 examples. The major emphasis is on Andean weaving in Peru and Bolivia. Most of the pieces were collected by Florence Dibell Bartlett during the second quarter of this century. They cover a time span from the Nazca culture of 400 A.D. up to the 20th Century. All the pieces are four-selvedge weavings made on backstrap looms. There are double cloths, warp and weft float patterns, tapestry weaves, and embroidery pieces.

Mexico. More than 70 examples of Mexican weaving and costume.

Central America & Caribbean. Over 200 examples, including a number of Panamanian molas.

Africa. Close to 150 pieces, including wovens and tie-dyes.

Asia-Indonesia. A varied group of 275 pieces with examples of Indonesian batik and ikat, as well as textiles and costumes from India, Australia, and the Pacific.

Eastern Europe & Russia. About 100 examples of peasant work.

Northern Europe. Also about 100 pieces including work from Scandinavia.

Far East. A small group of about 20 pieces of folk textile art from China and Japan, including a number of printing stencils.

Costume. Folk costumes from Palestine, Hungary, and Sweden.

Publications. From the Museum of New Mexico Press.
Popular Arts of Spanish New Mexico. By E. Boyd. 1973.
Navajo Weaving Today. By Bertha P. Dutton. 1973.
1500 Years of Andean Weaving.
Indigo. Catalog available.

SEATTLE, WASH.

Seattle Art Museum
Volunteer Park
ZIP: 98112   TEL: (206) 325-2000

Willis F. Woods, Director

The Seattle Art Museum has a small collection of textiles—about 450 pieces—but it has representation from more than 30 different areas. The strongest representation comes from China, Japan, pre-Columbian Peru, and the Islamic cultures of Persia and Turkey. Further details follow.

China. This is the largest single unit in the collection—just over 100 pieces. Among them are imperial robes, mandarin squares, sutra covers, embroidered sleeve bands, and silk tapestry hangings. Particularly interesting is a set of eight Buddhist symbols in woven silk squares, dating from the 17th Century.

Japan. Another large group of over 75 pieces. Among them are 30 examples of priest's robes (kesa). The rest are chiefly fragments of Japanese weaving art in damask, brocade, gauze, and ikat (kasuri). Also a number of embroideries.

Ancient Peru. From the pre-Columbian period in Peru the museum owns 58 textiles. Most are tapestry fragments, some from the Paracas and Chimu cultures.

Islam. From the Islamic cultures of Persia and Turkey come 38 examples. Some of the Persian pieces are early fragments of gold and silver brocading, compound silks, and several shawls. There are also five examples of work from Egypt, some with kufic script.

France. French textile art is represented by 23 pieces. Among them are brocaded satins of the 17th–18th Century, black Chantilly lace, and four 18th-Century tapestries.

India. Twenty examples of Indian textile art. Among them are ten Kashmir shawls (19th Century) and a representative group of woven, painted, and embroidered pieces.

Java-Thailand-Bali. There are 18 examples of Javanese batik work and five pieces of silk woven in Thailand. Also a double ikat from Bali.

United States. Seventeen examples of the early American woven coverlet in a variety of constructions and patterns.

Scotland. Thirteen examples of the paisley shawl, both the woven and printed varieties.

Coptic. Nine examples of Coptic tapestry weaving, some dating from as early as the 4th Century.

In addition to these groups there is token representation of textile work from Africa, American Indians, Austria, Belgium, Byzantium, Flanders, Germany, Greece, Italy, Korea, Latin America, Pacific Isles, Portugal, Russia, Spain, Switzerland, and Tibet.

SEATTLE, WASH.

Costume & Textile Study Center
University of Washington
ZIP: 98195   TEL: (206) 543-1730

Virginia I. Harvey, Curator

This collection is little known outside the University of Washington, where it serves the School of Home Economics as a research center. But it deserves to be far more widely known because it is a substantial collection of over 5,000 pieces, representing many of the world's cultures and covering a time span from 1500 B.C. to the present. It was established in 1958 and its first curator was Virginia I. Harvey, known for her fine books on macramé and basketry. She was later succeeded by Diane Sugimura but has now returned to the post.

Under the direction of these enterprising curators the whole collection has been

FAR LEFT. Double-ikat silk sari from India (Orissa, Cuttack, Nuapatna). The Elizabeth Palmer Bayley Collection. *U. of Washington—58.1-394 (5341-E).*

LEFT. Woven wedding sari in silk and gold thread from India (Uttar Pradesh, Banares, Varanasi). Bayley Collection. *U. of Washington—58.2-15 (6657-C).*

BELOW. Embroidered-cotton skirt piece from India (Kashmir, Srinigar). Bayley Coll. *U. of Wash.-—58.1-325 (6938-A).*

TEXTILE STUDY CENTER cont'd

made easily accessible to researchers and can boast one of the best storage and cataloging systems available anywhere. It is so good that it is worth describing in some detail.

Each piece in the collection is cataloged on a 5-by-8-inch card, and half of each card displays a 4-by-5-inch identification photo of the piece. The other half of the card contains a description of the piece, together with its provenance, registration number, function, dimensions, technique used, photo number, donor, and storage area.

The storage facilities are the most ingenious I have yet encountered for flat textiles. They consist of two large cabinets, each 7 feet high and containing six vertical compartments. The compartments roll out sideways on floor tracks to expose fabrics rolled on cardboard tubes and visible through a covering of polyethylene film. The system keeps the fabrics uncreased and well protected against dust and light yet leaves them clearly visible when the compartment is rolled open. The fabric rolls are held on wooden dowels and are easily removed for closer examination. Over 1,000 flat fabrics are stored in this manner, and the Center generously offers to supply other museums with the construction plans.

Clearly, the holdings comprise an excellent study collection. Out of the 5,000-plus pieces in the collection, about 3,500 are flat textiles or ethnographic garments, such as shawls and ponchos, which fold flat. The remainder are costumes and accessories.

Before 1958 the collection consisted of less extensive historic textiles and costumes personally collected by Professors Blanche Payne and Grace Denny. It was a small but representative study collection with pieces from Central Europe, the Balkans, Scandinavia, the Far East, the Pacific, and Latin America. This nucleus was later expanded by substantial gifts of textiles from India, Guatemala, and a small collection of Coptic textiles on permanent loan from Yale University. The Choate Collection of lace was also acquired from the Museum of Fine Arts in Boston, as well as a further study collection of historic textiles from the Chicago Art Institute. More recently there have been gifts and loans from the Garbaty Collection, including pieces from both Europe and the Far East.

Thus today the Center holds textiles from most of the important periods in textile history. A condensed breakdown of its holdings shows the following main groups.

India. This is a varied and representative collection of woven, embroidered, and printed textiles as well as costumes and jewelry, revealing work which is typical of the different states in India; also in some of the surrounding territories. The main strength lies in 19th- and 20th-Century work, but a number of pieces date from the 18th Century.

The Indian collection numbers well over 1,000 pieces, most of which were originally

collected by Elizabeth Bayley Willis. These were acquired from her by Mr. & Mrs. Prentice Bloedel and presented to the School of Home Economics in 1958.

A more recent addition to the Indian group is a collection of some two dozen Kashmir and "Paisley" shawls.

Japan-China. A substantial group of both flat textiles and costumes illustrating many different textile techniques and covering a long time span from the 17th Century to the present.

Balkans. A large group of peasant costumes and embroideries from the Balkan states.

Guatemala. The nucleus for this representative collection was presented to the Center by the Seattle Weavers Guild. It is an excellent study collection of Guatemalan weaving.

Europe. The strongest section of the European collection consists of velvets, brocades, and satins dating from the 14th to the 17th Century. There are also representative and more modern pieces from Poland, Germany, France, Spain, czarist Russia, Britain, and the Mediterranean area.

Lace. A good range of both bobbin and needle lace illustrating most of the important European types.

Peru. A small but important group of some 130 pieces, consisting of fabrics and weaving implements from ancient Peru. They were given to the Center by Harriet Tidball.

Research Facilities. Study tables and reference works on textiles are available at the Center. Special classes are given on historic textiles and costume, as well as in handweaving and textile design. The Center offers a unique service to undergraduates and graduate students working in this field. It also conducts seminars and workshops on various aspects of its collection.

RIGHT. Meetinghouse, one of many reconstructions at Old Sturbridge Village.

BELOW. Roller- and block-printed glazed cotton with a pattern repeat of 11⅞". *Old Sturbridge—26.30.353 (B8285).*

SHELBURNE, VT.

Shelburne Museum
U.S. Route 7
ZIP: 05482   TEL: (802) 985-3344

Sterling D. Emerson, Director

The Shelburne Museum—like Old Sturbridge Village—is a series of buildings, restored and set out in the pattern of an early New England settlement. The 35 buildings in the complex are spread out over 45 acres of grounds, and several of the period houses are furnished with textiles appropriate to the time. They cover the years 1733 to 1890.

For textile designers and students the most important attraction will probably be the building known as Hat & Fragrance Unit. Here Shelburne exhibits its outstanding collection of American quilts and rugs—some 300 pieces in all. The quilts are justly famous and are considered to form one of the most important collections of its kind in the country. It includes many fine examples of all the techniques used and a wide range of distinctive and handsome patternings. The majority of them were collected by Electra Havemeyer Webb, who, together with her husband, J. Watson Webb, established the museum in 1947.

In addition to quilts and rugs, Shelburne also owns a number of woven coverlets, samplers, laces, and toiles which were not made in America but which were imported for use in New England homes. It also has costumes, chiefly of the 19th Century.

The Shelburne Museum is closed during the winter months but is open daily 9 to 5 from May 15 to October 15.

STURBRIDGE, MASS.

Old Sturbridge Village
ZIP: 01566   TEL: (617) 347-3362

Jane C. Nylander, Curator of Textiles

Old Sturbridge Village is described as "a living museum of early New England." Its large complex of exhibit buildings reconstructs the patterns of life in New England villages during the 18th Century, and part of this interesting exhibit is a substantial collection of textiles and costumes covering a time span from 1790 to 1840.

In all, the textile-costume collection contains some 4,000 pieces, of which perhaps half are costumes and accessories. The rest are flat textiles and home furnishings—all made or used in New England during the period covered. The most notable groups are bed coverings, documentary textile samplers, and costumes. There are homespun and home-woven pieces, as well as goods imported from England, together with the commerical products of early American textile factories.

Among the more important holdings are the following: some 500 documentary textile samples; 200 bed quilts; 180 linen sheets; 200 nonquilted bed coverings; 200 blankets; 150 samplers; 20 sets of window curtains; 125 dresses; 60 men's shirts; and a large group of costume accessories ranging from shoes to aprons and underwear.

Among smaller groupings are bed hangings, pillowcases, cushions, slipcovers, towels, rugs, and bags of various kinds. There are also a number of stenciled fabrics used in bedspreads and curtains, as well as crewelwork and embroidered pictures.

Among other interesting pieces are examples of painting on velvet and an extensive group of costumes and accessories used by Early New England militia companies.

The collection is accessible to researchers, but an appointment must be made with the Curator of Textiles at least a week in advance.

Publication. *Textiles in New England—1790–1840.* By Catherine Fennelly. Old Sturbridge Village Booklet No. 13. An excellent illustrated review of early New England textile production both in the home and in the factory.

WASHINGTON, D.C.

Dumbarton Oaks
1703 32nd Street N.W.
ZIP: 20007   TEL: (202) 232-3101

Elizabeth P. Benson, Pre-Columbian
Susan Boyd, Byzantine

The Dumbarton Oaks Research Library and Collection (full title) is world-renowned for its holdings of Byzantine and pre-Columbian art. The latter collection was assembled by Robert Woods Bliss and was previously held by the National Gallery of Art in Washington. It was transferred to its present home in 1963.

Dumbarton Oaks is affiliated with Harvard University and devotes itself primarily to scholarly pursuits. It is housed in an elegant formal mansion, surrounded by gardens and situated in one of the world's most beguiling urban environments—the Georgetown section of Washington. This alone makes it worth a special visit. How-ever, quite aside from its ambiance, Dumbarton Oaks—among its large art holdings—owns superb examples of textiles in the two areas of its specialization, and these are accessible to designers by appointment.

The textile collections are not large in numbers, but they are exceptional in quality and they manage to convey more effectively than most such collections the past splendors of the regal cultures which produced them. Following is a brief description of the textile holdings.

Pre-Columbian Textiles. There are exactly 36 pieces—all from Peru. They cover a time span extending from the Chavin culture of 1100–400 B.C. through to the Inca Empire, which ended in 1532 A.D.

Among these pieces are 22 garments and fragments with tapestry or brocaded decorations dating from the Late Nazca/Wari to the Inca periods. Of the remaining 14 pieces, three are painted textiles of the Chavin and Paracas cultures; two are feather garments dating from the Late Period—650–1532; two are plaited tassels of the Late Period; four are cut-pile hats—Coastal Wari; and three are embroidered garments—two Paracas and one Late Period.

Out of the 36 pieces in the collection, 16 are on display in the galleries. The rest are in storage. Photographs of most pieces are available.

Byzantine Textiles. These holdings are much larger than those from Peru. There are exactly 217 pieces. Of these, 159 examples are Coptic—4th to 14th Century; twelve are Early Islamic and Sassanian; 20 are medieval silks; and 26 are examples of woven textiles from royal Tiraz workshops in Egypt, Yemen, Syria, and Iraq.

A few of these Byzantine pieces are displayed in the galleries, among them several exceptionally fine examples of Coptic tapestry weaving. A catalog of the whole collection was in preparation at this writing.

WASHINGTON, D.C.

National Museum of History & Technology
Smithsonian Institution
ZIP: 20560   TEL: (202) 628-4422

Rita J. Adrosko & Grace R. Cooper, Curators, Division of Textiles

The Smithsonian has a great complex of museums under its wing, but this is the one which most people associate with the Institution. Here, in a modern building, is the record of American civilization—its history, technology, crafts, industrial development, and contributions to design.

In this vast repository textiles as such play only a small though important role. Flat fabrics are held by the Division of Textiles, which owns a total of about 40,000 items. Of these, at most 5,000 pieces are actual fabrics. The rest are textile-related objects such as patent models of textile-processing

RIGHT. Detail of a Peruvian mantle from the late period, Central Coast. Cotton, brocaded with wool, with a tapestry border. Width: 48.1 cm. Bliss Collection. *Dumbarton Oaks—B-493.PT.*

BELOW. Entrance to the textile exhibit at the Smithsonian National Museum of History & Technology, Washington, D.C.

and sewing equipment (4,000 pieces), full-sized examples of textile machinery, hand-spinning and handweaving tools, sewing clamps (500), and other types of equipment.

All these various objects are related to the development of the American textile industry from its Colonial beginnings up to the 20th Century, and this whole developmental sequence is well illustrated through a permanent exhibit in the museum's Textile Hall on the ground floor. In addition to American textile products the exhibit shows some of the household and costume textiles imported for use in America during the 18th and 19th Centuries. Such products are also included in the textile holdings and were collected as important examples of processing or decorating techniques. The whole exhibit is an excellent teaching tool, which is extended through spinning and weaving demonstrations conducted in the Textile Hall.

Among the 5,000 pieces of fabric in the collection the strongest categories are American quilts and coverlets, many European laces, and a large collection of embroideries made both in America and Europe. A more detailed listing follows, together with the approximate number of pieces in each category: aprons, beadwork from 1800 forward, bedspreads (15), blankets (65), braids (30), carpets and carpet bags of the 19th Century (60), and counterpanes (60).

Coverlets. The collection of coverlets is an important one with over 175 examples representing all the different types made in America during the 18th and 19th Centuries. There are examples of overshot, double-woven, jacquard, summer-winter, and similar constructions.

Crewelwork, crochet (70), doilies, draperies, and curtains (60).

Embroidery. The embroidery collection is extensive—about 700 pieces, chiefly 19th-Century work. It is both American and European with one of the largest cate-gories coming from France (300). Another substantial group is Macedonian (75).

Garments, many with lace decorations (400), handkerchiefs with embroidered or printed designs (150).

Lace represents the largest single unit in the fabric collection—over 1,000 pieces. It holds examples of all the important types of lace from the European lace-making centers. It is particularly strong in examples of work from Chantilly, Valenciennes, and Brussels.

Linens with damask and embroidered decorations (100), nets and netting (25), pattern and sample books. The latter group contains more than 25 separate volumes showing patterns for knitting, embroidery and patchwork. In addition, there is a group of 19th-Century sample books from the Hamilton Print Works.

Prints. This is a substantial group of fabrics with examples of all techniques—block-print, copperplate, discharge, roller, and screen. Also some examples of batik work.

Quilts. This is perhaps the most important group in the holdings. There are over 200 examples of American quilt making—appliqué, patchwork, and all-white types. Among them is the famous Harriet Powers' Bible Quilt of appliqué and pieced work, made in Georgia about 1886.

Rugs and carpets in all the homemade techniques (65), samplers (125), sheets and pillowcases (50), tablecloths and napkins (125), tatting (15), towels (50), and upholstery (40).

Fibers and Yarns. In addition to the fabrics listed above the Division of Textiles holds an important study collection of fibers and yarns used in textile construction. Among them are examples of abaca, acetate, animals fibers of all types, asbestos, bamboo, bark cloth, glass fiber, ramie, and rattan.

Research Facilities. The Division's library holds an excellent collection of about 2,000

The Textile Museum is housed in a large private mansion on a quiet residential street of Washington, D.C.

HISTORY & TECHNOLOGY cont'd

volumes on all aspects of textile processing and many on textile design. Among these is a file of the Ackerman's Repository from 1809 to 1828, many with actual swatches of fabric from the period covered. Also a complete file of the *Ciba Review*. The textile study room owns a good file of B/W pictures of its most important pieces.

These facilities are available to researchers, but an appointment must be made.

Costume Collection. This is a major collection of American costume—some 18,000 pieces with its greatest strength in the 19th–20th Century. It is held by another museum department—the Division of Costume & Furnishings. Claudia B. Kidwell, Associate Curator, is in charge. Its focus is on the clothing worn by all American socio-economic groups from Colonial times to the present. It approaches costume as cultural history rather than as decorative art. This collection was the basis of an illuminating exhibit—*Suiting Everyone*—mounted at the museum in 1974. Its theme was the democratization of clothing in America, and it showed a representative range of middle-class ready-made clothing worn from 1920–70.

Publications. The following textile-related publications by Smithsonian staff members have been issued by the Smithsonian Institution Press. They are available from the Superintendent of Documents, U.S. Government Printing Office, Washington, D.C. 20402.

Natural Dyes in the United States. By Rita J. Adrosko. U.S.N.M. Bulletin 281. 1968. (A paperback reprint was issued by Dover Publications, N.Y. in 1971.)

The Copp Family Textiles. By Grace R. Cooper. Smithsonian Studies in History & Technology No. 7. 1971.

Women's Bathing & Swimming Costume in the

United States. U.S.N.M. Bulletin 250, Paper 64. 1968.

Floor Coverings in 18th Century America. By Rodris Roth. U.S.N.M. Bulletin 250, Paper 59. 1969.

WASHINGTON, D.C.

National Museum of Natural History
Smithsonian Institution
ZIP: 20560   TEL: (202) 381-5626

Clifford Evans, Chairman,
Department of Anthropology;
William C. Sturtevant, Curator

(NOTE. This museum should not be confused with the Smithsonian's National Museum of History & Technology. They are both on Constitution Avenue and next to each other.)

I must confess to a sense of frustration in my attempts to explore the vast resources of the Smithsonian's Museum of Natural History. It may conceivably hold the largest collection of ethnological textiles and costume in North America, if not in the world. But that is only a guess since no accurate statistics are available on these holdings—all in the Department of Anthropology.

The most that can be recorded with assurance is that the museum has extensive holdings of ethnographic textiles from the North American Indian cultures, from Asia and from South America, as well as more limited holdings from Africa and the Pacific.

A somewhat more detailed record is available for the North American material than for the other categories. Here, a guess would place the number of textiles-costume at a minimum of 10,000 pieces with a possible maximum of 25,000 or even more, depending on what types of materials are included. The strongest collections are from the Southwest, but most other regions of Indian culture are well represented. And one statistic is known: the

collection owns a little over 200 examples of Navajo rug weaving.

The problem in assembling statistics is that here (as in most anthropological collections) the material is cataloged by tribe or region and not by types of artifacts. Thus the North American Indian division owns perhaps 100,000 ethnological specimens and does not segregate textiles from other artifacts. For designers to dig out textiles of particular interest to them would be a major enterprise.

I therefore conclude—reluctantly—that the difficulties of exploring so vast a range of materials, much of it still unstudied, would be too discouraging for most designers and students, as it was for me.

Fortunately, however, there is an alternative. It is more limited in scope but it can be quite stimulating. The museum has mounted permanent displays of textiles in its public galleries—and they are excellent. They have much to offer designers, and if any particular exhibit is of special interest, an appointment can be made to explore the reserve stores from which the display material was drawn. At least the Anthropology Department seems agreeable to this procedure, provided that arrangemnts are made well in advance of a visit.

Among the textile exhibits I found particularly relevant were the following.

The Americas

A painted caribou skin from the Northwest Coast.

Tlingit (Chilkat) clothing from the Northwest, especially a painted buckskin dance kilt.

The exhibit of Chilkat and Salish blankets is outstanding. It explains the production process—designs painted on boards by men to guide the women weavers. It details the type of yarn used—mountain-goat wool wrapped on a core yarn of cedar bark. It demonstrates how the warp yarns on the

RIGHT. The two-story main gallery of the Textile Museum is generally devoted to changing exhibitions. This photo was taken during the exhibit of Joseph V. McMullen rugs in 1965.

BELOW. Wool rug from Transylvania, 17–18th Century. Size: 1.21 × 1.69 m. *Textile Museum—R.1.84.*

vertical blanket loom are tied into bladder bags to keep them clean. It explains that to weave a Chilkat blanket might take as long as six months so that they were expensive possessions which only the wealthy could afford.

This type of illuminating caption material is typical of the museum's approach to all its exhibits.

A Haida dance shirt with appliquéd pearl buttons. Also a Haida ceremonial robe with porcupine quill embroidery and very subtle painted motifs.

Painted moose-hide armor from the Northwest Coast.

Quillwork and beadwork designs are shown together with displays of the equipment used for each craft.

A fine exhibit of costumes worn by Plains Indians, including elegantly painted hides.

A spectacular painted buffalo robe which was worn with the fur side in and the decorated side out.

An intriguing man's outfit from the Seminoles, made of trade cloth with superimposed beadwork, which trasforms a formal 18th-Century English silhouette into a whimsical costume piece.

A finger-woven sash of the Woodland Indians.

The Pacific

Hawaiian feather cloaks, garments of the rulers, made only by men.

Tapa-cloth patterns and the process for making them in Hawaii from the bark of the paper-mulberry tree.

Some beautiful silk ikats from Cambodia.

Asia

An excellent display on the Kashmir shawl.

A flock-printed cotton sari from India and an embroidered shirt from Pakistan.

Embroidered quilting on pieced sari cloth and gauzelike saris—from East Bengal.

A marriage sari in the weft-ikat technique from Orissa, India.

Four elaborate saris with silver brocading from Uttar Pradesh.

Stenciled kimono cloths from the Japanese Ryukyu islands.

Examples of Chinese theatrical costuming.

Examples of Tibetan textile art, including a tanka (banner).

Africa

Fine examples of blue resist-dyed cottons from the Yoruba people of West Central Africa. Also Yoruba wild-silk cloth in a lovely undyed pale brown color.

Several other examples of West African textile craft, including strip-weaving from Dahomey, tie-dyeing from Liberia, Mandingo embroidery, Hausa ikats, and embroidered pile cloths from the Congo (Kasai velvet).

A most impressive chief's carpet of bark cloth from East Africa (Haya).

Handsome silk weavings (lambas) from Madagascar.

Altogether one of the most wide-ranging, informative, and stimulating group of exhibits I have seen on ethnographic textiles. Every designer visiting Washington should make it a point to see them.

WASHINGTON, D.C.

The Textile Museum
2320 S Street N.W.
ZIP: 20008   TEL: (202) NO 7-0442

Andrew Oliver, Executive Director
CURATORS: Louise W. Mackie, Eastern Hemisphere
Patricia L. Fiske, Assistant Curator, Eastern Hemisphere
Ann P. Rowe, Assistant Curator, Western Hemisphere

The Textile Museum is unique in North America and one of the few museums anywhere in the world devoted exclusively to the collection of historic textiles as art. Other comparable museums that come to mind are the French textile museums at Lyon and Mulhouse, the Calico Museum in Ahmedabad (India), and the Krefeld Museum in West Germany.

The Textile Museum was founded in 1925 by George Hewitt Myers to house and display his extensive private collection of rugs and textiles. It is a public museum privately administered by a group of trustees and is chiefly supported by an endowment left by Mr. Myers on his death in 1957. It is housed in a large private mansion on a quiet residential street.

To me—and no doubt to many others outside the inner circle of textile curators—the museum has chiefly been known for its superb collection of Near Eastern rugs. This was the field which evidently engaged Mr.

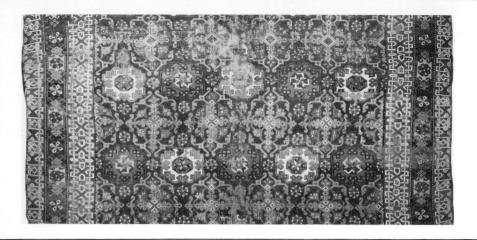

TEXTILE MUSEUM cont'd

Myers' major interest as a collector, and the museum does indeed own one of the world's outstanding rug collections. However, the international fame of the rug collection has tended to overshadow other facets of the museum's holdings which may be of greater interest to textile designers. These include important collections of ancient Peruvian and Egyptian textiles, as well as smaller but substantial holdings from Iran, India, Turkey, Indonesia, the Far East, Central America, and the American Southwest.

These wide-ranging textile holdings, together with its fine library, lead me to believe that the Textile Museum is one of the richest and most accessible research facilities for textiles now available in this country. I should add that in the past the museum has chiefly attracted scholars and is perhaps not as well adapted to the needs of designers. However, the material is there

and it is accessible. I would urge every textile designer visiting Washington to allow time for an exploration of this rich resource. It will be a rewarding experience, as it was for me.

In size The Textile Museum's holdings number just under 8,000 pieces. These are divided into three categories.

1. Eastern Hemisphere—3,105 pieces.
2. Rug Collection—671 pieces.
3. Western Hemisphere—4,000+ pieces.

It goes without saying that these statistics are not fixed. They are constantly expanding through new acquisitions.

A breakdown of these three categories follows.

I Eastern Hemisphere

Egypt. The collection of textiles from Egypt is one of the most important in the world. It includes many unique pieces and covers the full time range of surviving Egyptian textiles. In all, there are 1,276 pieces, assigned to the following periods: Ancient Egypt—8 pieces; Greco-Roman—143: Greco-Roman to Coptic—55; Coptic—264; Coptic to Arabic—28; Islamic Egypt—768.

Persia (Iran). There are 385 pieces in this collection. It is perhaps the most comprehensive of its kind in the world today. This judgment was made by the Shah of Iran in 1964 when he saw the collection on exhibit (together with rugs from Persia) and said it was more representative and important than any similar collection that could be assembled in Iran.

India-Southeast Asia. Another large holding of over 500 pieces, with the majority coming from India (380). The remainder represents Indonesia (136), and here the largest group comes from Bali.

Near East. The museum holds 292 pieces from the Near East, the largest units being Greek Island embroideries and textiles from Turkey (106). There are also two smaller groups from Syria (33) and Palestine (40).

Far East. A total of 225 pieces. The largest unit is from China (165) with smaller groups from Japan (35), Formosa (13), and Mongolia (12).

Europe. The museum makes no effort to cover European textiles in any systematic way, but it has a small group of about 100 pieces from European countries. The largest is from Spain (42). Smaller groups represent Italy, Sicily, Poland, and a number of other unidentified sources.

Central Asia. 68 pieces, including textiles from Turkestan (25), the Caucasus (22), and Mesopotamia (21).

Africa. 64 pieces, including work from West Africa (28), Morocco (26), the Congo (14), Algeria (7), and Nubia (3).

II The Rug Collection

At this writing (1975) The Textile Mu-

RIGHT. Detail of a linen curtain with silk embroidery from Asia Minor, 17th Century. Length: 101". *Textile Museum—1.42.*

BELOW. Detail of an 18th Century embroidery from India. Size: 2' × 1.78'. *Textile Museum—6.25.*

seum's rug collection numbers 671 pieces. The major part of it was assembled by George Myers during his lifetime, beginning in 1890. It is widely regarded as among the world's largest and most important collections in this area. Its greatest emphasis falls on work from Spain, North Africa, the Near East, and Central Asia. Perhaps its most illustrious holdings are its Hispano-Moresque rugs and its carpets from the Mamluk period in Egypt.

A detailed breakdown of the rug collection follows.

SOURCE & PERIOD	PIECES
Egypt—Cairene, c. 1500	26
Persia—all periods, 15th to 20th Century	100
Turkey—all periods, 16th to 20th Century	126
Caucasian—all periods, 17th to 20th Century	90
Turkoman—late 18th to 20th Century	66
Spain—all Islamic-Spanish types represented, 15th to 17th Century	34
Chinese—not strong group, 19th to 20th Century	27
Japanese—20th Century	1
Sinkiang-Khotan, late 18th Century	7
India—16th to early 19th Century	29
North Africa—Moroccan, Berber, late 19th to 20th Century	7
Miscellaneous	12
Stevens Collection—19th to 20th Century, Caucasian, Turkish, Persian, Turkoman, China	146

III Western Hemisphere

Peru-S. America. George Myers and his wife began to collect Peruvian textiles in the 1920s and were able to build what is considered to be perhaps the largest as well as the most representative collection of its kind in the world. There are over 3,000 pieces in the holding today, and it continues

to grow through purchases and gifts. Although this large number also includes a number of other archaeological and ethnographic textiles from South America, the overwhelming portion comes from Peru.

It is particularly strong in examples of the Paracas and Huari styles, as well as in work from the Spanish Colonial period in Peru after 1532. Its earliest examples are grave cloths dating from 2500 B.C., and its most recent acquisitions were woven by living Indians in the Andes region yesterday.

The collection demonstrates an incredible range of textile virtuosity, and it is a continuing revelation of beauty. For the contemporary designer it will be a breathtaking but humbling experience since it is difficult to think of anything our modern textile technology has created to match the beauty of these ancient artifacts.

It is also a pleasure to report that most of these quite marvelous Peruvian pieces are easy to examine. Many are stored under glass covers in a great bank of large art file cases in the library. I counted 80 full-size art drawers, each of them containing remarkable textile treasures.

Central America. This grouping is devoted chiefly to textiles from Guatemala, Mexico, and Panama. The largest number comes from Guatemala—about 400 pieces. It represents the traditional costume and weaving skill of the Guatemalan peasantry, and it is rich in design ideas for contemporary textiles.

From Mexico come about 200 ethnographic pieces, the strongest group being many varieties of the traditional Mexican serape.

From Panama comes a group of about 50 San Blas molas and guaymi bags.

LEFT. Section of tapestry-woven tunic from Peru, Wari Middle Horizon I-II style (500–700 A.D.). Probably cotton warp, wool weft. *Textile Museum—1962.5.1.*

BELOW. Section of a Peruvian mantle in late Paracas style, South Coast (500–400 B.C.). Wool and cotton yarns in plain weave, embroidered in stem stitch, 1.08 m. wide. *Textile Museum—1962.5.1.*

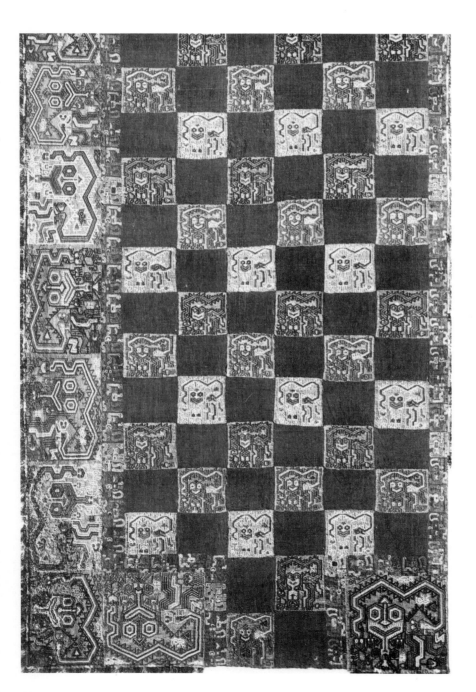

TEXTILE MUSEUM cont'd

North America. About 250 pieces. The Indian cultures of the Southwest are well represented; also those of the Northwest Coast. The collection includes about 75 Navajo rugs and blankets.

Exhibits. The museum has two main public galleries and attempts to change its exhibits every three to six months in order to show different facets of the collection.

Research Facilities. The library at the Textile Museum is almost as impressive as its fabric collections. It holds over 6,000 volumes and bound periodicals, as well as numerous monographs and bulletins from U.S. and foreign museums. It also owns many past and current catalogs of textile exhibits held in other museums. Among its hardcover volumes are a wide range of reference works on the cultures of South America, the Near East, and the American Indian. It has an exhaustive collection of written and illustrative material on rugs, and its shelves hold the key works on modern textile art and technology.

Altogether, The Textile Museum library is one of the two most important specialized textile libraries in the United States, ranking with that of the Cooper-Hewitt Museum in New York. It is well worth an extended visit, and this should be arranged in advance if possible, due to limited staff time.

Conservation Laboratories. The Textile Museum has long been a center for research on the conservation of ancient textiles. It maintains fully staffed research laboratories next to the museum building, and its Curator of Technical Studies—Irene Emery—is one of the country's leading experts in this specialized field. The laboratories have developed a number of techniques for textile restoration and have

RIGHT. Peruvian fragment, late Nazca style, probably Middle Horizon I (500–600 A.D.), South Coast. Cotton weave with wool embroidery. Height: 0.47 m. *Textile Museum—91.130.*

BELOW. Tapestry-woven wool tunic from Peru, Nazca drainage, probably Middle Horizon II (600–700 A.D.). Size: 0.67 × 0.94 m. *Textile Museum—91.150.*

published results of their experiments in the now-defunct *Workshop Notes* and in the museum's annual *Journal.* This department also operates an active apprenticeship program to train students in textile conservation and analysis.

Publications. The following publications have been issued under The Textile Museum imprint.

1. *The Primary Structures of Fabrics.* By Irene Emery. 1966. 339 pages with 378 B/W illustrations. This is a fully illustrated classification, the leading text in its field.

2. Six separate catalogs produced for exhibitions of museum holdings. They cover Peruvian textiles, Turkish rugs, flatwoven rugs from Central Asia, Turkish rugs in the Stevens Collection, molas of the Cuna Indians, and Turkish weaving. A detailed list is available from the museum.

3. Four gallery guides dealing with museum exhibits on Persian weaving, Spanish weaving, Peruvian textile traditions, and Turkish rugs from outside collections. A descriptive and detailed list is available.

4. A series of four *Workshop Notes* on the following themes: *Rug Preservation* (by George Myers), *Weaving Techniques in Egypt and the Near East, Rug analysis,* and *Peruvian Shaped Textiles.* Descriptive list on request.

5. *Textile Museum Journal.* Copies of this interesting and instructive publication are available for the years 1963, 1964, 1966, 1970, 1971, 1972, 1973, 1974.

Photographs. The museum maintains a comprehensive file of B/W photographs of its major pieces, and prints can be made to order.

Note: Galleries are open free to the public Tuesday through Saturday 10 A.M. to 5 P.M. except on legal holidays. The Offices are closed Saturdays.

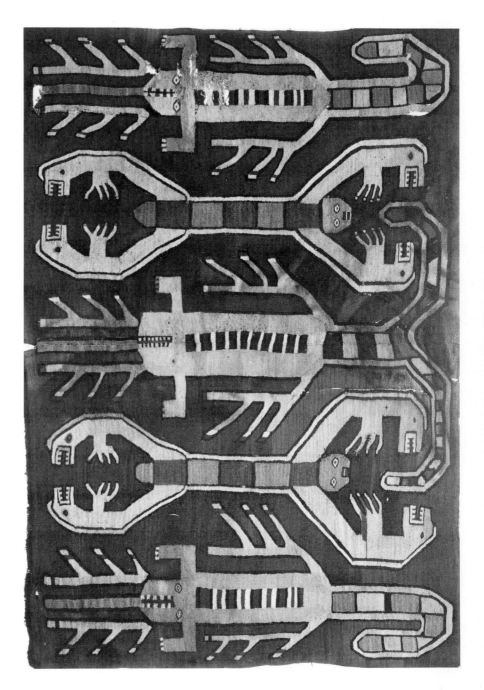

English needlework rug, about 1750. H. Randolph Lever Fund. *Brooklyn—65.143.*

WILLIAMSBURG, VA.

The Colonial Williamsburg Foundation
Drawer C
ZIP: 23185 TEL: (804) 229-1000

Mildred B. Lanier, Curator of Textiles

Colonial Williamsburg has a larger collection of textiles and costumes than most people suspect. It is estimated at between 10,000 and 12,000 pieces. That includes fabrics in use in the restoration buildings as well as much larger holdings of documentary textiles and costume housed in a climate-controlled storage facility.

Textile furnishings in the exhibition buildings are usually changed twice a year and are varied from time to time to expose different aspects of the collection. As a result the visitor is able to gain a documented picture of the furnishings used in Virginia homes during the 18th Century.

The larger part of the collection, however, is kept in storage and is not open to researchers. For the future a series of publications is being planned, and these will be devoted to different segments of the collection. In the meantime those interested can gain access to the comprehensive catalog file which contains photographs of most pieces in the collection. For this an appointment is necessary.

Highlights of the textile collection are the home furnishings which decorate the restoration rooms and which have been documented through Virginia records of the period. They consist of both original fabrics and reproductions. Among them the following groups are notable.

1. English and East Indian cottons. This is the largest category in the holdings and contains many examples of Indian mordant-painted cottons, as well as prints made with both wood blocks and copperplates. Much of the work dates from the 18th Century.

2. English wools, including blankets, cover-lets, and Norwich worsteds—calamancoes, damasks, and brocades in "silk" patterns.

3. Household linens of all types (damask, huckaback, diaper, etc.), as well as tablecloths, napkins, towels, pillowcases, sheets, mattress ticks, and grain sacks.

4. English and American needlework in crewels and silks. These are worked on household furnishings such as bed hangings, pictures, samplers, fire screens and upholstery. There is also a rare group of embroidered wool "rose" blankets.

5. A substantial collection of costumes and accessories for both women and men, chiefly of the 18th Century.

6. A representative collection of English Spitalfields silks.

Colonial Williamsburg also owns a detailed photographic record of a most interesting "textile" document. This is the album of Barbara Johnson (1738–1825), a North Country Englishwoman who kept a record of the fabrics she used for her dresses between 1746 and 1823. There are 122 samples in the album. It was originally acquired by Colonial Williamsburg and then graciously relinquished to the Victoria & Albert Museum in London.

Publications. *Copperplate Textiles in the Williamsburg Collection.* By Ruth Y. Cox. Williamsburg, 1964.

English & Oriental Carpets at Williamsburg. 1975.

WINTERTHUR, DEL.

Henry Francis du Pont Winterthur Museum
Route 52
ZIP: 19735 TEL: (302) 656-8591

John A. H. Sweeney, Deputy Director
Karol A. Schmiegel, Asst. Registrar

The word for Winterthur is "elegant." Here, in a vast, sprawling mansion set on rolling acres of immaculate parkland, Henry Francis du Pont assembled one of the world's largest and most comprehensive collections of early American decorative arts. Two hundred furnished interiors (over 100 rooms) document the decor of American homes from the 17th to the early 19th Century.

In addition to the textiles used as furnishings in these exhibits, there are five large climate-controlled storage rooms which hold reserve furnishings to replace those on display from time to time. This is maintained to avoid overlong exposure of the exhibit textiles.

Further, the museum maintains a large Textile Study Room which holds many examples of interior fabrics—predominantly prints.

These various holdings are sustained by one of the largest and best-equipped textile conservation laboratories in the world, with a trained staff and full-scale facilities for cleaning, repairing, and preserving both large and small pieces.

Winterthur also maintains an elegant research library which owns a major collection of historic swatched sample books. These may well be the high point of any exploration of the museum's resources.

Textile designers and researchers who contemplate a visit to Winterthur should understand that it cannot be casual or unplanned. A guided tour must be arranged in advance, and the visitor will be accompanied by a well-informed and white-gloved attendant. No textiles either on display or in storage can be handled.

Statistically, the textile holdings at Winterthur number between 4,000 and 5,000 pieces—aside from the important collection of sample books. Of this total perhaps 1,000 pieces of furnishings are on display in the exhibit areas. Another 1,000 pieces or thereabouts are held in the storage rooms. And the Textile Study Room contains at least 2,500 study pieces.

The Henry Francis du Pont Winterthur Museum. Library is on the right.

In content the textile collection is specialized. It concentrates on home furnishing fabrics either made in America or imported for use over a period of 200 years—from the 17th to the early 19th Century. Among the more important holdings is a major collection of about 200 patchwork, appliqué, and embroidered quilts, together with over 30 double-woven coverlets. There are also window hangings and domestic linens in great variety.

Following is a more detailed breakdown of the textile collection.

American Textiles

Unpatterned domestic fabrics in linen and wool—sheets, towels, blankets, tablecloths, napkins.

Printed and stenciled fabrics, including the earliest documented American print—a block print by Bedwell and Walters, Philadelphia, 1775–77.

Needlework in silk and crewels. This includes one of the country's finest and most comprehensive collections of American canvaswork.

Quilts and Coverlets. At least 200 important examples of patchwork and appliqué work, over 30 double-woven coverlets, and some unusual candlewick spreads. All these are stored on pullout rods so that the whole design is readily visible.

Floor Coverings. An important range, including woven-strip rag carpets (1790–1850), hooked rugs (1820–60), bed rugs, and an 18th-Century painted floor cloth.

Imported Textiles

Linens, particularly checked linens which were often called "furniture checks" in the 18th Century and were used as bed hangings, summer curtains, and slipcovers.

Cottons—printed and painted. This is one of the largest and most extensive collections in America, and many of the examples are known through Florence Montgomery's book, *Printed Textiles: English & American Cottons & Linens 1700-1850*. The range includes block prints (1700–1850), copperplate prints (1760–1820), and roller prints (1812–1850). There is also an important collection of French block and copperplate prints, including toiles de Jouy dating from 1770–1800. In addition, there are cottons from India, painted-and-dyed and embroidered.

Silks. Good examples of French, Italian, Spanish, and English damask, brocatelle, and brocade—used in upholstery and window hangings. Also hand-painted Oriental silks.

Wools. Among other pieces are some rare examples of English wool damask used as window and bed hangings.

Floor Coverings. English Axminster, Exeter, Kidderminster, and Wilton carpets of the 18th and early 19th Centuries. Also French Aubusson carpets, Oriental carpets (17th–19th Century), and one of the best collections of Turkish Ushak carpets in America.

Trimmings. A large collection of braids and border decorations used in home furnishings.

Library. Two particular sections of the Winterthur library should be of great interest to designers. One of these is the Rare Book Room, which owns primary French and American material on textile design and use, including works on printing and dyeing. There are also many illustrated volumes devoted to interior decoration, ornament, and furniture design. These works range in date from 1700 through the 19th Century and include books by Daniel Marot, Thomas Sheraton, George Hepplewhite, George Smith, Thomas Chippendale, William Hogarth, Thomas Webster, Rudolph Ackerman, and André la Méssangère.

The second and more important textile resource of the library is a large and important manuscript collection with at least 125 volumes containing some 50,000 swatches of fabric. Below are listed a few of the treasures in this major collection.

French textile samples, 1809–1845; English Manchester cotton samples, 1775–1785; a swatch book of printed calicoes and dimities, 1850–1900; sample books of French silks and velvets, 1830–52; a huge group of 90 large textile sample books from August Zindel, Mulhouse, France, 1825–52; a merchants' color order book with 200 samples of printed cotton, Rhode Island, 1858; a sample book of Japanese wools and cottons, 19th Century; a sample book of fabrics and ribbons from France, Switzerland, and England, 1750–1830; a sample book of ribbons from Coventry, England, 1826–30; a French sample book of printed challis, 1830; a sample book of silk weavings from Vienna, 1800–1849.

These specialized works are part of a total library collection which includes 50,000 printed volumes, 275 current periodical subscriptions, 3,700 bound periodicals, 5,000 manuscripts, 1,540 microfilm rolls, 50,000 slides, and 105,000 photographs.

Curatorial Training Program. Together with the University of Delaware, Winterthur sponsors what is considered to be perhaps the best curatorial training program in the decorative arts—and particularly in textiles. It is a two-year course leading to a Master of Arts degree.

The Name Winterthur. The name Winterthur was taken from the city of that name in Switzerland. This was the home of the Bidermann family, who built the original mansion in 1839. Mrs. James Antoine Bidermann was the great-aunt of Henry Francis du Pont.

Publication. *Printed Textiles: English & American Cottons & Linens, 1700-1850*. By Florence M. Montgomery. A Winterthur Book. Viking, N.Y. 1970.

CANADIAN COLLECTIONS

MONTREAL, QUE.

McCord Museum—McGill University
690 Sherbrooke Street West
ZIP: H3A 1E9   TEL: (514) 392-4778

Cynthia B. Eberts, Costume Curator

The McCord Museum at McGill University has only a small collection of some 200 flat textiles—chiefly domestic fabrics—but a large collection of about 5,000 costumes and accessories.

The domestic textile collection includes examples of bed linens, bedspreads, blankets, carpets (hooked and woven), coverlets (30), curtains, fur sleigh rugs, quilts (22), samplers (10), table linens and towels, Victorian embroidery and beadwork, chair covers, and cushions. All of these were either made or used in Canada.

The costume collection, in addition to many accessories, focuses on women's clothing worn in Canada. Among its holdings are about 500 dresses dating from the mid-18th Century to the present.

Since McCord is a museum of Canadian history, it also owns a collection of ethnological costume from the Eskimo and Indian cultures of the region.

MONTREAL, QUE.

Montreal Museum of Fine Arts
1379 Sherbrooke Street West
ZIP: H3B 3E1   TEL: (514) 842-8091

Ruth A. Jackson, Curator

The Montreal Museum of Fine Arts owns a textile-costume collection of modest size but of notable range and quality. In all, there are some 1,250 pieces, of which about 150 are costumes and accessories. It includes relatively large and important groups from Spain, Italy, ancient Peru, and Coptic Egypt, as well as smaller but significant holdings from England, France, India, and Persia. It is an international collection covering a wide span of time from the beginnings of the Christian era to the 20th Century and representing a full range of fabric types.

Following is a more detailed outline of the holdings.

America (Central).   About 40 examples, all early 20th-Century work. Among them are huipils, shawls, tzute, and belts. Some of the regions represented are Chichicastenango, Cotzal, San Juan Sactepequez, and Santo Domingo Xenacoj.

Canada.   About 45 pieces dating from the 18th to the 20th Century. Among them are coverlets and quilts, Eskimo batiks and weavings, as well as nine examples of ceinture fléchée—the colorful braided wool sashes worn by Canadian men in the fur trade.

England.   Over 100 pieces ranging from the 15th to the 19th Century. There are good examples of Opus Anglicanum embroidery, stumpwork, crewelwork, brocades, and printed cottons. Most of the pieces are in the form of women's and men's garments.

Egypt.   Some 60 fragments of Coptic tapestry weaving dating from the 3rd to the 10th Century.

France.   Over 100 pieces—17th–19th Century. Among them are toiles de Jouy, brocades, lace, ecclesiastical embroidery, chintz, painted linens, and woven silks.

Greece.   About 20 pieces—18th- and 19th-Century work. Most are decorative towels illustrating traditional patterns from several areas.

India.   More than 100 examples—17th–19th Century. They include saris, hangings, shawls, and many fragments from Hyderabad, Gwalior, Rajputana, Kashmir, Benares, and other regions. There are examples of many techniques—silk and gold brocades, embroidery, woven wools, painted cottons, gauze, muslin, and hand-stenciled cotton.

Persia.   About 55 pieces. Some are dated as early as the 11th, 12th, and 13th Centuries. Others are from the 16th–18th Century. They include brocades, compound cloths, silks, velvets, and brocaded taffeta. There is work from Rhages, Kashan, Isfahan, and from the Safavid and Seldjuk periods.

Peru.   This is an important collection with about 100 examples of ancient Peruvian textile craft representing most of the major styles in Peruvian iconography—Paracas Cavernas, Paracas Necropolis, Nazca, Chancay, Chimu, Tiahuanaco, and Inca. The museum is justly proud of this collection since it owns several large and outstanding mantles from Paracas, as well as some fine feather work and painted textiles from the Central Coast.

Spain/Italy.   The museum groups these two categories as one. It represents the largest unit in the holdings—over 400 pieces ranging from the 12th to the 18th Century. Much of the work is from the great weaving centers at Lucca, Sicily, Siena, and Venice. There are also many examples of the Hispano-Moresque style. Ecclesiastical pieces predominate in the form of chalice covers, copes, dalmatics, and other vestments. Among the many different techniques illustrated are brocatelles, voided and cut velvets, stamped wool velvets, silk-gold brocades, tapestry weaves, and a dozen other different types. An important study collection.

Other Countries.   The following twelve countries are represented with from two to twenty pieces each: Africa, Austria, China, Finland, Germany, Holland, Japan, Java, Palestine, Poland, Roumania, and Turkey.

Samplers.   An outstanding collection of 140 pieces from eight different countries—1700 to the late 19th Century in date.

Research Facilities.   The museum's library has a large section on textiles and

RIGHT. The Victoria Memorial Museum Building in Ottawa, home of exhibits for the National Museum of Man.

BELOW. White wedding bedspread with *boutonné* motifs. Height: 210.2 cm. Made in Ile aux Coudres, Charlevoix County, Quebec. *National Museum of Man—A-3389 (K74-1063).*

costume. Many of the textiles are permanently exhibited, and the departmental facilities are available by appointment.

OTTAWA, ONT.

National Museum of Man
360 Lisgar Street
ZIP: K1A 0M8   TEL: (613) 992-0483
Barbara Riley, History
Wesley C. Mattie, Folk Culture

Canada's National Museum of Man has two departments which own textile-costume collections—the History Division and the Canadian Centre for Folk Culture Studies. The combined holdings of these two collections number some 5,000 pieces, many of them exhibited at the Victoria Memorial Museum Building in Ottawa.

History Division. This department owns about 3,000 textiles, costumes, and accessories. The emphasis is on costume with about 2,500 pieces. Most of the work dates from the late 19th and the early 20th Centuries.

The flat textiles in this department (about 500) are chiefly fabrics for the home. They include quilts, coverlets, towels, blankets, bed linens, and samples of flannel, cotton, wool, linen, and silk. Among them are many examples of handspinning and handweaving, as well as crochet work. The largest groups illustrate handweaving in Nova Scotia and coverlets from Ontario and Quebec. The coverlet collection is a most representative one, particularly the examples from Ile aux Coudres in Charlevoix County, Quebec.

Folk Culture Collection. Most of the 2,000 textiles and costumes in this interesting and varied collection represent the textile crafts of many ethnic groups who have settled in Canada. The material has been divided into two groups: (1) textiles brought from the homeland and (2) those made in Canada following traditional patterns and motifs.

The work comes from more than 20 different cultural groups, including those from Bulgaria, Hungary, Iceland, Latvia, Lithuania, and the Ukraine. Perhaps the most interesting aspect of the holdings is a collection of 80 complete folk costumes—a literal treasury of the designs and motifs traditionally used in European folk craft. In addition, there are numerous examples of embroidery, lace, beadwork, crochet work, weaving, and sampler making. The pieces were originally used as wall hangings, tablecloths, shelf liners, antimacassars, and other types of decoration for the home.

For designers, this collection can become a rich and fascinating source of inspiration

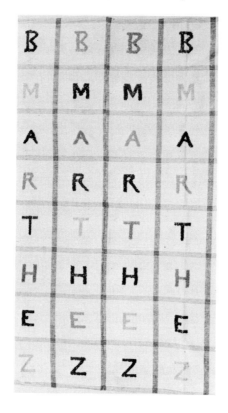

since it concentrates in one place the varied resources of many different cultures.

SAINT JOHN, N.B.

The New Brunswick Museum
277 Douglas Avenue
ZIP: E2K 1E5   TEL: (506) 693-1196
Valerie Simpson, Registrar

The New Brunswick Museum has a large collection of textiles and costumes, but it is difficult to assess its range since much of the material has not yet been catalogued or dated and there is no textile curator in charge. Nevertheless, even a general inventory of the holdings shows about 7,000 pieces of textiles, costume, and accessories from many different sources.

An analysis of the museum's extensive inventory list shows the following rough breakdown:

Costume—about 3,500 pieces.
Flat textiles—about 1,500 pieces.
Lace—about 1,900 pieces.

Among the 1,500 textile examples there are fabrics from Canada, Europe, and many other parts of the world, including about 250 pieces of damask weaving. There are good examples of Chinese and Japanese textile work, as well as a representative group of some 30 Canadian quilts of the late 19th Century. The laces are largely unnumbered, which means they have not yet been studied and no information about them is available.

The bulk of the costume collection consists of women's fashion clothing dating from 1860 to 1890. There is also a collection of ethnic garments of such diverse types as Chinese and Japanese robes, Greek peasant costumes, and Moslem and Indian dress. Also a good deal of Paris couture.

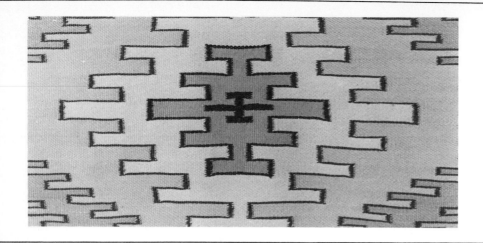

LEFT. Carpatho-Ukraine wall hanging in natural-dyed wool, 1870. Size: 3½' × 6'. *Ukrainian Arts & Crafts Museum.*

BELOW. Woman's shirt, woven, with embroidered collar and cuffs. From the Volyn region of N. W. Ukraine, 1870. *Ukrainian Arts & Crafts Museum.*

SASKATOON, SASK.

Ukrainian Arts & Crafts Museum
1240 Temperance Street
ZIP: S7N 0P1   TEL: (306) 242-0429

Linda M. Lazarowich, Director

The Ukrainian Arts & Crafts Museum in Saskatoon is a National Museum with branches in Toronto, Winnipeg, Edmonton, and Vancouver, sponsored by the Ukrainian Women's Assoc. of Canada. (It has no connection with the Ukrainian Cultural & Educational Centre in Winnipeg.)

The specialized collection of textiles and costumes which it holds is the largest in Canada and one of the largest in North America—with holdings estimated at over 40,000 pieces. They consist entirely of work made by Ukrainians either in the Ukraine or in Canada, and they cover a period from the early 1800s to the present.

The following materials predominate: wall hangings (kilims); bench covers (nalawnyks); sashes (poyas); skirts (plaxta-obhortka); shirts; decorative towels; table coverings; beaded neckbands (gerdans); block prints (vebeka); many types of embroidery; leather work with embroidery; jackets; and various other costume pieces.

This vast store of materials reflects the cultural diversity of the Ukraine, which has some forty provinces, each with distinctive design motifs, craft techniques, and colorings. This is particularly apparent in the embroidery work. For designers interested in Ukrainian folk art the collection is therefore an invaluable resource.

Edukits. The museum is currently developing a series of educational kits on Ukrainian art and culture. Costumes, weavings, and embroideries will be an important part of this program. They will be presented through color slides and cassette tapes in both English and Ukrainian. And the kits will be accompanied by catalogs with appropriate color plates.

Traveling Exhibitions. Another facet of the museum's active educational program is concerned with traveling exhibitions which will tour Canada. The first of these exhibits will be concerned with Ukrainian embroidery; the second, with costumes and weavings.

Research Facilities. The museum owns an extensive library of ethnographic works and journals published in the Ukraine, in Canada, and in the United States. Many of these date from the turn of the century, and a few rare volumes go back to the mid-1800s. Most of the material is in the Ukrainian language. Photography is permitted in the museum, but arrangements for research visits must be made in writing.

Publication. *Ukrainian Embroidery Designs & Stitches.* 1958. Published by Trident Press, Winnipeg, for the Ukrainian Women's Association of Canada. 130 pages with color plates and 219 illustrations of designs, giving their regional origins. Under the same title the museum has also published an album with 12 color plates of embroidery designs taken from the book.

TORONTO, ONT.

Royal Ontario Museum
100 Queen's Park
ZIP: M5S 2C6   TEL: (416) 928-3655

John Vollmer, Asst. Curator-in-Charge, Textile Dept.
Veronika Gervers, Assoc. Curator
Mary Holford, Asst. Curator

Even a casual stroll through the galleries of the Royal Ontario Museum makes it abundantly clear that the museum management has a high regard for its textile collection. Four major galleries are assigned to the Textile Department, and they are effectively used to mount textile-costume exhibits which change frequently. In addition, there are displays of important art fabrics in the galleries devoted to China, Japan, India, Greece, and Ethnology.

The collection itself justifies this attention. It is one of the most important of all U.S. and Canadian collections. It holds about 13,000 pieces, of which 9,000 are flat textiles and 4,000 are costumes or accessories. It is international in scope, owning many and fine examples of art fabrics from most parts of the world and covering a time span from ancient Peru and Coptic Egypt to contemporary textiles and fashions.

The ROM collection owns excellent examples of the textile art one would expect to find in any well-rounded international collection, but it also owns unique pieces which are seldom if ever found in most general collections.

For example, it has a representative collection of costume and textiles from many ethnic minorities in Southeast Asia. These were acquired through Canadian missionaries who sent examples of material culture to their home churches or to local universities with religious affiliations.

Another example is the unique collection of Latvian and Estonian textiles brought to Canada by immigrants and gathered by

RIGHT. The Royal Ontario Museum (ROM) at the junction of Bloor Street and Avenue Road in Toronto, Canada.

BELOW. Painted-and-dyed cotton from the Coromandel Coast, India, 1720–40. Probably made for the Dutch market. *ROM—934.4.54. (67Tex180).*

them as a permanent record of their cultural roots.

Equally unique is the large and noteworthy collection of early Canadian weaving and quilting—undoubtedly the finest of its kind anywhere.

It thus becomes apparent that ROM combines the types of textile resources usually found separately in museums of art and museums of natural history. Researchers will therefore find here a remarkably wide range of textile inspiration.

Add to this my personal impression that the Textile Department at ROM is blessed with one of the most cooperative, knowledgeable, and enthusiastic staffs it has yet been my pleasure to meet. The curatorial members and the departmental assistants make it a pleasure to work at the museum and explore its resources. The fact that ROM is in Toronto is a bonus, for I find this one of the most pleasant cities in North America, with a human dimension which is rare in a high-rise urban environment.

Here, then, are brief notes on the chief holdings which make up this notable textile-costume collection of some 13,000 pieces.

Canada. The record of early Canadian handweaving is large and representative— about 1,000 pieces. A great many come from Ontario, but there is also good representation from Quebec and the Maritime Provinces. There are many woven coverlets and other domestic textiles, as well as a comprehensive collection of handweaving equipment.

This collection of early Canadian handweaving is the subject of a definitive work *Keep Me Warm One Night* by Harold and Dorothy Burnham, University of Toronto Press, 1972.

Canadian quilting is another important category in the collection. There are about 75 pieces, a well-balanced group illustrating the different types and designs made in Canada.

Both the Canadian weaving and quilting collections are backed by good comparative material from other countries.

Latvia/Estonia. As noted earlier, the textiles in this unique collection were acquired from two of Canada's national minority groups who assembled them as a record of the folk arts in their homelands. There are several hundred pieces in the group. They include woven, embroidered, and knitted fabrics such as blankets, shawls, and household linens.

Printed Textiles. This is one of the strongest groups in the whole textile collection—about 650 pieces, most of which are French. These, together with the Indian painted-and-dyed cottons for the European market (noted below), are part of the Harry Wearne Collection given to the museum by Mrs. Harry Wearne.

From the 18th Century the museum holds about 250 examples of French cottons printed by wood block. They provide a comprehensive picture of work done at Jouy and Nantes, as well as other important print centers in 18th-Century France.

Also from the 18th Century come 50 examples of early French copperplate printing, some of them quite rare.

From the 19th Century—about 300 pieces of French work. One famous example in the collection is a large wood-block print made for the Great Exhibition of 1851 in London. At the time it was reviewed as an outstanding example of good taste.

English print work of both the 18th and 19th Centuries is represented by some 40 pieces, two or three of which are rare early copperplate prints.

Painted & Dyed. Though not large in numbers, this is an outstanding collection of painted-and-dyed cottons made in India for the European market during the 18th Century. There are some 75 pieces in the group, and they are carefully described in a most interesting research work which brings them together with similar Indo-European cottons held by the Victoria &

ROYAL ONTARIO MUSEUM cont'd

Albert Museum, London. The book is *Origins of Chintz*, listed at the end of this ROM review.

Woven Fabrics. The woven collection is chiefly European and also numbers about 650 pieces. Its major strength lies in European silks, of which there are some 500 examples representing England, France, and other silk-weaving centers in Europe. The emphasis is on 18th-Century work, but there are also examples of earlier work as well as pieces from the 19th Century. Because of its range and variety this unit is considered an excellent study and teaching collection.

Another important grouping among the woven fabrics comes from Turkey. It holds about 100 examples of Turkish towel weaving with brocaded and tapestry-woven decorations.

A smaller collection of towels comes from Transylvania (Roumania), and there are

also a few examples of Hungarian weaving skill.

Among more ancient fabrics in the woven group are two important examples of Persian velvet weaving from the period of the Safavid Dynasty (1499–1736). Finally, there are important groups of Coptic and early Islamic wovens, which are listed at a later point in this review.

Embroidery. The embroidery collection (excluding Asiatic embroideries) has about 800 pieces—chiefly from England, Continental Europe, Turkey, Greece, and Hungary.

English embroideries cover the 16th to the 19th Century—about 175 pieces, some outstanding, especially in early blackwork and crewelwork.

Continental Europe is represented by some 200 pieces, chiefly from Italy, France, and Spain.

Turkish embroidery is the largest group in this category—over 200 pieces, chiefly

18th- and 19th-Century work but also including some earlier work.

Greece and the Greek Islands—over 100 pieces. There are good examples of work from Rhodes, Cos, Naxos, and several other areas.

Hungary—about 100 pieces, with especially good examples of 19th-Century needlework from Transylvania.

Lace. The curatorial staff at ROM regards its laces as a good study collection. There are over 900 pieces dating from the 16th to the 19th Century and representing most of the important types of needle and bobbin lace from the great periods of Italy, France, Belgium, and England.

Far East. The Far Eastern collection at ROM covers China, Formosa, Japan, Korea, India, Tibet, Bhutan, Burma, Central Asia, and at least eight regions in Southeast Asia. In all it holds over 2,500 pieces of textiles and costume from these areas, the strongest groups from China Japan, and India. A more detailed listing follows.

China. In numbers this is the largest unit in the ROM textile collection—1,350 pieces. The majority are small accessories—about 1,100 pieces. However, there is also an outstanding collection of 70 court robes and 150 more informal costumes. Among the court robes is a notable example of a 17th-Century dragon robe, as well as several 18th- and 19th-Century 12-symbol dragon robes.

Aside from these costume pieces the collection owns a substantial group of mandarin squares and a range of woven silks and embroidery pieces. Among them is a unique panel of 17th-Century velvet made from a length intended for an Imperial robe of state.

Finally, there is a group of about 30 pile carpets, six of which are considered important pieces.

Formosa. About 75 pieces of Atayal cos-

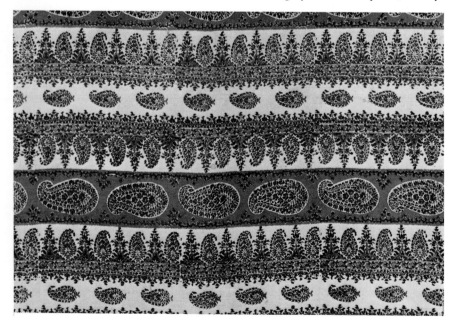

RIGHT. Toile de Jouy copperplate print by Oberkampf titled *Children's Games*, about 1780. Harry Wearne Collection. *ROM—934.4.441 (65Tex297).*

BELOW. Painted-and-dyed cotton, Coromandel Coast, India, 1775–1800. Gift of Mrs. W. B. Harris. *ROM—972.260 (72Tex311).*

tume from the northern aboriginal people, collected in the 1890s by Rev. G. L. MacKay.

Japan. There are close to 800 pieces in the Japanese collection. It is strong in folk costume and textiles of the 19th Century—about 300 pieces. Also about 75 other costume (not folk) of the 18th and 19th Centuries. The remainder of the Japanese group (about 400 pieces) consists of woven silks in many designs and constructions and these may on the whole prove more valuable to the working designer than the more elaborate costume pieces.

Korea. About 75 pieces representative of Korean textiles and costume during the 19th and early 20th Centuries.

Tibet. About 30 pieces of Tibetan costume and flat textiles.

Central Asia. About 50 pieces, chiefly from Afghanistan, including both embroidery and woven fabrics in costumes.

India. About 250 pieces, not including the painted-and-dyed cottons noted earlier. There are embroideries, decorative woven panels, and costumes. The costume pieces date from both the 18th and 19th Centuries. The embroideries are chiefly 18th Century work made for the European market.

Assam/Bhutan/Burma. About 30 pieces representing the different cultures in this area.

Southeast Asia. The textiles from this part of the world were chiefly acquired through Canadian missionaries, as noted earlier. In all there are about 740 pieces, but the overwhelming majority (600) come from Indonesia. These are dominantly ikats and batiks from Sumatra and Java—superb decorations to inspire every print designer.

The other groups in the Southeast Asian collection are much smaller but equally rich in design ideas. There are 45 pieces form Thailand, 30 silk ikats and other silks from Cambodia, 15 pieces each from Laos and

Vietnam, 8 pieces of Iban material from Borneo, and a representative group of 25 pieces from the Philippines. The latter are mostly from Mindanao and are part of the collection which was assembled in the 1906 Louisiana Purchase Exposition. (The Field Museum in Chicago owns the bulk of this material.)

Central & South America. Though this is not a particularly strong group, it represents some of the most important textile cultures in the region. In all there are about 230 pieces divided between Mexico, Guatemala, Chile, Bolivia, and Peru, including ancient Peru.

From Mexico come about 50 pieces, chiefly regional costumes from South Mexico.

From Guatemala—30 pieces of highland costume.

From Chile, Bolivia, and Peru—about 50 pieces of contemporary textiles and costume.

From pre-Columbian Peru—about 100

pieces, including two large Paracas mantles and half a dozen decorative ponchos.

Africa. About 180 pieces, most of them from Nigeria (150) and the Congo (30). There is also a large and interesting hanging from Gondar (Abyssinia). It was made by the card-weaving technique and probably dates from the 17th Century.

Coptic. An important and diversified collection of over 200 pieces dating from the 4th Century. It includes several complete tunics with tapestry-woven decorations (claves). It also includes a large and most impressive curtain or hanging of the 3–4th Century in a remarkable state of preservation. The design is a tapestry-woven widely spaced repeat of moving animals and equestrian hunters on a natural linen ground. The piece is about 88 by 136 inches in size and is permanently displayed behind glass in the gallery devoted to ancient Greece. The only similar piece I have seen in North America is one owned by the Field Museum in Chicago, and it is a fragment.

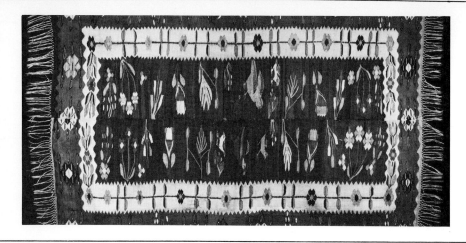

LEFT. Tapestry-woven rug from Rumania (Oltenia), 20th C. Gift of Alice M. Calverley. *ROM—941.22.217 (72Tex351).*

BELOW. French woodblock-printed cotton, 1851. Exhibited by Japuis et Fils of Paris at the Great Exhibition. Harry Wearne Coll. *ROM—934.4.445 (64Tex39).*

ROYAL ONTARIO MUSEUM cont'd

Early Islamic. A group of 30 woven Islamic textiles dating from the 8th to the 12th Century.

Regional Costume. Over 500 pieces of folk costume and festival garments from 14 different countries. Most of the countries are represented by from 5 to 20 pieces, but from Roumania the museum owns a much larger group of some 400 pieces. There are complete festival and everyday costumes, embroidered leather pieces, embroidered blouses, and many other examples of Roumanian folk textile craft.

Other countries with smaller representation in the collection are Hungary, Greece, Yugoslavia, Albania, Turkey, Persia, Palestine, Sudan, Bulgaria, Slovakia, Spain, and the U.S.S.R.

Fashionable Clothing. This is one of the major collections of fashion costume in North America. It owns over 4,000 pieces and covers changing fashions in both Europe and North America from the 18th Century to the present. Accessories reach back further to the 15th Century, and there are shoes from Anglo-Saxon times. The collection is especially strong in Canadian women's fashions from 1780 to the present.

Rugs. About 50 pieces (not including China) with good examples of flat-woven rugs from the Caucasus, Anatolia (Turkey), Persia, Afghanistan, and the Balkans.

Ethnology. The Ethnology Department at ROM holds a small collection of textiles for which no exact count is available. The group includes a fair representation of American Indian costume from the Plains, the Woodlands, and the North Pacific Coast. From the latter region come several fine Chilkat blankets.

From Africa, the ethnographic textiles are chiefly drawn from the Kasai region of the Congo. They are the work of the Bakuba or Zappa Zap people, who make a distinctive embroidered cloth from palm fiber. There are also woven textiles and tapa cloths from Angola and Nigeria.

From the South Pacific region (chiefly New Zealand) the department owns some examples of flax weaving and tapa cloth. Also some bags of plaited grass from Samoa and netted string bags from New Guinea.

Publications. The Textile Department at ROM has maintained an active publication program. Works by the curatorial staff are listed below.

The following have all been published under the ROM imprint.

1. *English Embroidery—16th to 18th Centuries.* By Katharine B. Brett. 1972. Describes the ROM collection. 94 pages.

2. *Haute Couture.* By Katharine B. Brett and the Fashion Group, Inc. of Toronto. 1969. Notes on fashion designers and their clothes. 68 pages.

3. *Women's Costume in Ontario (1867-1907).* By K. B. Brett. 1966. 16 pages.

4. *Women's Costumes in Early Ontario.* By K. B. Brett. 1965. 16 pages.

5. *Modesty to Mod.* By K. B. Brett, with 12 patterns and related notes by Dorothy K. Burnham. 1967. Describes clothes worn in Canada 1780–1967. 72 pages.

RIGHT. Section of Taoist priest's robe in green silk satin with couched design in gold thread. Chinese, late 18th C. *ROM— 950.100.570 (74 Tex 294).*

BELOW. Woven Ukrainian Sluts'k sash, about 1780. *Ukrainian Cultural & Educational Centre, Winnipeg, Canada.*

6. *Chinese Velvets.* By Harold B. Burnham. 1959. A technical study. The late Mr. Burnham was Curator of Textiles at ROM.

7. *Costumes for Canada's Birthday.* By D. K. Burnham. 1967.

8. *Cut My Cote.* By D. K. Burnham. 1973. A pioneer study and a most interesting one of the different ways in which lengths of cloth were cut up to make different types of garments in different cultures. Illustrated with diagrams by the author. 36 pages.

9. *The Hungarian Szur.* By Veronika Gervers-Molnar. 1973. Describes an archaic mantle of Eurasian origin. Dr. Gervers is a member of the Textile Department curatorial staff at ROM.

10. *Japanese Art.* By John E. Vollmer and G. T. Webb. 1972. Describes Japanese holdings at the Art Gallery of Greater Victoria. Mr. Vollmer is a member of the Textile Department curatorial staff at ROM. 241 pages.

The following three works were issued by other publishers.

11. *Origins of Chintz.* By Katharine B. Brett and John Irwin. London,' 1970. H. M. Stationary Office. 134 pages, 166 plates.

12. *Keep Me Warm One Night.* By H. B. and D. K. Burnham. Toronto, 1972. University of Toronto Press. 416 pages, fully illustrated with photographs and weaving charts. A definitive treatment on early handweaving in Eastern Canada.

13. *Japanese Country Textiles.* By K. B. Brett and H. B. Burnham. Toronto, 1965. University of Toronto Press, Catalog for a ROM exhibition. 40 pages, illustrated

Research Facilities. The museum has a large library on the decorative arts, and the Textile Department has a comprehensive file of B/W photographs which can be ordered. Unfortunately, until the museum's expansion program is completed, there are no research facilities.

VICTORIA, B.C.

Art Gallery of Greater Victoria
1040 Moss Street
ZIP: V8V 4P1   TEL:(604) 384-4101

Colin D. Graham, Director Emeritus

The Art Gallery of Greater Victoria has only a small collection of textiles—about 300 examples—but among them is a special group of Japanese pieces which should interest designers.

It consists of about 100 large squares (18 by 24 inches) of stenciled fabrics taken from 19th-Century folk costumes. Complementing these pieces are 120 stencils (katagami) which were used in making the designs for such fabrics.

In addition to this notable group, the museum owns 13 large screens made from 19th-Century folk bed coverlets, as well as several pieces of ritual costume. Also a dozen 19th-Century Chinese robes and about 20 batiks made in the early part of this century.

Other holdings include 30 pieces of 18th- and 19th-Century lace, and a 17th-Century French tapestry.

WINNIPEG, MAN.

Ukrainian Cultural & Educational Centre
184 Alexander Avenue E. Box 722
ZIP: R3C 2K3

Sophia Kachor, Curator

The Museum of the Ukrainian Cultural & Educational Centre in Winnipeg owns a specialized collection of close to 900 pieces —fabrics made or used in the Ukraine. They date from the 17th to the 20th Century and are of two types: (1) silks and brocades of the 17th–19th Century belonging to the Ukrainian upper classes; and (2) linen and wool fabrics common to the Ukraine's rural population.

The first category includes about 70 examples of silk and brocade work, mostly imports from France, Italy, Persia, Turkey, and Russia. Also five 19th-Century silk shawls with gold and silver decorations. In addition, there is a large group (350 pieces) of silk and wool ribbons made or used in the Ukraine during the 18th–19th Century.

The second category of folk textiles consists mainly of homespun wool or linen fabrics, many with embroidery. They include some 40 hangings, dating from the 17th–20th Century; about 50 skirts and skirt fragments; 35 wool sashes; 100 linen shirts; 75 linen towels with woven or embroidered designs; 30 wool vests and other types of outer garments; 40 examples of ecclesiastical embroidery; and about 100 miscellaneous pieces.

Some of the material is on display in the Centre's Museum.

The Centre maintains a research library of some 20,000 volumes, chiefly in the Ukrainian language but with a good many works in English. Among these are special publications which reveal Ukrainian weaving methods, patterns, and design samples, as well as Ukrainian costumes.

Coptic textile, 5–6th Century. *Newark Museum—16082A.*

COLOR PAGES . . . The section of color photographs beginning on the

facing page is token of the rich source material held by textile collections in North America.

AMERICA. Appliqué quilt with embroidered detail, signed P.W. Early 19th Century. Usually referred to as the Phebe Warner quilt and a superb example of the type. Gift of Catherine E. Cotheal, 1938. *Met—38.59.*

AMERICA. Silk quilt in "bow-tie" pattern, about 1920. Purchase, Sansbury-Mills Fund, 1973. *Met—1973-205.*

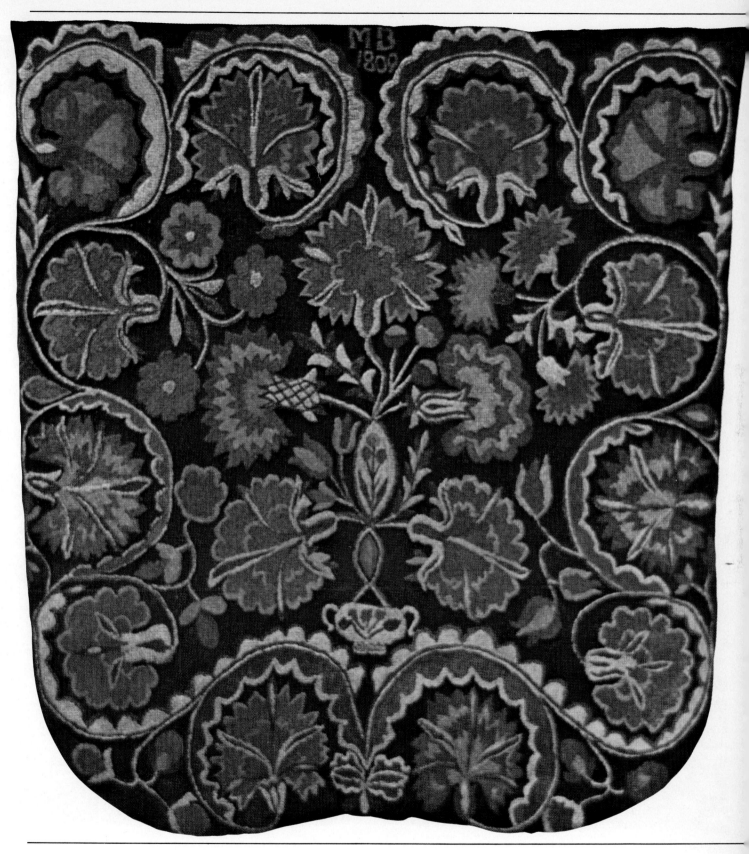

AMERICA. Bed rugg. Canvas tufted in wool, dated 1809. Purchase, Rogers Fund, 1913. *Met — 13.207.*

AMERICA. "Sunshine and Shadow," pieced quilt, Lancaster, Pa., 1900-1910. Amish quilts are known for their distinctive and interesting color combinations. Eva Gebhardt-Gourgand Foundation Gift, 1973. *Met—1973.94.*

TOP. **AMERICA.** "Friendship Quilt," appliqué. Baltimore, 1845-50. It is made of cotton with embroidered silk detailing. Purchase, Sansbury-Mills Fund, 1974. *Met — 1974.24.*

BOTTOM. **AMERICA.** "Crazy Quilt" by Aletta Davis, c. 1850. Gift of Rev. & Mrs. Karl Nielsom, 1962. *Met — 62.143.*

AMERICA. Sampler from the huge Whitman Sampler Collection. Silk on canvas, 18 x 21½ inches. Made by Mary Wiggin in 1797. Given by Pet Incorporated. *Philadelphia Museum of Art—'69-288-18.*

AMERICAN INDIAN. Man's shirt of mountain-goat hair in the dramatic Chilkat pattern weaving. The design represents the brown bear. It is from the Tlingit tribe of Alaska. *Museum of the American Indian—19/9098(1831).*

TOP. **AMERICAN INDIAN.** Navajo (Yeibichai) blanket, sand-painting design. *Museum of the American Indian—(2451).*

BOTTOM. **AMERICAN INDIAN.** Navajo blanket of woven wool. *Museum of the American Indian—(2447).*

AMERICAN INDIAN. Beaded shoulder bag from Lenape, Oklahoma. *Museum of the American Indian—(1896).*

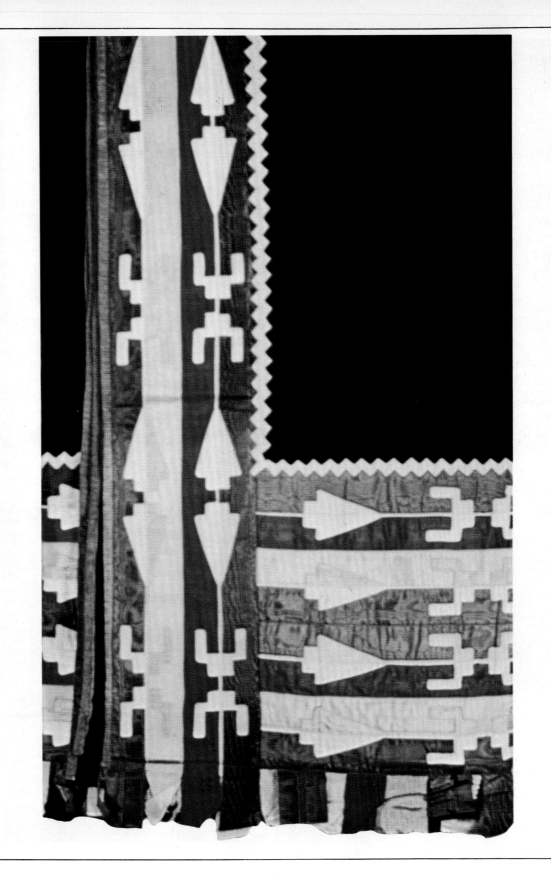

AMERICAN INDIAN. Detail of a ribbonwork appliqué blanket, Osage. *Museum of the American Indian—(2215).*

AMERICAN INDIAN. Detail of ribbonwork blanket on stroud cloth, Sauk-Fox. *Museum of the American Indian—(2671).*

TOP. **AMERICAN INDIAN.** Woman's beaded cape, Cree, Canada. *Museum of the American Indian—(2676).*

BOTTOM. **AMERICAN INDIAN.** Painted tipi lining, Teton, Dakota. *Museum of the American Indian—(3774).*

AMERICAN INDIAN. Embroidered design on a Hopi blanket. *Museum of the American Indian—(4274).*

PANAMA. Man's beadwork collar, Guaymi. *Museum of the American Indian —(3343).*

PERU. Tapestry hat from Nazca, Coast Tiahuanaco, about 500 A.D. *University Museum, Philadelphia —(221).*

PERU. Detail of embroidered textile, Paracas, about 300 B.C. *University Museum, Philadelphia —(222a).*

PERU. Textile from the Nazca culture, 200-800 A.D. *University Museum, Philadelphia—(230).*

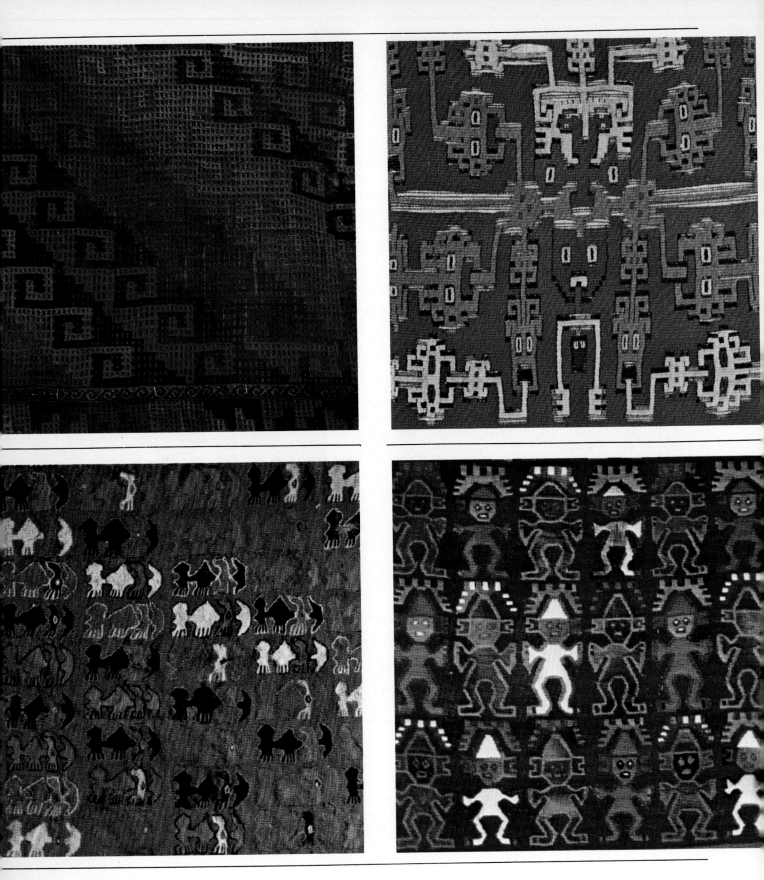

TOP LEFT. **PERU.** Chancay textile, 1000-1400 A.D. *Duke University Museum of Art—20.*

TOP RIGHT. **PERU.** Detail of Nazca textile, 100 B.C.- 400 A.D. *University Museum, Philadelphia—234a.*

BOTTOM LEFT. **PERU.** Wool-cotton tapestry panel, coastal region, Late Chimu, 10-11th Century. *Met—33.149.95.*

BOTTOM RIGHT. **PERU.** Tapestry breechcloth panel. Chancay, 1000-1400 A.D. *Duke University Museum of Art—P941T.*

LEFT. **PERU.** Paracas textile, about 300 B.C. *University Museum, Philadelphia—(227).*

RIGHT. **PERU.** Textile fragment, Ica, 1000-1400 A.D. Cotton-wool slit tapestry weave with embroidered outlines, 4¼ x 15 inches. *Cranbrook Academy of Art/Museum—1939.153.*

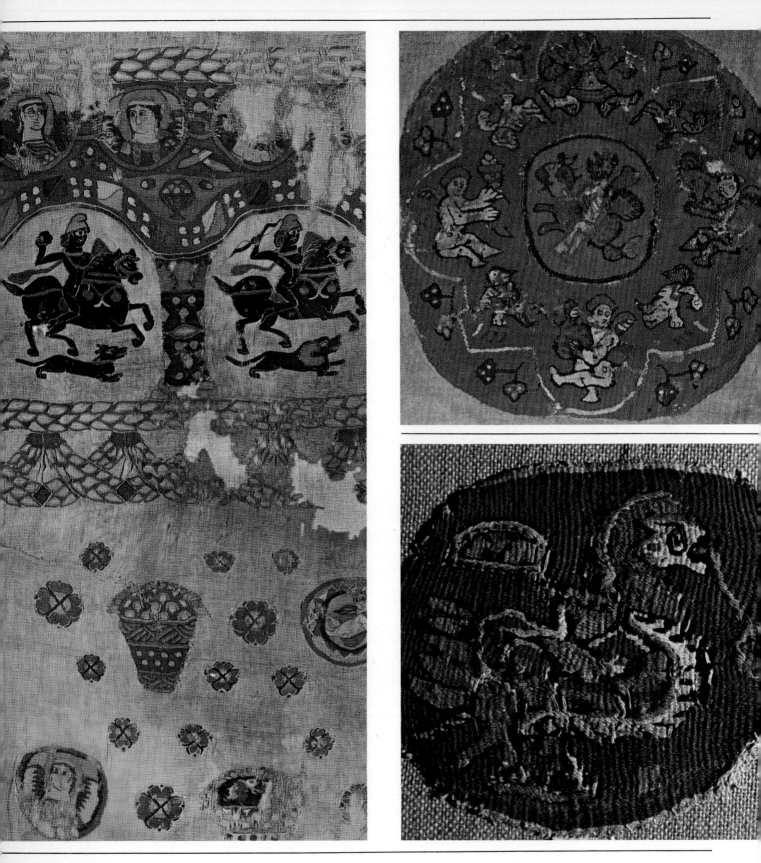

LEFT. **EGYPT.** Portion of linen hanging with tapestry-woven wool ornament, Coptic, 5th Century. Gift of George F. Baker, 1890. *Met—90.5.905.*

TOP RIGHT. **EGYPT.** Medallion, Christian-Egyptian, 4th-6th Century. Linen-wool weft-faced slit tapestry weave, 11¼ x 12 inches. *Cranbrook Academy of Art/Museum—Temp. 1004.*

BOTTOM RIGHT. **EGYPT.** Coptic tapestry weave, 6th-7th Century. Gift of George Pratt, 1933. *Met—33.19.2.*

EGYPT. Coptic tapestry roundel, wool on linen, about 13 x 12¼ inches. *Textile Museum—11.18.*

ENGLAND. Woodblock-printed cotton with inscription of royal wedding, 1816. Similar designs were often printed by the yard to be used as center motifs in pieced quilts. Gift of William Sloan Coffin, 1928. *Met—28.153.5.*

MANUFACTURE. DE OBERKAMPF.
PRÈS VERSAILLES. BON TEIN

TOP LEFT. **FRANCE.** Early 18th-Century fragment of brocaded compound tabby weave. Linen, silk, and metallic gold thread wrapped around silk core, 13½ x 20 inches. *Cranbrook Academy of Art/Museum—1927.444.*

TOP RIGHT. **FRANCE.** 18th-Century woodblock-printed cotton from the Oberkampf printworks at Jouy. Gift of William Sloan Coffin, 1926. *Met—26.265.111.*

BOTTOM. **ENGLAND.** Embroidered coverlet dated 1728. Linen-cotton embroidered with wool, about 50 x 54 inches. Gift of Mr. & Mrs. Edgar J. Stone in memory of Gerard Brett. *Royal Ontario Museum—970.128.*

TOP. **SPAIN.** Silk curtain, Hispano-Moresque, 15th Century. Purchase, Fletcher Fund, 1929. *Met—29.22.*

BOTTOM. **NORTH AFRICA.** Early 19th-Century bolster cover, linen tabby embroidered with colored silks. Purchase, Everfast Fabrics, Inc. Fund, 1970. *Met—1970.272.*

TOP LEFT. **GREECE.** 18th-Century embroidered Ionian valance. Gift of George D. Pratt, 1931. *Met—31.42.*

TOP RIGHT. **TURKEY.** Silk embroidery of the late 16th-early 17th Century, 90 x 31 inches. *Textile Museum—1.22.*

BOTTOM LEFT. **GREECE.** Embroidered skirt border, Crete, 18th Century. Purchase, Rogers Fund, 1914. *Met—14.62.2.*

BOTTOM RIGHT. **TURKEY.** Woven silk, late 16th Century, about 44 x 24 inches. *Textile Museum—1.68.*

CENTRAL ASIA. This magnificent 18th-Century embroidery is from Samarkand. Like similar pieces from the region, it was probably a girl's dowry, made by herself and members of her family over many years. The work is done with silk thread in a chain or couched (Bukhara) stitch through two layers of cloth—one silk, the other linen. The ground cloth is completely covered with the intricate embroidery. *Artweave Textile Gallery, NYC.*

TOP LEFT. **CENTRAL ASIA.** Detail of a 19th-Century silk ikat woven in Turkestan. *Artweave Textile Galley, NYC.*

TOP RIGHT. **CENTRAL ASIA.** Another example of Turkestan ikat design. *Artweave Textile Gallery, NYC.*

BOTTOM LEFT. **CENTRAL ASIA.** Detail of the Samarkand embroidery at left. *Artweave Textile Gallery, NYC.*

BOTTOM RIGHT. **CENTRAL ASIA.** Typical motif in a Turkestan ikat design. *Artweave Textile Gallery, NYC.*

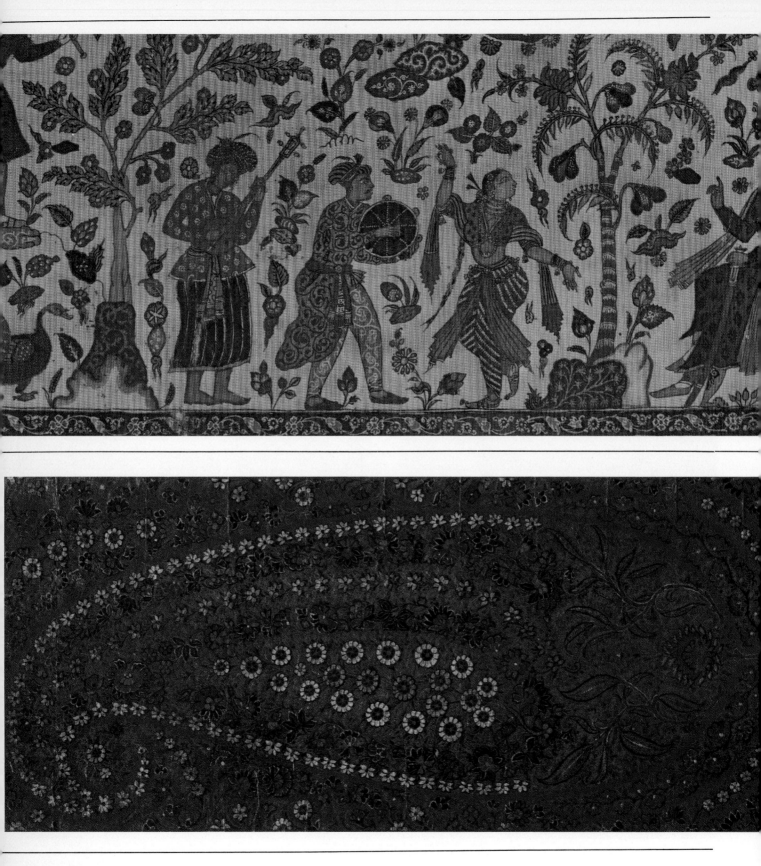

TOP. **INDIA.** Painted-and-dyed cotton cushion cover, 1640-50. Purchase, Rogers Fund, 1928. *Met—28.159.2.*

BOTTOM. **INDIA.** Painted design for a Kashmir shawl motif, gouache on paper. This is one of eight such designs brought to England from India in 1823 by William Moorecroft. They can be examined in the Department of Prints and Photographs at the Met. Elisha Whittelsey Collection, 1962. *Met—62.600.235.2.*

CHINA. Imperial dragon robe embroidered in silks and couched, wrapped gold. First half of the 18th Century. Bequest of Wm. Christian Paul, 1930. *Met—30.75.79.*

CHINA. Mandarin square from the early Ch'ing Dynasty, 17th Century. Military rank badge with Lion of India embroidered in silk and couched, wrapped gold on satin. Purchase, Fletcher Fund, 1936. *Met — 36.65.4.*

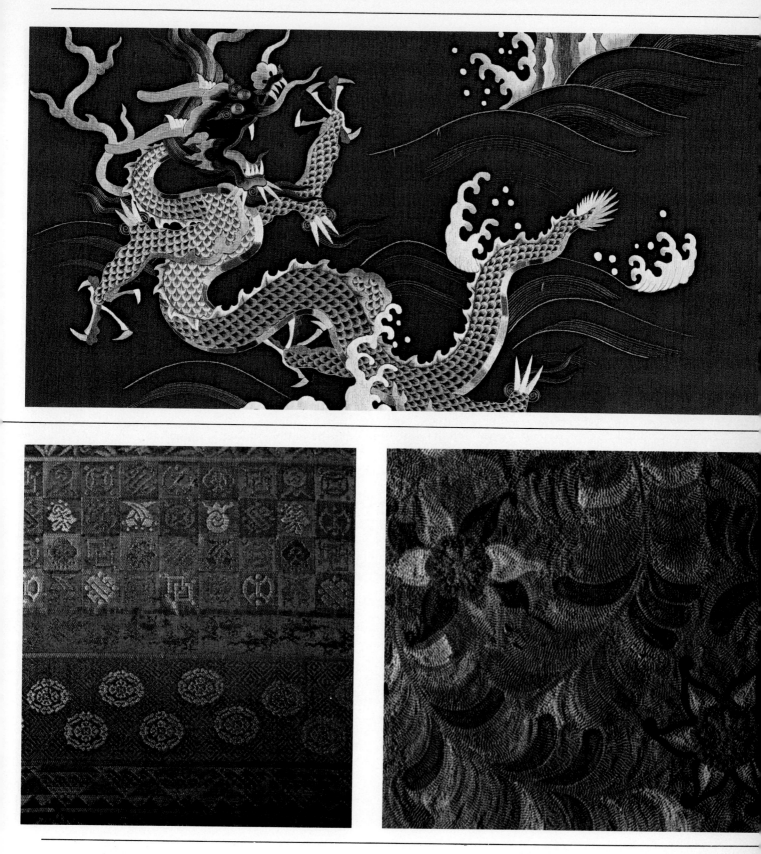

TOP. **CHINA.** Embroidered chair back, early 18th Century. Bequest of Wm. Christian Paul, 1930. *Met—30.75.49.*

BOTTOM LEFT. **JAPAN.** Brocaded silk, 19th Century (?). Gift of Mr. & Mrs. H. O. Havemeyer, 1896. *Met—96.14.632.*

BOTTOM RIGHT. **JAPAN.** Woven silk, 19th Century (?). Gift of Mr. & Mrs. H. O. Havemeyer, 1896. *Met—96.14.1916.*

JAPAN. Detail of early 19th-Century ceremonial coverlet made in the shape of a kimono. The fabric is cotton tabby. The lobster design is painted and resist-dyed. Purchase, Seymour Fund, 1966. *Met—66.239.3.*

TRADITIONS OF NORTH AMERICAN TEXTILE DESIGN

Painted buffalo robe, Oglala Dakota (Sioux). *Am. Mus. of Nat. Hist.—411497.*

American patchwork, c. 1830. Gift: Mrs. M. M. Fogg. *Phila. Mus.—24-11-5.*

Ontario coverlet, 1840–60. Gift of Evelyn G. Follett. *ROM—961.96 (70 Tex 103).*

The cultural melting pot which is North America could hardly be expected to foster a homogeneous tradition of textile design—except in the cultures of American Indians. The New World acquired a composite of older traditions born and nurtured in the Old World, then adapted to the needs of a developing society.

Because of this fragmented cultural past it seemed inadequate to discuss the traditions of North American textile design in a single survey. Instead I have divided the discussion into three distinct parts: (1) United States traditions; (2) Canadian traditions; and (3) American Indian traditions.

In the pages which follow each of these subjects is treated by specialists:

1. U.S. Textile Traditions. An essay by Robert Riley, a specialist who is himself a link between the separate worlds of museum and commerce. His long association with the Brooklyn Museum Design Lab as its Consultant to the Textile/Fashion industries has made him thoroughly familiar with the major traditions of U.S. textile design. His more recent appointment as Director of the F.I.T. Design Lab places under his jurisdiction the world's largest facility for textile/fashion research. He writes of U.S. textile traditions from a point of view which will be understood immediately by textile designers and students.

2. Canadian Textile Traditions, by Dorothy K. Burnham, is the work of a creative scholar whose long curatorial association with the Royal Ontario Museum has given her the opportunity to explore all facets of the Canadian textile experience. She is the author of a fascinating pioneer study on the different ways in which lengths of cloth were cut into garments by past cultures—*Cut My Cote.* She is also co-author of *Keep Me Warm One Night*, a definitive work on early handweaving in Eastern Canada.

3. Fabrics of the North American Indians. This comprehensive essay was written by the anthropologist Prof. Andrew Hunter Whiteford, who has spent more than 30 years studying the archaeological remains and the living cultures of Indians in all the Americas. It is the longest of the three essays and the most detailed, since I believe this to be an area about which too little has been written, though its significance is large in the world of textile design. As background for further study of Indian textiles it should prove invaluable.

U.S. TEXTILE TRADITIONS

When human beings first started living with their fellow humans to protect themselves, to hunt for food, and to raise their young, they expressed their feelings and their history in stories, in magic ceremonies, in drawings and sculpture, and most particularly in the crafts of everyday life: their pots, their ornaments and badges, the clothes they wore. Each people established its identity through its art. The weaving of the ancient Egyptians, the Chinese, and the West African tribes may have technical similarities, but the concepts and designs of each are unique, as separate as culture and distance can make them.

As the Spanish, English, Dutch, and French colonized the New World, they brought their arts from the old countries. These took root in the new soil whenever a group stayed in one place. Some of them even developed new forms, adapted to the rigors of life in a wilderness. But shortly, as successive waves of colonists appeared, as settle-

ments grew into towns of many different peoples, the arts began to lose their identities. By the time machines and mills replaced handicrafts, the American arts were homogenized, a reflection of European fashions.

After the Revolution broke England's colonial rule, Noah Webster exhorted the new American citizens to find an American way of life. "America must be independent in *literature* as she is in politics, as famous for *arts* as she is for *arms*," he urged, and she must stop "mimicking the follies of other nations." But a few years later Abigail Adams, on a trip to London, remarked so many Americans on the streets that she thought she had never left home.

Dominant European Influences

And, as the still-existing bills of lading show, the visiting Americans brought back calicos, damasks, fine woolens, and linens. From France they brought silk brocades and laces and dolls dressed in miniature clothes, made of French fabrics and trimmed in the latest styles. From these fabrics they made their finer clothes and furnished their best rooms, for goods of like quality were not made in the New World. The designs and constructions of novel European garments and fabrics were carefully studied by American tailors, dressmakers, and weavers, many of whom were very skilled at their trades and very clever at adapting the ideas they saw.

Merchants and early textile firms ordered sample books from England and Switzerland, Holland and France. Yardage was ordered from the books, but the samples themselves were especially prized as designs which could be adapted for domestic manufacture. One such sample service,

Claude Frères, existed in 1805, is still in business and widely used by our modern mills.

The fact that American fabric designs have followed the European mode may be ascribed in large portion to our colonial past. English ships took lumber, indigo, cotton, and raw products from the New World. They returned with manufactured goods to sell the colonists. Rival American manufacturing was actively discouraged by the mother country through both destructive taxation and violent controls. John Hewson, sponsored by Ben Franklin, set up a calico printworks in Philadelphia in 1774. The "insurrection" of 1775 gave General Howe the excuse to demolish his buildings, and the British offered 5 guineas for his "body dead or alive."

No Time for Luxuries

The art of textiles is an art of leisure produced by a settled people. There was no leisure for the colonial American. Life in a wilderness left little time for luxuries. The broad, unexplored acres of the new land, which could be had for the asking, lured adventurous families from settlements and towns. Even indentured servants, having served their time, could set up as free farmers instead of going through the arduous and long training required for a trade in the town. Consequently, skilled workmen were scarce. So long as land was free, America's arts could not match the long-established craftsmanship of Europe.

And yet there were arts in early America. The cultures which came with the settlers put out new roots in the new land. The painting, the pottery, the woodworking, and the homespun cloths might have been crudely utilitarian, but they were often marked by a rugged beauty. The forms and colors remembered from their past were translated by the colonial craftsmen,

RIGHT. Pa. embroidery sampler, 1777. Rogers Fund. *Met—59.20 (168006).*

FAR RIGHT. American "Star of Bethlehem" patchwork quilt, 19th Century, 94½" × 96". *Brooklyn Museum—57.154.7.*

limited in skills and materials, into new concepts and a new aesthetic.

Products of Necessity

Very little survives of our first textiles. Every scrap was used and used again. Even Martha Washington unraveled the yarn in her old gowns and in the General's stockings and wove them once again into chair seats or other practical articles. But America's patchwork quilts are a veritable museum of calicos, damasks, and homespuns. Odds and ends of fabrics were hoarded by families for generations to be used in making covers against the cold. More often than not, the fabric designs were usual enough—paisleys, dots, small florals or stripes—but the layout of the patches was generally imaginative and sometimes startlingly beautiful. Their geometric patterns, quite properly, are currently popular as examples of abstract art. Both quilting and patchwork were ancient crafts, but the limitations and the skills of our early needleworkers gave them a vigorous new interpretation which was distinctly American. That these needleworkers regarded their work with a certain wry humor is indicated by the names they gave their patterns: *Duck's Foot in the Mud, Robbing Peter to Pay Paul, Drunkard's Path, Hearts and Gizzards,* and other fancies.

Also products of necessity, ingenuity, and the saving of fabric scraps were hooked rugs and rag carpets. And the need for warmth against bitter New England winters produced the "bed rugg," a heavy, tufted coverlet of homespun wool dyed with indigo and other herbs into unusual colors and bold, handsome patterns.

The Blue Resist Print

A special type of blue resist print was unique to early 18th-century America. This was a discharge print, usually in two shades of indigo blue on a soft linen or linen/cotton ground and in a pattern of leaves and birds. The source of these patterns has never been satisfactorily established. They may have been taken from an East Indian *Tree of Life* design or from an English calico, yet in their flowing drawing and restricted colors they have an oddly oriental aspect. Again one is led to suspect that the limited facilities and unsophisticated skills of colonial printers had developed a new form while adapting an old design. Certain it is that many of the blue resists are singular and beautiful fabrics.

Home Work & Professionals

As early as 1640 Massachusetts required families to grow and spin flax and wool. Flax was important in the making of linen, and it was strong enough to be used as warp threads on a loom. Linen with wool filling produced the ubiquitous "linsey-woolsey," which was a staple in every home. It was used for everything from clothes to curtains. In an effort to duplicate the elegance of imported silks, the colonists embossed linsey-woolsey in designs taken from moiréd taffetas and satin damasks. The results were far from a duplication; the "moreen" had an artless and rough elegance of its own.

Not all weaving was done at home in the kitchen or attic. There were professional weavers in most sizable communities. Itinerant weavers covered the countryside, setting up their looms in barns to weave the linens and woolens spun by the household. Our textile museums have splendid examples of their work, most particularly the woolen coverlets with intricate geometric patterns of indigo and white. As looms became more complicated, designs followed suit. Analysis of one coverlet dated 1817 indicates that it was woven on a loom with 40 harnesses. After 1825 the Jacquard loom (described by one viewer as "looking like a threshing machine") enabled the weaver to produce double-wovens with charming flower, bird, feather, and gallant patriotic motifs, many with mottos and improving verse woven into the border.

Plain fabrics were decorated by wood-block printing, often done at home with blocks either borrowed or bought when the family lacked a skilled carver. Embroideries were worked in traditional, fanciful, and political patterns. The Brooklyn Museum possesses a coverlet embroidered by a patriot needleworker with the Battle of Bunker Hill. Stencils were used on coverlets, curtains, and walls. Instead of expensive carpeting, floor cloths were stretched and painted like marble, parquetry, or Wilton patterns. Painted fabric, "oilcloth," made table covers and rain capes. Our ancestors' ingenuity in "making do" with style was remarkable.

Homespuns vs. Imports

Fabrics became a weapon in the days leading up to the Revolution. The Daughters of Liberty pledged to boycott British goods and to wear only garments made of homespun. Not to be outdone by their sisters, the class of 1768 at Harvard graduated in homespun suits. Colors once called by British names such as Kendall Green, Lincoln Green, or Bristol Red were supplanted by Independence Green, Congress Brown, and Federal Blue.

But the changes brought about by the Revolution affected American fabric production more fundamentally than political activism or descriptive words. The severing of colonial ties meant that America was free to develop her own industry—if she could.

A Native Textile Industry

The industrial revolution had begun in England, and the great inventions there had completely changed the manufacture of textiles. John Kay's flying shuttle had quadrupled loom production. With the

Lafayette commemorative print by the Germantown Print Works (Pa.), c. 1824. Rogers Fund. *Met—44.109.5 (133307 LS)*.

U.S. TEXTILE TRADITIONS con't

introduction of Hargreave's spinning jenny in the 1760s, Arkwright and Strutt's mechanized mills in the 1770s, and Crompton's spindle carriage in 1779, English mills could outproduce any in the world. So jealous were they of their mechanical monopoly that Parliament enacted stringent laws against the export of machinery or "any knowledge of its form."

America, economically drained by the Revolution, could not compete against British goods. And yet the enthusiasm of the new nation, as well as the foresight of James Madison, was reflected when he declared in 1786 that "The United States will one day become a great cotton producing country." There was little to bolster his optimism. Small amounts of cotton were growing in Maryland and Virginia, but the farmers of Georgia and South Carolina found prices so depressed that they were literally abandoning the land.

However, in the same year the legislature of Massachusetts passed a resolution encouraging the introduction of machinery for carding and spinning cotton. More significantly, a well-to-do merchant of Providence, Silas Brown, sponsored a British immigrant by the name of Samuel Slater. This young man, so he said, had worked for Arkwright and Strutt and could reproduce their machinery. Brown's confidence—and money—were well placed. By 1793 the Slater mill in Pawtucket was spinning cotton mechanically. Both the original company and the mill exist today.

Whitney's Cotton Gin

In 1793 Madison's prophecy was transformed into fact, for it was then that Eli Whitney perfected the sawtooth cotton gin. By mechanically removing the seeds from short-staple American cotton, Whitney's invention established the immensely profit-able cotton economy of the South. In the year of Whitney's invention 487,000 pounds of cotton were exported to England. In 1794 exports leaped to 1,601,700 pounds. The following year six times that amount was sold to the mills of Lancashire. On the eve of the War of 1812 the figure had grown to the amazing sum of 62,186,081 pounds. So, by the time he was President, James Madison's prophecy had become an enormous business fact. The industrial revolution had taken over America and cotton was king.

Mills began to proliferate wherever there was water power. Despite the economic slump following the War of 1812 and ruinous foreign competition, by 1840 the cotton business alone employed 53,476 workers in 922 mills.

America Competes

In 1840 (so Edward Field's *History of the Providence Plantations* relates) an agent of a Rhode Island printworks saw a French *mousseline de laine* selling for 14¢ a yard in the New York market. He bought a piece and sent it to his factory. In 16 days he was selling a copy of the challis print in New York at 10¢ a yard. He was an enterprising agent, but he was typical of the industrial expertise which had replaced the American handcraft tradition.

Now it was easier and cheaper to buy commercial fabrics, which came in many types: paisley and floral printed calicos; chintzes like Indian hangings; prints that looked like stipple and stencil-painted "theorems"; spidery geometrics called "excentric" prints, which enjoyed a great vogue in the 1840s; cotton tickings; coarse wool coatings and suitings in practical shades; sturdy ginghams. Luxurious silks and the finer fabrics still came from abroad, and the imports could still compete with domestic manufacture. Because of the chronic shortage of skilled workers, Ameri-can mills were forced to pay higher wages than their European competitors.

Prosperity in Ready-mades

Free land in the West was the basic reason for the scarcity of trained labor, but, ironically, it was the opening of free land to settlement that gave the American textile industry its first great prosperity. As American families began their trek westward, unlike their colonial ancestors, they could not stop to raise cotton, wool, and linen or set up spinning wheels and looms. Fabrics were bought from peddlers or in scattered village stores. By the days of the great California Gold Rush of 1849, there was a large shifting population in this country which had neither time nor tailors but needed clothes. The Oak Hall Store of Boston was one of the earliest manufacturers of ready-made clothing. Using Irish immigrant labor and the tailoring and sizing procedures which had been established in making army uniforms, they produced clothing for men, women, and children to sell at wholesale and by mail order.

It was a profitable trade, and, naturally, other manufacturers followed suit, notably the firm of Levi-Strauss in San Francisco. When the sewing machine was brought into use, the ready-made clothing business was booming hand-in-hand with the fabric business. For a time, at mid-century, the textile business was the largest industrial enterprise in the country.

Fashion & Opulence

In addition to the ready-made clothing business, a new element was introduced into the selling of fabrics—the fashion magazine. *Godey's Lady's Book*, *Harper's Bazaar*, and *Leslie's Weekly* carried fashion plates, drawings, and descriptions of clothes and furnishings from all the places that were considered fashionable. Even during the

RIGHT. Worth costume of Cheney velvet. *Wadsworth Atheneum—1957.47 (184D).*

FAR RIGHT. American printed silk by Cheney Bros., designed by Candace Wheeler, about 1885. Gift of Mrs. Boudinot Keith, 1928. *Metropolitan—28.70.15 (70949LS).*

devastation of the Civil War, the gowns of Worth and the Versailles revival of Eugenie's court were duly reported to dressmakers and mills. America's homes and the crinolines of her women began to blossom in congested Victorian versions of 18th century rococo designs. Morning glories battled cabbage roses on organdies, taffetas, plushes, and repps. The rather turgid colors of the 1850s gave way to an 1860s range of pastels accented with bright pinks, greens, and yellows. For the 1870s, following the grim days of Reconstruction, the fall of France's Second Empire, and the world financial panic of 1873, fabrics reverted to sober patterns of greens, browns, and blues. These changes were faithfully and often well recorded in the "home" magazines, and their influence on the buying public was tremendous.

Perversely, it was the financial debacle of 1873 which marked the emergence of the vast American investment fortunes gained in railroads, steel, and oil. Where once the ownership of land had been a mark of respectable wealth, by 1885 money had become the badge of power and social distinction. Opulence was the order of the day. Satins, velvets, and brocades in increasingly visible patterns were worn by those who could afford them. Well-to-do parlors were stuffed with cut plushes and faconné velvets, braided with gilt and hung with fringe.

In American mills silk and woolen production was growing. With the increasing facility of steam transport, top wool clips and raw silk were imported from Australia and Japan. Over the years domestic manufacture had vastly improved, and firms such as Cheney Brothers turned out first-quality goods. Needless to say, they reflected the current mode of ostentation, and Cheney velvets became a household word. In Hartford's Wadsworth Atheneum there is an 1888 suit of green Cheney velvet made for Mrs. Cheney by Worth. It is cut in the manner of a Louis XIV redingote, embroidered in sufficient gold and silver to dazzle the Sun King himself.

The Crafts Movement

There was bound to be a reaction against the overrich diet of commercial banality. It came in a back-to-the-crafts movement centered around the English designer, William Morris, who had been producing fabrics and wallpapers with a strong medieval flavor since 1859. Morris' flowing patterns of stylized flowers, grasses, and trees became a strong influence in England and Europe. It was not until they were commercially produced and accepted abroad that the Morris influence was introduced into America. It was a singularly potent design force which lasted until World War I and resurrected a popular interest in handicrafts such as blockprinting, stencils, and pyrography.

A logical outgrowth of Morris' graceful line was the Art Nouveau movement of 1895–1905. It was most successfully employed in Europe in architecture, furnishings, and glassware. Its twining and convoluted shapes were applied to all manner of objects. But art nouveau had a short life. It was killed by commercial overexploitation on both sides of the Atlantic.

A close follower of Morris and art nouveau was the American Louis Comfort Tiffany. His decorating firm did some splendid interiors and fabricated a remarkable iridescent glass called, properly enough, "Tiffany glass." His interiors, with custom-built furniture, handwrought ironwork, and specially woven fabrics, were perforce expensive. The design concept was equally individual: Each piece was interdependent and meant for that interior alone. His glass was also expensive and made by a secret process. Therefore much of Tiffany's work was uncopyable, and his impact on the commercial market was small.

Along with art nouveau and medievalism, the turn of the century saw a revival of "classic" design. This grew out of Beaux Arts eclecticism, seen on the "Greek" facades of Chicago's Columbian Exposition. It resulted in fabrics with pallid colors and vaguely Greek patterns of keys and nymphs and daffodils.

Modern Design Emerges

When the vivid Bakst costumes of the Ballets Russes danced before an astonished world, a whole new color spectrum was born. American manufacturers looked in amazement at their Fall 1908 color card from Claude Frères. They could not believe the oxblood reds, electric blues, poison greens. When Paul Poiret created a sensation with outsize oriental shapes in vibrant shades, the American market was clearly skeptical. And well they might be, for they were faced with more than a change of color and pattern: "modern" design was coming to life.

The Wiener Werkstätte, the Bauhaus, and Scandinavian design ideas, which culminated in the Finnish Pavilion at the 1939 New York World's Fair, opened new vistas on the relationship of design to people and material. Their work was as much philosophy as design, and it is no wonder that the commercial world lagged behind. The fabric mills contented themselves with adaptations of Poiret's stencil-like roses, the skeletal drawing of the Bauhaus, and sweetened versions of Scandinavian abstractions and sold them very well to an increasingly educated public. What the mills were forced to overlook, since they could not afford it, was the time spent in schools and laboratories on endless experiments in matching new materials to new techniques for new uses.

Beginning at the end of the last century and gaining momentum with the years was a trend towards informality in social rela-

Section of a handwoven window blind designed by Dorothy Liebes in 1963. It was made with aluminum strips and reeds, woven together with rayon and metallic yarns. *Museum of Contemporary Crafts.*

U.S. TEXTILE TRADITIONS con't

tions. The old ethic and its adherents were waning. On the rise was an interest in activity, in new ideas and relationships, in speed of communication. The ideal person—particularly the American ideal—changed from Victorian solidity to an ever younger, more unceremonious breed. The breezy Gibson Girl and her escort became Fitzgerald's 20-year-old heros and teenage heroines in the 1920s. Sports grew to be an important part of young life. Dress reflected the new outlook, and informal, washable cotton and linen shirtings, crashes, and ducks were made into shirtwaists, jackets, pants, and skirts.

The Industry Moves South

The cotton business—in fact, the entire textile industry—had been changing. New England's mills still produced most of the nation's goods, but the boom years of World War I and the 1920s found southern mills gaining almost half the market. The long decline of the northern mills was hastened by the depression of the 1930s. The production needs of World War II boosted the industrialization of the South and spelled the end of the antiquated mills of the North. By 1950 the once-prosperous textile towns of New Bedford, Fall River, and Lowell were looking for other businesses to fill their empty factories. With the aid of government money and local subsidies, textile firms had built giant modern mills in the South, equipped with the latest automated machinery and capable of enormous production with a minimal work force.

The Man-Made Fiber Revolution

During this period chemical advances played an important role in American textiles. Solvents, acids, starches, oils, and dyes were essential to textiles and to important products of the new giant chemical

industries. In the 1920s a new chemical product was introduced: chemical fibers. Acetate yarn had been invented by the Comte de Chardonnet in France in 1889. During the silk shortages of World War I and later, it was revived as "artificial silk." In an effort to popularize the yarn it was rechristened "rayon" and given to the French textile manufacturer Colcombet to develop. He turned out novel sculptured fabrics: blistered crepes, raised brocades, and mixtures of rayon and wool for textural contrast. Schiaparelli used the materials in her Paris couture collection of 1936, and rayon became as fashionable as silk.

After the restrictions on essential goods were lifted following World War II, plastic fibers were added to the cellulosic yarns, and chemical yarns usurped a major part of the market. Nylon, polyester, and acrylic are now household words, and fabrics made from them are everywhere in every price bracket. As usual, the weaves and patterns of the new fabrics follow the prevailing mode in home and clothing fabrics. Crease-resistant knits for travel clothes and sheer curtains which wash without stretching have been logical developments. But aside from some industrial uses, such as filters and heat-sealed packaging, surprisingly little advantage has been taken of their unique properties. Not much that is new in construction or individual in design has appeared on the commercial market.

Full Circle to Handicrafts

In the 1950s, postwar attitudes began to make themselves felt. The Beat Generation turned into the Youth Revolution, and their rumbles still echo in the halls of history. Essentially, the revolt was against commercial mores.and manners, and it was remarkably successful in shattering outdated myths. One of the characteristics of this anticommercialism was an interest in handicrafts. So strong was the interest that

commercial firms were soon machine-producing bleached designs, patched and embroidered jeans, and batik T-shirts in imitation of handwork. The new handicraft workers were, in some instances, fairly adept at their job, but they were less interested in arriving at new designs than in declaring an antiestablishment viewpoint. Their viewpoint, interestingly enough, affected commercial design. New "homespun" woolens and "hand knits" have appeared in French couture collections and American mills. The vogue for handicrafts has made prizes—very expensive prizes—of patchwork quilts, hand-blocked prints, blue and white coverlets, bed ruggs, crewelwork, and all those early creations of our ancestors when textile making was an art. We have come full circle in our appreciation, if not in our abilities.

Certainly, American mills have produced many fine fabrics over the years. Their capability is unquestioned and unsurpassed. There are also important textile artists on the scene who have deservedly made their mark here and abroad. Pioneers like the late Dorothy Liebes created a new genre of fabrics. Lenore Tawney and Sheila Hicks handle yarns in sculptural ways which have never before been attempted. All three mastered the handloom and developed their ideas there. Another craftsman is Jack Lenor Larsen, the catalyst for a group of designer-craftworkers who have made advanced contributions to the world of textiles. Their impact has been singularly forceful because Larsen has the ability to translate the handwoven experimental art form into commercial mill production while still preserving the integrity of the original. It is this unique combination of artist and mill technician which points to the future of American textile design.

Robert Riley
Director, Design Laboratory
Fashion Institute of Technology

RIGHT. Detail of a "Star & Diamond" coverlet, Ontario, 1850–70. Gift of the Ontario Spinners & Weavers Cooperative. ROM—952.46.2 (70Tex29).

FAR RIGHT. Detail of doublecloth coverlet, Ontario, about 1820. Gift of Mrs. F. A. Ballachey. ROM—960.118 (68Tex86).

CANADIAN TEXTILE TRADITIONS
FOUR BASIC SOURCES

From the Atlantic Coast to the Detroit River in the agricultural areas of the older settled parts of Canada, there is a strong tradition of hand textile techniques. Further west the country was not opened up to permanent settlement until after the impact of mass-produced goods had rendered local spinning and weaving of little importance. In Ontario and Quebec the older settlements clung to the southern parts of the provinces, and handweaving went no further north. In Nova Scotia, Prince Edward Island, and parts of New Brunswick locally made textiles played an important part, but Newfoundland's economy was based on fishing and lumbering rather than agriculture and there is little record of textile production there. In spite of the vast size of Canada these hand techniques were important in a small area only, but where they did occur they had significance both economically and socially.

Canada's textile traditions stem from four basic sources. The first settlers to come from Europe were French. Small precarious settlements were established in the Maritime Provinces and Quebec early in the 17th century, and these grew slowly, spreading their influence as the country opened up with the flourishing fur trade.

The second source resulted from the American War of Independence, when those who declared their loyalty to the Crown were forced to flee their homes. They went by sea to Nova Scotia and New Brunswick, while others traveled overland to become the first settlers in Ontario. Many followed as the 18th century came to a close and the 19th century began. Most were of British stock, but there were also people of

Pennsylvania Dutch, Swiss, and German origin.

The third wave of immigration came directly to Canada from the British Isles in the early part of the 19th century. The English had already been so much affected by the Industrial Revolution that they had lost the skills of spinning and weaving. There were not many Irish who produced textiles after coming to Canada, but among the Scots textile traditions were strong. Those who had been displaced by the turnover to large-scale sheep farming in the Highlands were well accustomed to supplying their own spinning and weaving needs. Wherever they settled, the same strong traditions of pattern and technique are found. Also among the Scottish settlers there were many highly trained weavers

from southwestern Scotland where the textile trades were in a depressed state due to the disruptions of the Industrial Revolution. Seeing no future at home, they came to Canada intending to farm but found that their skills could be used to provide their neighbors with clothing, linens, blankets, and decorative coverlets.

The fourth source of Canadian textile techniques was German. The earlier Pennsylvania Dutch influence was vastly strengthened by immigration from Germany, particularly in the 1840s. Trained handworkers were hit by the depression following the Napoleonic Wars which, coupled with mechanization, produced heavy unemployment and led to a steady stream of skilled artisans crossing the Atlantic in search of a better future.

Canada now has a culture which comes from many other sources. Practically every part of the world has contributed to the makeup of the cosmopolitan society that forms the vital modern Canada. But most of this varied population has come since

Detail of twill diaper coverlet, Ontario, 1840–60. Annie R. Fry Collection, lent by Fry family. ROM—L965.11.20 (70Tex76).

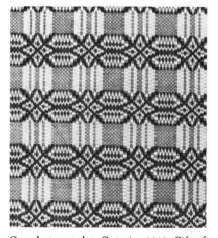

Overshot coverlet, Ontario, 1840. Gift of Mrs. O. D. Vaughan. Royal Ontario Museum—955.10.1 (70Tex18).

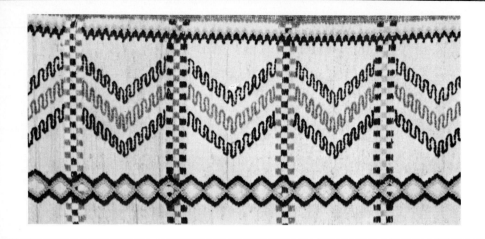

CANADIAN TEXTILE TRADITIONS con't

hand production of textiles died out as a commercial force. Much traditional weaving, embroidery, and knitting is carried on by various ethnic groups, but it is a survival of the old ways from the "old country" and is used by that limited cultural group for nostalgic reasons rather than as a living, growing tradition which will eventually become Canadian.

French Traditions

As with other colonies, the early French settlements in Canada were not encouraged to produce manufactured articles. The fish and fur trades were lucrative, and with the proceeds the colonists were able to purchase what they needed from France. Some attempts were made to grow flax and hemp and to raise sheep, but it was with the depression at the beginning of the 18th century when the bottom dropped out of the beaver market that, of necessity, textile production became important. New France was ceded to Britain in 1763, and with increased population and more peaceful times the demand for locally produced materials continued.

Spinning and weaving became part of the domestic occupation in most rural homes. The old loom of the French areas had only two shafts, limiting production to plain tabby weave. For decorative coverlets two hand methods of patterning were used: *à la planche*, in which a thin board, inserted through the warp behind the heddles, could be turned on edge to open a special pattern shed; and a freer technique, *boutonné*, where an extra pattern weft was pulled up to form a pattern of small loops.

Ecclesiastical embroidery was introduced from France, and beautiful work was done in the convents. When silk threads were scarce, Indian women taught the nuns to use dyed moose hair. Moose-hair em-broideries in floral patterns, done in satin stitch and French knots, were made by both nuns and Indians and sold for the support of the convents. They became the great Canadian souvenir carried back to Europe by many 19th century travelers. A flourishing cottage industry produced another typically French Canadian textile, the complex braided arrow sashes, or *ceintures flèchées*, which were worn wrapped tightly around the waist by the men who paddled and portaged the canoes of the fur traders on their long journeys across Canada.

The "Loyalist" Tradition

Many of the Loyalists who arrived to take up their grants of free land were destitute, and the first years of settlement were exceedingly difficult. Among other things the government provided blankets, but for clothing many had to turn to deerskin until the first flax crop could be harvested and a few precious sheep raised and guarded from the dangers that were all too close with uncleared land. Among the first settlers there were weavers, and as life became a little

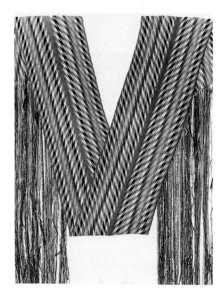

more civilized, they started to produce plain materials for themselves and on a barter basis for their neighbors.

By about 1800 a few of the more highly trained had managed to establish themselves with multiple-shaft looms such as they had used in their old homes. A limited production started in linens and decorative bed coverings woven with complex techniques such as double cloth, "Summer and Winter" weave, and twill diaper. This work does not differ from that produced in the United States, but as life was much closer to the edge, it tended to be simpler and was far from common.

Scottish Traditions

The Scottish tradition of weaving was dominant among people who came directly from Great Britain. The standard loom had four shafts. On it they made checked and striped materials for clothing, plain linens, twill blankets, carpets, and decorative coverlets in overshot weave. This is the most flexible patterning technique, with only four shafts, and it was used with a colored wool weft passing over and under a plain white ground to produce a great variety of geometric designs. Coverlets woven in this way are not only attractive but are practical, for air is trapped between the cotton ground and the woolen pattern weft, making a very warm covering with an economic use of the frequently scarce wool. In this tradition spinning and much of the plain weaving was done in the farm homes, but making the coverlets was usually professional work.

The German Tradition

In the areas where German people settled, particularly Waterloo County in Ontario, spinning and dyeing were done at home, but handweavers were plentiful and professional. In many small villages there were

RIGHT. Detail of Jacquard coverlet, Ontario, 1842. Gift of Adelaide Lash Miller. *ROM—965.190.4 (70Tex100).*

BELOW. Patchwork quilt of handwoven woolens, Ontario, mid-19th Century. Gift of Mrs. J. T. Burt-Gerrans. *ROM—948.157 (75Tex4).*

trained men, often two from one family working together with varied looms for different purposes. They made all sorts of useful materials, but techniques requiring multiple shafts were especially popular: twill diaper, complex point twills, "Star and Diamond" weave, and to a lesser extent double cloth. Some of the most effective productions were for horse blankets.

It was among the highly trained German weavers that the Jacquard loom took hold. Men who were accustomed to weaving on complex looms invested in one of the new Jacquard heads, mounted it on a loom, and informed their neighbors that they were now ready to supply "Fancy Coverlets on the New Improved Loom." The Jacquard mechanism, worked by a series of punched cards, allowed the warp threads to be controlled individually rather than in groups and permitted fairly realistic designs. Jacquard coverlets were only produced in Ontario; the first one known to have been made is dated 1834, while the last dated example is 1902. The patterns differ little from those used in the northern United States.

Local handweaving in all the older parts of Canada started slowly with the first settlements but increased enormously as supplies became less limited. It held its own through much of the 19th century, even when imports were readily obtainable and local mills were coming into production. It slowly died out in the beginning of the 20th century, with pockets of survival continuing almost to the present day.

Sewing, Embroidery, Knitting, Crochet, Quilting

Fine sewing was an attribute necessary for every well-brought-up girl. She was expected to be able to sew a fine seam at a very early age. Apart from samplers, which were used for teaching and the mark-

ing of linens, there was little effort expended on useless embroidery until well on in the 19th century when life became easier and some women had time on their hands. Much the same is true of knitting. Purely practical knitting was an essential part of women's work in the early stages of settlement, and it wasn't until later that fancy collars, openwork stockings, and lace edgings for linens were finely and painstakingly knitted. Crochet also is a late development, and all these fancy techniques belong to the international Godey's Lady's Book style rather than to Canada.

In English-speaking areas from the beginning until the present day, quilts have been made whenever materials were avail-

able. Many are similar to examples from elsewhere, but some that are rather unusual and very appealing are made from patches of handwoven woolen materials saved from worn-out clothing and carefully pieced to form a pleasing pattern. All Canada's textiles tell something of her spirit, but in these humble productions with their sturdy thriftiness, their warmth of texture and color, and their determined making of something good out of unpromising material, there is the essence of the hardy spirit that built the country.

Dorothy K. Burnham
Associate Curator, Textile Dept.
Royal Ontario Museum, Toronto

FIG. 1. Pueblo ceremonial robe (detail), wool embroidery on plain cotton. Hopi, Arizona. Logan Collection. *Logan Museum of Anthropology—7039.*

FABRICS OF THE NORTH AMERICAN INDIANS: TECHNIQUES AND DESIGNS

The use and production of fabrics by the American Indians north of the Rio Grande has long been much more highly developed than is generally known. They date back to a very early time, were distributed practically from coast to coast, and were made in an enormous variety of vegetal and animal fibers.

The Archaeological Evidence

Yarn or cordage twisted from sagebrush and cedar bark, native hemp, flax, and yucca leaves; twined or looped to make sandals, nets, bags, and belts—such materials have been found in dry cave sites associated with the Old Desert culture stretching from Baja California into Wyoming and Idaho. They are dated as early as 3000 to 5000 B.C. (Danger Cave, Utah). Robes made of fiber cords wrapped with strips of rabbit fur or soft feathers and twined together with fiber were made as early as 1000 B.C. and continued to be made throughout most of North America into historic times.

The regional history of fabrics is difficult to reconstruct because their delicate nature precludes archaeological recovery of ancient examples except under the most favorable and fortunate circumstances. In many parts of the eastern United States the early production of fabrics is indicated by impressions on pottery fragments. The mound-building Hopewell people of Ohio and Illinois made small pottery figurines showing women wearing long wraparound skirts apparently of cloth. Fragments of cloth preserved by burial with copper ornaments show that between 300 B.C. and 100 A.D. these people used various basts and buffalo hair to produce skirts and mantles, bags and belts in plain and twilled plaiting (interlacing), plain and twilled twining, and looping. The cloth was decorated with

resist-painted geometric designs or with applied shells and copper plaques. This tradition may have continued through the centuries and eventually into the cultures of the historic tribes of the east. We know that fabrics were made throughout the years, but the actual archaeological links are meager.

Evidence of fabrics has been found in the great Middle Mississippi mound sites (700–1600 A.D.) such as Moundville (Alabama) and Etowah (Georgia). The many fragments from the Spiro Mound in Oklahoma were made of rabbit and buffalo hair in fine plaiting (interlacing) and open twill twining (spaced alternate-pair weft twining). Some of the pieces are quite large (19 × 53 inches) and have resist-dyed designs in red, yellow, and black. Throughout the Southeast, fabrics were produced from the fibers of mulberry bark, basswood, wild hemp, and palmetto leaves.

FIG. 3. Early Navajo "Chief" blanket—Third Phase. Indigo blue and red bayeta. Herbert & Sonia Zim Collection. *Logan Museum of Anthropology—9034.*

The scribes who accompanied Hernando de Soto in his long exploration of the area between 1539 and 1543 were impressed by the quality and the quantity of fabrics used by the Indians and describe how the Spaniards acquired them to make mantles, cassocks, and gowns for themselves. In the Creek Village of Cofitachequi they saw "...large quantities of clothing, shawls of thread, made from the barks of trees and others of feathers, white and gray, vermilion and yellow, rich and proper for winter" (*Narratives of the Career of Hernando de Soto in the Conquest of Florida as told by a Knight of Elvas*, translated by Buckingham Smith, New York, 1866, p. 52).

In another place the same writer describes the clothing of the Indians: "These are like shawls, some of them are made from the inner barks of trees, and others from a grass resembling nettle, which by threading out, becomes like flax. The women use them for covering, wearing one about the body from the waist down-ward, and another over the shoulder, with the right arm left free, after the manner of the gypsies; the men wear but one, which they carry over their shoulders in the same way..." (ibid. p. 52).

These observations are important because they link fragments of evidence from the prehistoric archaeological sites to the early contact period of the middle sixteenth century and also with the later colonial period of the eighteenth century. Two centuries after de Soto and his wandering Spaniards passed through the Southeast, a Frenchman, Le Page du Pratz, described fabrics being worn in the same fashion by Natchez women of the lower Mississippi Valley. He tells something of their manufacture: "Then they set up their frame, which consists of two stakes extending four feet out of the ground, between the tops of

FIG. 2. Pueblo ceremonial sash, cotton with embroidery weaving. Hopi, Arizona. Herbert & Sonia Zim Collection. *Logan Museum of Anthropology—8402.*

which runs a large thread on which other threads are double knotted. Finally they make a cross texture which has a border worked in patterns extending all the way around. This stuff is at least an ell (ca. 36") square and a line in thickness. The mantels of mulberry bark thread are very white and very neat" (Antoine S. le Page du Pratz, *Histoire de la Lousiane*, 3 vols., Paris, 1758).

This is one of the only descriptions of the weaving process among early tribes of the Southeast. It seems to refer to suspended warps hung from a cord between two uprights, a method which was widely used for mats and bags by many eastern tribes into the twentieth century. Various reports describe the belts, garters, and sashes which were woven by Indians of the Southeast and most of the Mississippi Valley in the 18th century, but one description of weaving among the Chickasaw in 1775 has led to considerable speculation and research. It seems to detail something resembling a true loom: "When the coarse thread is prepared, they put it into a frame about six feet square, and instead of a shuttle, they thrust through the thread with a long cane, having a large string through the web, which they shift at every second course of the thread. . . . . They paint each side . . . with such figures, of various colours, as . . . images of birds and beasts . . . and of themselves . . . . They passed the woof with a shuttle; and they have a couple of threddles, which they move with the hand so as to enable them to make good dispatch, something after our manner of weaving. (They make) broad garters, sashes, shot-pouches, broad belts, and the like, which are decorated all over with beautiful stripes and chequers" (James Adair, *The History of the American Indians*, London, 1775).

In any case with or without a true loom fine fabrics were produced and used over a large part of the eastern United States, and it is tragic that the once-powerful tribes of this area were so quickly affected by European military and commercial influences which destroyed their rich native culture. Their long-developed skills in weaving were among the first crafts to disappear as cheap trade textiles in bright colors were introduced by the traders.

In the western United States archaeologists have uncovered fabrics thousands of years old. The earliest materials, dated 3000–5000 B.C., in Danger Cave, Utah, indicate the use of twisted cords of hemp, cedar bark, flax, bullrush fiber, and, later, sagebrush bark to make bags, nets, and traps. About 1000 B.C. these same materials were being twined and looped into blankets, bags, and sandals in Nevada (Lovelock Cave) and southeastern Oregon (Fort Rock Cave). Bird skins and fur strips were made into the kind of soft, warm covering which is still made occasionally by the Hopi Indians of Arizona and some of the tribes of central Canada.

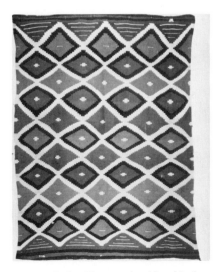

FIG. 4. Early Navajo shoulder blanket. Horatio N. Rust Coll., J. B. Wheat photo. *Logan Museum of Anthropology—1846.*

The Basket Makers

The early art of finger weaving in the Southwest becomes linked directly to the textile arts of modern Indians in the region around the beginning of the Christian era when the people known as the Basket Makers appeared. Even in their earliest phases these people produced excellent baskets, and they also used bark and the fibers from yucca leaves to make plaited (interlaced) sandals, bags, and mats and fur and feather robes, which were fabricated with twined wefts of yucca cord. In recent times the Pima and other tribes used a vertical frame with the fur and/or feather warps suspended from a crossbar; it is possible that the Basket Maker robes may have been made in the same manner.

The complex fabric sandals of the Basket Makers were made with twined or wrap-twined wefts on warps which were probably suspended from a cord loop, although some archaeologists feel certain that they could have been made only on a warp frame so that the wefts could be battened tightly against each other. Wide sashes, often decorated with colored designs, were twined on stretched warps of fine yucca fibers, and examples have been found with the warp bars still attached. These could have been suspended vertically or even stretched like a belt loom. Looping was still a favorite technique and was used to make large storage bags. As the Basket Maker culture developed into the Pueblo culture about 600 A.D., looping was used even more extensively for bags, blouses, socks, and fabric tops for sandals. Many of them were brightly colored with elements dyed blue, red, and buff.

At this same period two very important fabric elements were introduced into the area, probably from Mexico: these were native cotton and the true loom, which was in the form of a backstrap loom with

FIG. 5. Early Navajo rug, J. B. Moore Trading Post design, Crystal, New Mexico, about 1900. Native yarn, aniline, and natural-wool colors.

AMERICAN INDIANS con't

stretched warp elements and heddles to separate the warp into sheds for inserting the weft.

As the cultivation of cotton spread and displaced almost all the earlier fibers, large pieces of decorated fabric were produced, which suggest that the two-bar blanket loom had appeared. Pieces roughly six feet square have been recovered, with elaborate geometric designs which may have been copied from the pottery of the period. In southern Arizona the prehistoric Hohokam and the modern Pima and Papago wove cotton blankets with the large loom set horizontally about 10 to 18 inches above the ground. The more northerly Pueblo people set it up vertically. One authority suggests that they did this to save space in their underground ceremonial chambers (kivas) where most of the weaving was done. Archaeological remnants of weaving and spinning equipment suggest that the historic loom and the techniques of its use were identical to those still used by the contemporary Hopi and Navajo.

Weaving was a highly developed art from around 700 A.D. through the ensuing centuries until the coming of the Spaniards in 1539. Its products were important for daily use and for ceremonial garb. Complex weaves, plain and twilled plaiting (interlacing), and openwork were made with dyed wefts; other weaves were tie-dyed, painted, or decorated with embroidery or a unique wrapped embroidery weaving (brocading) still used on ceremonial sashes among the Pueblos.

* * *

When Francisco de Coronado entered the Pueblo towns along the Rio Grande in 1540, there were three groups of Indians in the Southwest actively engaged in weaving: (1) the southern desert tribes, (2) the Pueblo villages, and (3) the Navajo.

Southern Desert Tribes

The first group included the Pima, Papago, and Maricopa of southern Arizona, who probably inherited the tradition of cotton textiles and the horizontal loom from the preceding Hohokam and continued to make large rectangular cotton blankets until the beginning of this century. These were generally undecorated, although sometimes dyed red. However, cotton belts were also made with distinctive designs which perhaps reflected the complex motifs of their excellent coiled baskets.

The Pueblo People

The second and much more important weaving group was the Pueblo people, who continued the tradition of cultivating cotton and weaving fine fabrics begun by their ancestors more than a thousand years before the coming of the Spaniards. This ancient tradition continues today and is the most important indigenous weaving complex to be preserved from prehistoric times in the entire area north of Mexico. The ubiquitous belt loom was once used in most of the villages along the Rio Grande in New Mexico as well as in the western Pueblos to make distinctive cotton warp-faced belts with warp-float designs in central panels. The red, black, and green warps are now respun commercial wool; the thin weft element is usually black or white cotton.

Today almost all Pueblo belts, garters, and hair ties are woven in the Hopi villages. Generally the back loom has been superseded by a small vertical suspended loom on which the warp elements are set in a tubular arrangement. Weaving with the belt loom was done by the women; the suspended tubular loom is used by Hopi men.

Fabrics were once woven in all the Pueblos, but, as clothing styles changed and factory clothing and textiles became available, most weavers abandoned their looms. Some Zuni women continued to weave until about 1940, but today all the native fabrics, which are still important for the costumes in all Pueblo ceremonials, are woven by men in the Hopi villages to be sold and traded throughout Arizona and New Mexico. Except for sashes these articles are all woven on the vertical two-bar loom. The upper, or yard, beam is hung from the house rafters, either inside the kiva or out in a patio, and the lower, or cloth, beam is anchored to pegs or loops set into the floor.

The Wedding Blanket

Cotton has been the traditional weaving fiber among the Pueblo since about 700 A.D. Although the native plant has been almost completely replaced by commercial cotton string, most of the fabrics used in ceremonial dance costumes are still of cotton cloth. The largest item produced is the woman's "wedding blanket," which she receives from her husband's family at the time of the nuptial celebration. Later her husband decorates it with embroidery for use as a ceremonial robe. The conventionalized patterns—incorporating motifs symbolizing butterflies, rain, fields, clouds, squash blossoms, and dragonflies—are applied also to the cotton dance kilts, breech cloths, and fringed sashes used by the men and to rectangular shoulder shawls for the women.

All embroidery is now done with modern needles and commercial wool yarn, using a simple back stitch with the pieces stretched on a frame. The bands on the lower edges of the shawls are done in standardized colors: broad bands of black with vertical stripes of green and medallions in combinations of red, green, and yellow (Fig. 1). The edges of men's ceremonial kilts and breech

FIG. 6. Contemporary Navajo Yei rug with figures in sand-painting style. Native yarn, vegetal dyes. Shiprock area, New Mexico. *Logan—2041.*

cloths are embroidered with a band of terraced rain clouds and other symbols in red, green, and black.

The wide sashes worn by the men are also embroidered at the ends with a broad band; on some of them the colored wool yarns are worked into the sash during the weaving process. The technique by which this is done seems to be unique among the Hopi. It has been referred to as "embroidery weaving" and sometimes as brocading. The colored yarns are wrapped around one or more warp elements and floated over others to bring the desired color to the front of the fabric (Fig. 2). A thin "tabby" weft of white cotton is woven in at the same time to hold the cloth together. The result of this weaving is similar to embroidery but with a distinctive ribbed appearance.

Most of the cotton cloth is woven with a plain, or "basket," weave (interlacing), in which warp and weft show equally; a diagonal twill occasionally appears. The exception to this is the distinctive Hopi "wedding sash" with its parallel rows of herringbone pattern, which result from the complex braiding process by which it is made. These long (four to five feet) ceremonial sashes are generally about six inches wide and have long fringes of heavy twisted cords, which are held at their upper ends with large rings made of corn husks and twine. They are produced by "frame braiding," an ancient mode of finger weaving in which a cord is wound spirally between two rigid horizontal rods and each strand is pulled under three others and held with a retaining rod. The finished sash is carried by a woman at her marriage and later worn by men in ceremonial dances.

Pueblo Wool Weaving

The Pueblo Indians did not have wool until sheep were brought into the area by the Spaniards, and it did not become available

FIG. 7. Chilkat ceremonial tunic of cedar bast and mountain-goat wool, native dyes, 44¾" long. *Museum of the American Indian—19/7902 (20961).*

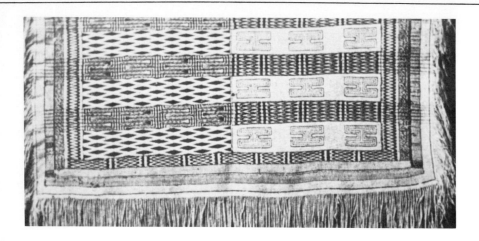

AMERICAN INDIANS con't

in any quantity until 1600 A.D. Another hundred years passed before wool weaving was fully established. It is mentioned in Spanish documents, although they were mainly concerned with exacting an annual tribute of 33 inches of cotton cloth from each Pueblo household. Little is known about the early woolen textiles, but it is clear that the Pueblo weavers simply transferred almost all the techniques they had used for cotton to the new and more easily produced fiber. The only implements they adopted from the Europeans were metal carders and clipping shears.

It is in woolen fabrics that the full range of variety and sophistication of Pueblo weaving appears. Cotton was woven largely in plain weave (plain interlacing, basket weave, or checker weave) with warp and weft elements showing equally: only occasional use was made of diagonal twill. Archaeological evidence indicates that more elaborate weaves of openwork, damask twill, and even slit-weave tapestry were once done in cotton. These had disappeared by 1600 A.D., but for unknown reasons, some of them were revived in weaving with wool. The most important weave made possible by the softer quality of wool yarn was tapestry, in which the weft elements are tightly battened down against each other so they completely hide the warp and produce a weft-face, closely woven textile. A wide variety of twill weaves were produced in this same way, and many articles were made or decorated with diagonal tapestry weave, diamonds, or herringbone patterns.

At one time garments for daily use were woven in all the Pueblos but by 1880 little or no weaving was being done in the Rio Grande towns of New Mexico. Through most of the first half of the twentieth century some textiles were made at Zuni and Acoma, but the art has survived today only in the Hopi villages, where all garments used by the Pueblo people in their ceremonial costumes are now woven. No fabrics were ever made to be cut or tailored. Shawls, robes, skirts, kilts, and other garments were simply rectangular pieces of cloth which were wrapped around the body and held in place with ties or sashes. Even the relatively rare shirts were no more than rectangular ponchos with additional rectangles sewn at the shoulders to serve as sleeves. Men's shirts were usually plain black or dark blue; they also wore short, sleeveless red wool ponchos decorated with horizontal stripes.

Both men and women wore robes, and soft woolen blankets are still woven by the Hopi men for their own use and for trade to other tribes. Some are made for sale, but few reach the tourist market. Pueblo blanket design is simple, consisting generally of parallel bands or stripes across the width, usually the greatest dimension. One type of coarse, loosely woven white blanket has dark stripes. Dark blue or black blankets are more tightly woven and decorated with

narrow white or red stripes which are sometimes broken into blocks, and occasional pieces are woven with bands of simple geometric motifs.

A different type of man's blanket is woven in a complex combination of diagonal and diamond twill weaves with a pattern of light and dark stripes crossing each other at right angles to produce a checkered design, something like a Scottish plaid. They are made in various sizes, usually with black, sometimes brown, over white. Young women also wear shoulder shawls but with quite different patterns. Although they consist mostly of white cotton woven in diagonal twill, they are always decorated with broad bands of deep blue and red on the upper and lower edges. The colored bands are created by substituting wool wefts for the cotton weft elements used in the center part of the shawl. The blue outer bands are generally woven in diamond twill.

The "maiden's shawls" and the traditional Pueblo woman's dress are no longer worn except on ceremonial occasions. The dress consists of a single wide piece of soft wool fabric, which is wrapped around the body with the center line under the left shoulder and the two upper outside corners tied together over the right shoulder. The open edges along the right side are held together with silver brooches and a colored belt around the waist. Natural black or dark brown wool is used in a diagonal twill weave, and the upper and lower edges are decorated with a wide band of diamond twill in bright blue. These large pieces of soft cloth were often used as shawls, and in the Rio Grande villages the edges were sometimes embroidered with red and blue geometric patterns.

Navajo Weaving

The third group of weavers in the Southwest is the large and growing Navajo tribe.

Their history in this region is much shorter than that of the Pueblo. They are relative newcomers from the North, who were apparently nomadic hunters until they began to copy some of the things the Pueblos did and gradually adopted agriculture and a more settled mode of life. It has often been assumed that they acquired sheep from the Spaniards but did not begin to weave until about 1700 A.D. when many Pueblo families took refuge among them to escape punishment for their revolt against the Spaniards in 1680. There is accumulating evidence to suggest that Navajo weaving was already well developed by the beginning of the 18th century and may have begun considerably earlier. Whatever the date may be, it is clear that the Navajo adopted the techniques, tools, and designs of Pueblo weaving: the only change was that the women began to weave instead of the men, as was the case among the Pueblo.

Because Navajo houses (hogans) are smaller and somewhat less permanent than Pueblo villages and because the Navajo move around with their sheep, the large two-bar looms are not suspended from house beams and anchored in the floor but are fastened between two convenient trees or tied to vertical framing posts and set into the ground. When the family moves, the two warp bars are unfastened and the unfinished fabric is rolled up until the weaver can resume her work. The original function of weaving was simple: to provide clothing and sleeping blankets. The woman's traditional dress is like the Pueblo dress—but different. It is tightly woven of black wool with broad bands of bright red at the top and bottom, but it consists of two rectangles which are worn in front and in back, fastened at both shoulders, laced up the sides, and tied at the waist with a woven sash. Few such dresses have been made or used during this century, and one old trader is quoted as saying that the Navajo women were "going calico" as early as 1895.

European Influences—Bayeta

As in the Pueblo dresses the black is usually achieved with native dye and natural dark wool, but the bright red bands represent an important aspect of European influence in Southwestern weaving: the introduction of new colors. Many vegetal dyes were used in early times, producing for the most part colors which were fast but were rarely brilliant or intense. Indigo blue and cochineal red were brought to the Southwest from Mexico and quickly became treasured favorites because of their intensity and durability. Because they were scarce, they were used with care and restraint—primarily for narrow stripes. Red was more rare than blue until the beginning of the 1800s when "bayeta" came into use. This is the Spanish name for English baize, which was traded to the Pueblos and Navajo, who carefully unraveled it and either respun the threads or used them in groups of two or three to produce a brilliant cochineal-red fabric which did not fade. Bayeta was used until about 1875 and was a major factor in giving Navajo textiles their particular brilliance.

The finest weaving was done by these people between 1850 and 1875: women's dresses, men's shirts, saddle blankets, and shoulder shawls, or body blankets, for both sexes. The earliest blankets known date from the beginning of the 19th century and are very similar to Pueblo blankets: nearly square, with parallel bands of brown, black stripes, and touches of other colors, including red bayeta and indigo blue, on natural white. These examples, unfortunately, are few and fragmentary. Beginning about 1850 Navajo blankets changed rapidly as the weavers responded to new influences and began to produce many pieces for their own use and also to sell and trade to Mexicans, American soldiers, and even to the Pueblos, whose weaving was diminishing rapidly. More color was added as bayeta became somewhat more plentiful, and they also acquired between 1850 and 1860 a silky, three-ply commercial Saxony yarn in vegetal colors, especially red and green, which was used to provide bright details in design.

Chief Blankets

A particular example of the finely woven Navajo shoulder blanket illustrates the design changes which took place during this time. It is the so-called Chief blanket. There were no chiefs as such among the Navajo, and these shoulder blankets were worn by anyone who could afford one, women as well as men, and were commonly traded to the Plains tribes. Their Pueblo derivation is indicated by the simple striped pattern in the first phase, with strong weft stripes running across the greatest dimension of the textile. Some are simply natural white and brown with touches of indigo blue, but the typical Navajo touch is often shown in additional narrow stripes of red bayeta. In the second phase rectangular blocks were imposed upon the stripes at the edges and the center, first as long narrow shapes and

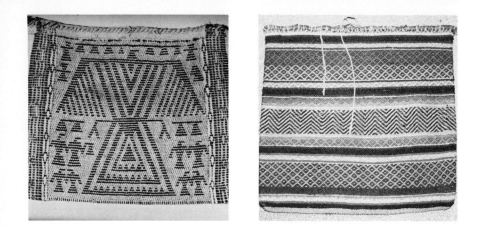

AMERICAN INDIANS con't

then as squares which were occasionally decorated. Although all variants were used in the 1870s and 1880s, the third phase is the most elaborate, with complex diamond shapes imposed upon the striped background (Fig. 3).

Although the shape and the basic striped pattern of the Chief blankets were derived from their Pueblo teachers, a longer rectangular "serape" shape was probably the result of Mexican influence. Many of the serapes were made with simple stripes or bands of stripes woven with the weft across the width of the blanket, but design and color elaborations were soon added to produce "Moki-style" blankets with center diamonds or with geometric figures added to the bands. The bands of geometric figures became increasingly complex and evolved into frets and terraced meanders, which eventually merged into overall patterns of terraced concentric diamonds (Fig. 4). In many of these, vestiges of the original striped pattern were retained as hatchings on the edge of the design.

Navajo Weaving After 1863

The Navajo are a tenaciously independent people who fought off the Spanirds and Mexicans and continued to raid the Pueblo and Mexican villages until 1863. In that year the U.S. Army burned their crops, killed their sheep, and drove the people to Fort Sumner, where they were imprisoned for five years in a small reservation called Bosque Redondo. This experience taught the ever-resilient Navajo many things. It pacified them and it also introduced them to the many changes which were coming to the Southwest. Unlike many of the Pueblo and other Indians, who gave up weaving when trade cloth became available, the Navajo women began to produce textiles

for the market and instituted major innovations to meet the new demand. New materials and new colors became available as soldiers, placing orders for "souvenir" blankets, gave the best weavers at Bosque Redondo brilliant aniline-dyed commercial Germantown yarns. The aniline colors faded, but the even, four-ply yarn was easy to work with, and the weavers produced tightly woven fabrics with complex designs and a completely new combination of colors; the blankets are sometimes referred to as "eye-dazzlers." Similar gaudy, colorful pieces were woven also in native yarns dyed with the new chemical aniline colors.

It was several years after their release from imprisonment at Bosque Redondo (in 1868) before the Navajo were able to build up their flocks and begin weaving on a significant scale. Then everything changed when the arrival of the railroad in 1880 opened up a vastly expanded market for Navajo textiles. Designs became complex, and colorful, serrated patterns with sawtooth edges displaced the simple terraces. Bands and borders were used for the first time, and the weavers began to copy foreign motifs or arrange them lengthwise in the fabrics. About 1885 some trader conceived the idea of weaving thicker fabrics, like the saddle blankets, to be sold in the East as rugs. From this time the famous "Navajo rugs" have been the most important products of their looms, and they have become a major factor in the economic life of the tribe.

A Weaving Renaissance

As demand increased and weavers rushed to meet it, quality declined in many instances. Rugs that were poorly spun, poorly designed, and poorly woven almost swamped the market. A considerable amount of indifferent weaving continued from 1890 until nearly 1930, but even as early as the beginning of this century other forces were at work which led to

improved quality and eventually to a real renaissance of Navajo weaving. The influence toward improvement came from a number of reservation traders who were interested in creating and stimulating a market for the Navajo goods they were offering to tourists and attempting to sell in the eastern market; they were concerned also for the welfare of their Indian neighbors. Some traders simply refused to buy poorly woven rugs, but others, such as Lorenzo Hubbell and J. B. Moore, worked with the Indians to improve the cleaning, spinning, and dyeing of their yarn and even created designs themselves—or with the help of European-American artists—which they passed on to the weavers. The patterns were rarely copied entirely, but many of the elements were adopted and became standard in the reservation (Fig. 5).

The influence of these early traders also stimulated the development of local styles as weavers produced rugs which would bring good prices at the nearest trading post. Some of these styles continued into the 1920s when a new series of changes came about and Navajo weaving began what has been called the "Revival Period." Once again reservation traders and other interested people collaborated with some experimental Navajo weavers to study the old traditional patterns and attempt to produce fabrics with soft, subtle hues instead of the usual strong aniline colors. New commercial dyes were procured, and a period of diligent search and trial began to reveal an extensive series of native vegetal products which could be used to give fast, economical, and desirable colors. These have been used in a variety of ways, and the past fifty years have seen Navajo ingenuity, technical skill, and aesthetic creativity develop in ways which the general public is just beginning to appreciate. There is not space here to describe or to illustrate the range of Navajo design: a few samples will have to represent the whole vast variety.

Variety in Navajo Design

The "Two Gray Hills" style arose from the use of natural colors emphasized by the earlier trader J. B. Moore. It still combines natural white, black, and brown wools with blends to make grays and tans. The designs are complex geometric overall patterns, and the weaving is the finest. They are far too fine to be used as rugs: wefts often exceed 120 threads per inch, and good examples cost thousands of dollars.

Complex geometric designs characterize two other distinctive styles: the "Teec Nos Pos" from the northern part of the reservation, which is woven with aniline colors and some commercial yarn, and the rugs from "Burnt Water" at the southern edge of the reservation.

Completely different from these and representative of designs which concentrate upon the use of vegetal colors are the "Crystal" rugs with simple patterns and subtle, earth colors, and the rugs from "Wide Ruin" and "Pine Springs," generally in banded designs of pastel colors.

The bold designs with strong aniline reds and jet blacks, which are often regarded as "typical" Navajo rugs, are still woven at "Ganado," and "Yei" rugs, depicting groups of figures in the style used in ceremonial sand paintings, are woven in several parts of the reservation (Fig. 6).

Whole sand-painting designs have been depicted on rugs since 1896 but are still rare. There are also double-face rugs, twilled rugs, rugs with pictorial designs, and an endless variety which reflects local styles, the tastes and skills of the individual weavers, and the constantly changing state of contemporary Navajo life.

North Pacific Coast

Along the Pacific coast, from Puget Sound to southern Alaska, Indians fished and hunted in the ocean and lived in large villages of rectangular gabled houses built of broad cedar planks. They were supreme woodworkers who carved complex towering totem poles, elaborate dance masks, and canoes capable of carrying fifty men. Art permeated their existence, and everything was decorated with the elaborate, highly conventionalized symbols which reflected their mythologies and family legends. Housefronts, canoes, wooden storage boxes, baskets, and even clothing were covered with tightly interlocking patterns depicting animals and mythological beings. Their anatomical parts were rearranged to form an overall design, but the identifying symbols were always apparent to those who understood them. Especially in the North, figures were split ventrally and spread over the decorated area, and all blank spaces were filled with eye symbols and curved figures. The effect is intriguing, puzzling, and totally unique.

The Chilkat Blanket

The people wore very little clothing because the climate was generally moderate, but ceremonialism was central to their lives and elaborate ceremonial costumes were woven in the form of blanket capes, long shirts, dance kilts, and leggings. The shoulder capes, which are known as "Chilkat blankets"—because many of them were woven by the Chilkat band of the Tlingit tribe—are famous for their intricate designs and as superb examples of fine finger weaving. The loom was not known to these people: the warp elements were simply hung over a wooden bar and the weft was twined across them. The yarn was twisted from the wool of the mountain goat and wrapped around shredded cedar bark for the warp elements. The wool from three goat pelts was needed to make one blanket, and the animals were difficult to procure because they lived only in the mountains back from the coast. Some wool was picked from the bushes in the spring when the goats shed their winter coats. It was saved carefully and was an important item for intertribal trade.

The colors in the textiles of this area were

FAR LEFT. FIG. 16. Burden strap of twined-weft bast fibers decorated with beads and false embroidery of dyed red and blue moose hair. Iroquois. *Field Museum—155574.*

LEFT. FIG. 17. Buckskin bag with embroidered design of "Underwater Panthers" in dyed porcupine quills. Ottawa Tribe, Michigan, about 1800. *Cranbrook Institute of Science—3690.*

AMERICAN INDIANS con't

limited and traditional: natural white, black or very deep brown, a bright, clear yellow dyed with barks and roots, and elements of brilliant blue-green. This distinctive color was achieved with a dye made by soaking copper in urine. In recent years some blankets have been woven with commercial yarn, but their colors and texture are quite different from the older pieces. At one time the blankets were woven by all the tribes of the North Coast, but by the beginning of this century only a few Chilkat women were still weaving. Woven garments were never abundant. The fine costumes were worn only by major chiefs, and they are increasingly rare.

The Chilkat blanket is distinctively pointed or rounded on the lower edge and is decorated with a long, thick fringe, an important element of the dance costume. At an early time the designs appear to have been nonsymbolic geometric figures similar to those the women used to decorate their fine baskets. Sometime about the beginning of the 19th century the symbolic, stylized patterns were introduced. They may have been done by the men because the new designs are similar to the kind they used in their painting and carving, and from this time on the textile designs were woven from wooden pattern boards which were painted by the men. The pattern board was done only in black paint because the weaver was limited to the four traditional colors, and only two-thirds of the pattern was presented because the side panels were mirror reflections of each other.

The technique of weaving used was twining, but the twined wefts cross completely from one edge to the other only in the solid borders. For the body of the blanket the weaver worked from one panel to another, literally weaving each one separately, joining them together with a special weaving stitch, and covering some of the junctures with a kind of false embroidery. The weft elements were twined back and forth within each panel until that section of the design was completed. It was then outlined with a bordering stitch and attached to the adjacent sections of the pattern.

The most common pattern consists of a central panel flanked by two vertical panels which are mirror reflections of each other. Two basic arrangements for the central panel have been distinguished. In the first type a large face can be discerned at the top with rectangular ears and large eyes. Below is the body of the animal, and the eye rec-

FIG. 20. Elk-skin pouch with a design of woven porcupine quills, 10¾" long. Chipewayan Tribe, Central Canada. *Mus. of the Am. Indian—5/3105 (20586).*

tangles at the bottom are identified with the feet or flippers. The space around these identifiable elements is occupied by conventionalized "fillers," said to represent eyes, flicker feathers, ears, etc., which have little or no relationship to the mythological figures in the design.

The second basic pattern has one or more rectangular faces at the center, but the head of the motif animal is at the bottom of the panel, where two central circles are said to stand for its nostrils. The central face represents the body, and the elements at the top of the panel may depict legs or flippers. The side panels usually contain an upright or seated animal shown in profile.

The Indians themselves do not always agree on the interpretation of these complex designs. Franz Boas, commenting on this, said, "In the art of the North Pacific coast a definite totemic meaning is given to conventional figures. There is no general agreement as to their significance, but to many forms is assigned a meaning according to the totemic affiliation of the owner for whom it thus attains a value based on its meaning." The distinctive signs which identify certain animals in carving and painting occasionally appear on textiles: the parallel incisor teeth and hatched tail of the beaver, the arching dorsal fin of the killer whale, the protruding tongue of the bear.

In most examples the identifying cues are obscure.

The same designs, colors, and techniques were used to weave dance kilts and aprons, as well as dance shirts or tunics which reached to the dancer's knees or slightly below. Because the back of the shirt was usually covered with a decorated blanket, the back surface was generally quite simple, with elements such as geometric bands. The elaborate, totemic designs were reserved for the front where they would be visible to the spectators (Fig. 7). The cos-

RIGHT. FIG. 18. Birchbark box decorated with dyed porcupine quills. Micmac Tribe, Nova Scotia, about 1860. Becker Fund Collection. *Logan Museum—7405.*

FAR RIGHT. FIG. 19. Birchbark box covered with porcupine quills in natural colors. Ottawa Tribe, Michigan. Heath Collection. *Logan Museum—31200.*

tume was completed with woven or leather leggings and a crown with a carved front, a frieze of seal whiskers, and a fall of white ermine skins at the back.

A much less common type of design on Chilkat blankets consists of rectangular panels each containing a motif figure such as a killer whale. A much earlier blanket, which is so rare that it is included here only because of its interesting designs, is rectangular in shape and decorated with panels of rectangular figures and zigzag borders (Fig. 8). The weaving in these blankets is very fine, and they are made of pure mountain-goat wool without the additional cedar bark used in the warp elements of the later Chilkat type. The weaving techniques are also different: full-turn weft twining is used as well as tapestry twilled twining, and the weft elements cross from one edge to the other instead of beginning anew with each motif in the design. Only a few of these blankets are known, and it appears that they were made only by the northern Tlingit and probably died out about the end of the 18th century.

The Salish

South of the Tlingit and Tsimshian (who wove the Chilkat-type blankets) little weaving was done except for some shoulder blankets of Chilkat shape with the same long fringe but with simple designs which consist of a few patterned bands crossing from one edge to the other. They are made of white mountain-goat wool, rather loosely woven of thick yarn, a type of textile which is typical of their southern neighbors, the Salish.

These people, living around Puget Sound and up the Columbia River, possessed a unique textile complex. They wove on a two-bar roller loom unlike anything else known in the Americas. Two upright posts, frequently decorated with carving, held two parallel roller rods which fitted into slots and could be moved up or down by setting them with wedges. The warp elements were arranged in a unique way: cord was strung between the uprights, and a continuous warp element was tied to the cord, passed over the top bar, under the lower bar, around the cord, and then reversed to retrace the route until it again reached the cord, where it was reversed again. The warp was thus wound discontinuously, and when the textile was completed, the loom cord was pulled out and the ends of the fabric came apart without cutting.

The materials used were also unique. The fine wool of the mountain goat was used, but duck down and giant fireweed fibers were also spun into yarn, and these people kept packs of fleecy dogs which were sheared for their soft, wooly hair. The various fibers were often mixed with each other, and the hair of lynx, bear, and other animals was sometimes added. The yarn they produced was usually rather thick and soft, and it was spun on large spindles, almost four feet long, which passed through enormous wooden whorls, ten inches in diameter and decorated with finely carved designs (Fig. 9).

The products of this unique weaving complex were of great utility but not of decorative significance. They were almost all robes or blankets. The robes were approximately five by six feet in size, but some of the soft blankets, which were used for bedding, were ten or twelve feet in length. The color was generally white, and the only decoration consisted of occasional borders, brown or tan crossbands, or cross-hatching of widely spaced narrow lines. In spite of the rigid frame on which the warp was stretched it was not a true loom: no provision was made to separate sheds and the weft was threaded back and forth with the fingers. Some blankets were twined like those further north, but most were woven

FIG. 21. Moccasins of dyed black buckskin with embroidery of colored moose hair, 9″ long. Huron, Quebec, Canada. *Museum of the American Indian—19/6346 (29148).*

AMERICAN INDIANS con't

in rather loose twilled plaiting (interlacing) with warp and weft showing equally.

For a short time, apparently about the beginning of the 19th century, the early traders brought in European woolen yarns, and some of the Salish women combined the bright colors with native fibers to produce a distinctive blanket which has been called the "nobility," or "organized," robe. Not only were these much finer in texture than the usual Salish blanket, but they were tightly twined instead of interlaced (twilled) and were decorated with complex geometric designs unlike anything seen in this area—before or since (Fig. 10).

The native peoples of this area made magnificent baskets in a variety of shapes and materials, as well as in several techniques. The developmental sequence of influence from baskets and fine mats to the soft cedar bark robes and the wool blankets is apparent, and it is an arbitrary decision whether the bark robes and some of the soft, flexible bags should be regarded as textiles or a form of basketry. South of Puget Sound was an area of fine baskets, but the only fabrics here were sashes of vegetal fiber, and the broad netted and braided bands which the Hupa and Karok painted with simple designs and hung from their ceremonial headdresses. Up the Columbia River the Wasco and Wishram twined flexible "sally bags" and decorated them with strange figures. Further east on the Plateau the Nez Perce twined soft bags of rushes and decorated them by completely covering their surfaces with corn-husk fiber and designs of woolen yarn (Fig. 11). These, of couse, are not really from the North Pacific Coast and they may not be fabrics, but they represent a distinctive type of decorative technique and an interesting series of designs.

The Eastern Weaving Area

In the 16th century various kinds of fabrics were being produced by the Indians throughout most of the eastern part of North America, from Florida into Canada and slightly beyond the Mississippi River. The varied products of the southeastern tribes, which were described by the early Spanish and French explorers, have been mentioned previously, as well as the evidence that some of their textiles may have been woven on a true loom. Because of the rapidity with which these tribes changed after European contact and their forced removal to territories west of the Mississippi River, their traditional weaving did not persist long into the historic period.

FIG. 24. Beaded bandolier bag, late naturalistic designs. Chippewa, Wisconsin. Heath Collection. *Logan—30566.*

Further to the north, among the Iroquoian-, Algonquian-, and Siouan-speaking tribes, fabrics continued to be produced and a few are still made in the region of the western Great Lakes. These are the last vestiges of the once-rich eastern fabric area, and they will be described as examples of styles, techniques, and materials which were once distributed throughout the larger region.

It is clear that they have been known for a very long time: examples have been recovered in Salts Cave, Kentucky which were made and used between 1200 and 250 B.C. The Hopewell Mound Builders were producing fabrics in Ohio and Illinois between 300 B.C. and 100 A.D., and archaeological pottery fragments with fabric impressions have been recovered from sites of the Effigy Mound culture in Wisconsin, which carry the craft from 300 A.D. up to 1642, at which time the French arrived in the area of the western Great Lakes. Here and throughout the East fine fiber mats have long been made, but no sheets of fabric which could be used as robes or blankets have been produced in the past 225 years. The unique products of this highly developed finger-weaving complex are rectangular bags and a variety of sashes and straps.

Indian Bags

The materials used were similar to those described for the early Southeast. Various nettle fibers were common, as well as apocynum (spreading dogbane) and bast fibers from the inner bark of basswood, cedar, linden, and slippery elm. They were often combined or used with bison hair, sometimes moose hair, or, farther to the south, opossum hair—rolled on the thigh to make two-ply yarn. The last bison moved west of the Mississippi about 1833, but even before this time the Indians had added a new material by unraveling the woolen trade blankets which came into the area

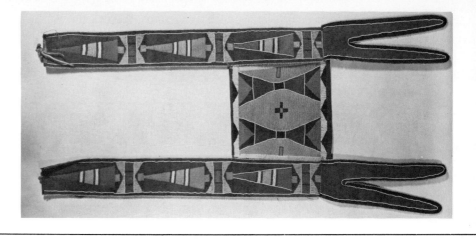

RIGHT. FIG. 25. Breast ornament for a horse, decorated with trade beads in spot-stitch technique. Crow Tribe, Montana, 42" long. *Museum of the American Indian— 20/7717 (29354).*

BELOW. FIG. 26. Vest covered with trade beads in spot-stitch patterns typical of the Plateau Area. Flathead, Idaho. Heath Collection. *Logan—30412.*

about 1690. It is probable that only fragments or well-worn blankets were used for this purpose: they were much too important as robes and bedding to be destroyed for the production of bags. Wool yarns did not become available until about 1800, but when they could be procured they were enthusiastically adopted and quickly resulted in new types of bags, made with new techniques and new designs.

The aboriginal bast fibers were rolled into two-ply yarns (cords) or used in slender untwisted hanks or bundles to make open-mesh rectangular bags for storage or for washing corn. The warp elements were hung over a suspended horizontal rod, and the weft element was twined across one side and then the other in a continuous spiral. The rim of the bag was finished by gathering the free-hanging ends of the warps into a stout braid. Finally the suspending rod was pulled out from the bottom of the bag, and the holes in the lower corners were sometimes closed with stitching. The infrequent decorations of colored vertical stripes were produced with dyed warps which showed between the separated wefts. The wefts were always spaced or compact, depending upon the use for which the bag was intended. The warps were straight and parallel in most storage bags, but cedar-bark bags for hulling corn were made with transposed warps in which the adjacent elements crossed and recrossed each other between the wefts, producing an open-diagonal crosshatch effect.

The famous yarn bags of the western Great Lakes fall into two distinct types. The earlier type, usually made of aboriginal native materials, is often decorated with figures of animals and such mythological forms as thunderbirds (Fig. 12) or the underwater panther. These figures occupy the large central panel; the narrow border panels are filled with geometric figures

such as triangles, stars, or the lines of diamonds known as "otter tracks." In almost all bags from this area the designs are different on the two sides.

These early bags were made in the same way as the bast-fiber bags, generally with two-ply yarns of tan nettle fiber or darker bison hair until these materials were displaced by commercial cotton string about 1870. The complex designs were produced by using double warps of different colors, which were exposed as desired in a process of spaced alternate-pair weft twining. Colors used were natural tan, brown, and black, as well as dyed elements in red, green, and yellow. Most bags are slightly wider than high, although some are practically square. Their dimensions vary greatly, from large storage bags nearly 36 inches across, which held a family's clothing or ceremonial paraphernalia, to very small pouches no more than three or four inches in width, which were used to hold ceremonial medicines and charms.

A few bags of this particular style were made with cotton-string weft and com-

mercial-wool-yarn warp, but the acquisition of wool yarn brought about marked changes in technique and design, and a different style of fabric bag came into being some time about the middle of the 19th century. These bags were not only of different materials, but they were made in a different technique and with quite different designs. Instead of hanging the warp elements over a suspended wood rod, a cord was passed around two springy sticks set vertically into the ground, and the warp elements were attached around the cord with half-hitch knots. As they hung from the cord in a loose tubular formation, the double-yarn wefts were twined across and around in a continuous spiral. The ends of the warps were braided to the form of the bag, the tube was lifted from the stakes, the two sides were sewn together across the bottom, and the bag was complete.

The design field on these bags, instead of being divided into three vertical panels, consists of three or four broad horizontal bands which are filled with repeated geometric motifs consisting of arrangements of triangles, diamonds, lozenges, and zigzag lines. The colors used are generally quite dark—red, green, blue, yellow, orange, brown—and the designs on the two sides of the bag are usually different. The complex geometric patterns are formed by the weft elements, which are worked in tightly compact twining, sometimes countered to produce a chevron or herringbone pattern. The fabric surface is distinctly different from the spaced alternate-pair weft twining of the older style (Fig. 13).

New Twining Techniques

A completely new twining technique appears in these bags and was used to manipulate the colored weft elements in producing the designs. In this technique, known as full-turn weft twining or wrap-twine, one

AMERICAN INDIANS con't

of the weft elements remains relatively passive while the other turns around it behind the warp, then around the warp and on to the surface of the fabric, returning to turn again around the passive weft and then over the next warp. In this way a particular color can appear over contiguous warps and then be replaced by the formerly passive weft, which then brings a different color to the surface. The origin of this twining technique is not known: it appears in the many soft and semirigid bags of the Wasco of the Columbia River and in the fine baskets of the Makah of the Olympic Peninsula in Washington. It was also a distinctive technique in the early geometric-patterned mountain-goat blankets which the Tlingit of Alaska once made.

A different technique was used to produce another style of bag with a distinctive design and rather limited distribution. These bags are associated primarily with the Winnebago and Potawatomi of the western Great Lakes and were made in a compact twined tapestry technique to create horizontal bands of interlocking diamonds (Fig. 14) or bands of "otter-track" design—

chains of diamonds and elongated hexagons. Unlike the more common yarn bags, in which the weft elements were carried continuously and completely around the bag, the wefts in these particular bags were worked back and forth in countered twining within a single color segment until it was completed; the second color was then worked in to fill the intervening spaces. The technique is similar to that used in the Chilkat blankets of the Northwest Coast, but otherwise it is extremely rare and its use here seems to be additional demonstration of the high development and unique attainments in the finger-weaving arts by the Indians of the Great Lakes.

Assomption Sashes

None of the techniques used in making bags were used by the Indians of the Great Lakes and the Northeast to produce any articles of clothing, but many early paintings show them wearing decorated sashes around their waists or over their shoulders in bandolier style. Some of them also wore knee garters to hold their leggings in place, decorated bands on their upper arms, and elaborate turbans.

The earliest explorers in the area saw the Indians making a variety of belts and bands with colored yarns of buffalo hair or other fibers, and the French voyageurs quickly adopted them for their own costumes. They were so popular with both Indians and French that the Hudson Bay Company introduced a European imitation, and the French women of some villages in Quebec began to make them. The French-Canadian sashes (*Ceintures Flèchées*), which are sometimes known as Assomption Sashes in reference to one of the villages where they were made, are still occasionally produced and are identical to those made by the Indians, except that they are usually bigger and the respun worsted yarn is generally finer. With their brightly colored zigzag patterns these braided sashes were esteemed by Indians from the Seminoles of Florida to the northern Iroquois. They were especially popular among the tribes of the Great Lakes (Winnebago, Chippewa, Sac, and Fox), as well as such Prairie relatives as the Omaha and Osage. The buffalo hunters of the Central Plains did not make sashes themselves, but they were always eager to trade them from the eastern tribes.

The technique of "braiding" is actually a type of diagonal plaiting, or over-and-under procedure, which Emery calls "single element oblique interlacing." As in simple three-strand braiding the elements were tied or hung parallel to each other, and each one in turn became the active element as it was interlaced over and under the others. No loom, heddle, or other instruments were used, and there were no separate weft elements. As many as 150 hanging yarns could be used in making a sash four inches wide; some are as much as a foot in width and from three to fifteen feet in length, almost always with a long fringe at each end. The larger sashes were tied around the waist with the long fringes hanging at the side, or wrapped around a man's head and topped with a feather.

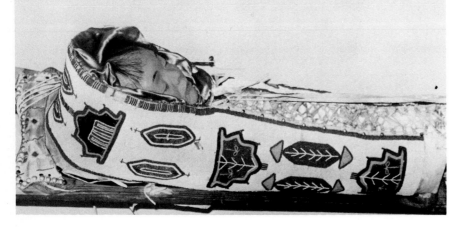

FIG. 29. Beaded cradle cover decorated with lazy-stitch and stylized floral motifs. Kiowa Tribe, Southern Plains. *Milwaukee Public Museum.*

RIGHT. FIG. 30. Loom-beaded bandolier bag, yellow ground with red, blue, and green decoration. Chippewa Tribe, Wis. Heath Collection. *Logan Museum—30564.*

BELOW. FIG. 31. Appliqué panels of silk ribbon on the front edges of a wool tradecloth shawl. Winnebago Tribe, Wis. Heath Collection. *Logan—30419.*

Three or more colors were usually combined: deep red, sage green, yellow, blue, etc. The yarn was two- or three-ply commercial wool, which was often redyed with native materials to produce the desired colors. The design reflected the particular braiding or interlacing technique employed. Patterns of interlocking chevrons resulted from double-band braiding, in which the strands at the center of each band were plaited across to the outside edge and back to interlock in the middle of the sash. Parallel diagonal stripes resulted from single-band plaiting, in which the strand on the left edge was braided through the others, and each strand was dealt with in the same manner as it moved outside.

The most popular designs were concentric Ws or zigzags which resulted from braiding with a number of double bands, each of which produced a pattern of interlocking chevrons. The double bands were then looped together along their edges (Fig. 15). Some sashes were started at the center and woven first to one end and then to the other, but the ends were invariably finished off with a few rows of twining, and the yarns then knotted and left to form a long fringe. In some of the old sashes of the southeastern tribes the fringes were formed into narrow braids, and white trade beads were added during the braiding process. Similarly, beads were often added to produce patterns in the body of Iroquois and other eastern sashes, and the Osage of Oklahoma, who still occasionally make excellent sashes, usually ran a zigzag line of white beads along the edges.

In addition to the very large and ornate sashes used as belts and turbans, a great quantity of smaller strips was produced by the same techniques for use as garters, arm bands, and even as straps to tie around medicine bundles. Braiding was the most popular technique, but sashes and other items were also made in a looping, or netting, technique which Emery defines as "interlinking with a single set of elements." This finger-weaving procedure is very ancient and widespread, occurring beyond this area among some tribes of central California. Because each element is connected only to its immediate neighbors, this technique produces a pattern of longitudinal parallel stripes.

The Fiber Bands

A still different group of techniques was employed by the eastern tribes to make stout bands or straps which were used as tumplines. These consist of a broad band which was passed across the forehead and long, narrow ties at each end which were used to secure burdens such as firewood and other materials. The central band is usually about a yard in length; the ties are five or six feet long. The three sections were made separately, with the six-strand flat-braided ties hitched through loops in the ends of the central band (Fig. 16). The materials used were bast fibers of slippery elm, basswood, and occasionally nettle.

These fiber bands are notable for the excellence of their construction, but it is their mode of decoration which most clearly marks them as important examples of North American Indian art. On many specimens the outer surface of the brow band was covered with geometric patterns in red, blue, green, and white. In some cases the designs were applied with woolen trade yarn, but the best examples are those in which the designs were done in the dyed hair of moose or, less frequently, deer and elk. In other cases fine porcupine quills were used. In each case the decorative materials were worked into the fabric in the process of manufacturing by a technique known as "false embroidery," in which the colored strands were twined around warp or weft elements as they were turned to the surface of the fabric.

Applied Decoration

Porcupine Quillwork. Clothing made of textiles was restricted to a few areas of aboriginal North America, but almost all the Indians decorated their skin garments with paint or with sewn designs in porcupine quills, moose and caribou hair, beads, shells, seeds, and ribbons. Their use of the hollow porcupine quills is unique: it dates from the pre-Columbian past and was spread over a large part of the continent, with a concentration which extended from the St. Lawrence valley across the Great Lakes and the northern Plains into the Mackenzie Valley and Alaska.

The smooth, hollow quills range in size up to five or six inches; they take dyes easily and become flexible when soaked in water or held in the mouth. They are flattened and applied to skin by wrapping or folding them in a variety of ways around a single sinew thread or between two threads. Techniques and designs vary from one region to another.

AMERICAN INDIANS con't

In the eastern area and among the tribes of the Great Lakes, quilled designs tended toward linear depictions of mythical forms such as thunderbirds and underwater panthers (Fig. 17), which were embellished with geometric and floral motifs. A somewhat similar linear approach, utilizing a simple wrapping technique, was used on the North Pacific Coast to create the traditional totemic designs of that area. Solid designs of quillwork are rare, but the Micmac of Nova Scotia covered birchbark boxes with lose patterns (Fig. 18).

Quilled bark boxes are still made by the Ottawa and Chippewa for sale to tourists (Fig. 19). The massive use of quillwork on clothing was most typical of the tribes of the northern and central Plains, where the flattened quills were folded or plaited between two threads to decorate shirts, pipe bags, and moccasins. They were also wrapped around cut slats of rawhide for pectorals and plaited between two stretched threads to be wrapped around ceremonial pipe stems.

A rare and different quill technique was used by the Chipewayan and Cree of central Canada, who wove the quills over and under the weft elements of simple fiber bands. When the wefts were compressed against each other, the quills were bent to produce an appearance of small cylindrical beads (Fig. 20).

Hair Embroidery. An aboriginal craft, which once spread from the lower St. Lawrence across Canada and into Siberia, utilized the longer hairs of moose and caribou in two basic manners. The first was most typical of the Iroquois and the Huron, who wove burden straps and tumplines of native hemp and decorated them in colored geometric designs with the technique known as "false embroidery." The same materials and techniques were sometimes used to make rectangular pouches.

The second use of moose hair was practiced primarily by the Huron, who from the beginning of the 18th century produced quantities of articles elaborately decorated with floral patterns in moose-hair embroidery (Fig. 21). The evident European style in many of the designs reflects the influence of the Quebec Ursuline nuns who taught Indian girls in their seminary from the middle of the 17th century until about 1875. Under their direction the Europeanized Huron produced moccasins and many other articles which were widely traded.

The western tribes did some hair embroidery also, but today the craft is preserved by Indian women of the Mackenzie area, where floral designs, sometimes trimmed with piping of dyed horsehair, are applied to gloves, belts, and moccasins. The wide-traveling French *voyageurs* and their Indian companions were probably responsible for the introduction of the craft.

Beadwork. This important Indian craft is related to quill and hair embroidery because it served the same functions and largely displaced them. Small, spheroid porcelain beads were brought to the eastern Indians about 1675 and quickly spread to the tribes further west and north. They were sewn to every kind of garment.

The early beadwork was often done in linear geometric patterns or in the outlined abstract forms which were particular to the eastern tribes (Fig. 22). Formalized floral patterns were continued by some of the Great Lakes tribes (Fig. 23), and others (such as the Chippewa) developed the floral motifs into exuberant naturalism (Fig. 24). To the north the floral patterns of the Cree were both formal and gracefully asymmetric.

In all these decorations the many-colored beads were sewn in a spot-stitch technique: they were threaded and laid out in the desired pattern to be attached to the cloth or skin backing with a loop stitch every three or four beads. This technique was used throughout the East and the Great Lakes area and also by the Blackfeet and Crow of the northern Plains, whose early beadwork designs were geometric (Fig. 25). Their later designs emphasized floral motifs, a

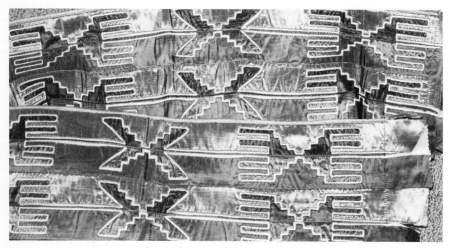

FIG. 32. A contemporary appliqué of moiré ribbon in finely detailed geometric patterning from the Osage Tribe. *Logan Museum of Anthropology—30415.*

style which was employed to the fullest by the Nez Percé (Fig. 26) and Flathead of Idaho. The Indians of the North Pacific Coast used this sewing technique to decorate ceremonial costumes with beaded totemic designs (Fig. 27).

A different bead-sewing technique was employed by the Sioux, Cheyenne, and other tribes of the central Plains. It is distinguished by a ribbed surface, produced by "lazy-stitch" sewing in which six or seven beads were strung on long parallel stitches which were fastened to the backing only at their ends. Massive geometric patterns were typical of this area: diamonds, terraces, and bands in various colors were worked in solid beading to decorate formal dresses, women's buckskin "anything" bags, pipe bags, vests (Fig. 28), and practically every other type of garment and container. In the southern Plains, the Kiowa used the same sewing technique but preferred isolated geometric or stylized floral motifs (Fig 29).

The southern Plains people also made "netted beadwork," as did some California tribes. The Mohave and Apache made openwork collars, and the Apache created neck decorations for the young women. There were various netting techniques, but all consisted of crossing a series of fiber threads with beads serving to hold them together instead of knots.

"Woven beadwork," which is simply plaiting (interlacing) fiber warps stretched on a frame or to the waist of the weaver with beads strung on the weft elements to create a design, was a specialty of the tribes of the Great Lakes. It is the most popular technique in craft classes and in Indian schools, and as a result it is now done in many areas. Weaving is done both with needles and with the European heddle. Long sashes with yarn fringes, garters, and arm bands were common. The most notable products were the large "Friendship" bandolier bags with

bold stylized leaf or floral motifs (Fig. 30), and complex overall patterns.

Ribbonwork, or Silk Appliqué. This technique was another specialty of the Lakes tribes and their Prairie relatives such as the Osage and Oto. It started about 1800 when traders began to import silk ribbons, and the Indian women used their trade scissors to cut ribbons into designs and sew them onto others of different colors. The resulting pattern was then sewn to dark blue or red robes, dresses, moccasins, and other garments. The ribbons are sewn with blind- or cross-stitches, and several bands are combined to create the desired pattern. Both curvilinear designs with floral motifs (Fig. 31) and geometric patterns (Fig. 32) were popular, often with mirror images in different colors. Wider silk ribbons became available during the 19th century and were eventually replaced with yard goods. About 1930 moiré and rayon satin and taffeta replaced scarce silk and to this day continue to be worked into elaborate powwow costumes by Osage, Mesquakie, and other tribal craftswomen.

Ribbon Patchwork. This technique of the Florida Seminole is an entirely different art. Cloth appliqué was once produced here, but since the beginning of the century sewing machines have been used to join small units of brightly colored cotton cloth into geometric bands which are then sewn into dresses and shirts (Fig. 33). The Seminole still do some patchwork for their own use and a great quantity for sale to tourists; it is generally much less complex than the older pieces.

Epilogue

As is true in all parts of the world the native traditional arts of North America have dwindled and disappeared. Handwrought materials and decorations have been displaced by plastics and prints—generally, but not always. Although craft revivals often begin with urban artists, their effects have sometimes helped to sustain the struggling remnants of native arts. The Pueblo and Navajo Indians of the Southwest have been encouraged to expand their traditional work in pottery, weaving, and silver jewelry to a level of artistry and acceptance which represents a new era. Other tribes are producing pottery, wood carvings, and excellent baskets. The level of tribal artistry should not be judged by the cheap items produced to sell to casual visitors but by the rare and exquisite pieces which the Indians make for their own use or for the appreciation of the connoisseur. These art objects blend directly into the stream of inventive nontraditional painting, sculpture, pottery, and weaving of the contemporary Indian artists of North America.

FIG. 33. Machine-sewn patchwork, Seminole Tribe, Florida. Herbert & Sonia Zim Collection. *Logan Museum—8801/2.*

Prof. Andrew Hunter Whiteford
Former Director, Logan Museum
of Anthropology, Beloit, Wisc.

Peruvian woven fabric from the Coastal Region, Inca Period, 14–16th Century. Gift of George D. Pratt, 1933. *Met—33.149.44 (97498).*

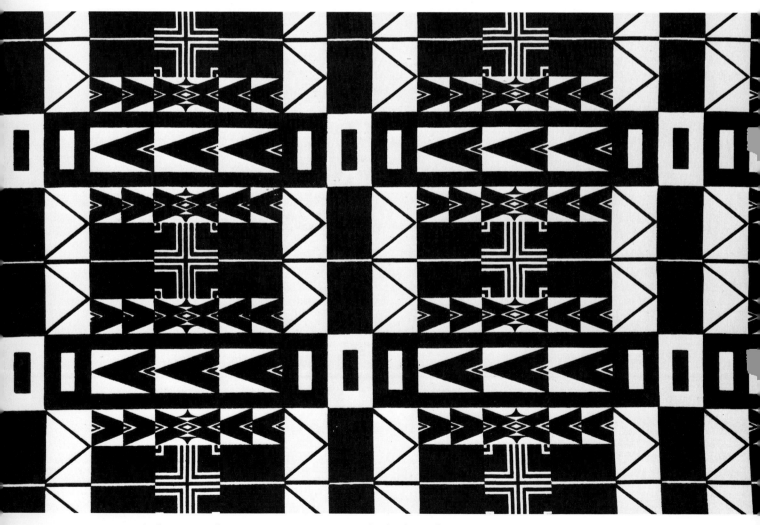

Screen-printed silk, Austria, about 1924. Size: 52½" × 45". Gift of Robert Allerton. *Art Institute of Chicago—1924.217 (C32879).*

TEXTILE DESIGN IDEAS

The photographic section which begins overleaf reveals the rich source material available in U.S. and Canadian museums. These B/W photographs cannot hope to offer more than a sampling of the half million or more pieces preserved in collections all over North America. But even the most casual viewer must be impressed by the range and excellence of these holdings. ¶ ¶ ¶ The photographs have been selected with a designer's eye; that is, they have been chosen for their pattern interest and only secondarily for their provenance or historical importance. They have been arranged alphabetically by region. No attempt has been made to group them in chronological sequence. The aim, rather, has been to suggest design themes for contemporary fabrics by selecting the best representative pieces from thirty different regional sources. ¶ ¶ ¶ In this sampling it is my hope the designer will find themes of sufficient interest to be followed up with research visits to the museums themselves. The photographs, as I have said before, can only offer ideas. They are no more than tokens of the much richer source material available in the collections themselves. ¶ ¶ ¶ And this point, too, should be emphasized: the selection is a personal one, based on my own experience in the design field. The pieces I have chosen please my eye and I hope they will please others. But *chacun à son gout* applies here as in all questions of taste, and I would hope each designer would go to the sources to find that particular example, that special motif, which alone can evoke a personal and creative response.

AFRICA. TOP. Indigo resist made with cassava paste. Nigeria, 1950s. *Cooper-Hewitt—1959-36-1 (9312).*

BOTTOM. Embroidered headcloth from Algeria, Central Western Sahara (Tuarega tribe), late 19th Century. Silk yarns on a linen ground. Gift of Mr. & Mrs. J. H. Wade. *Cleveland Museum—16.1225 (32193).*

RIGHT. Ashanti Kente cloth from Ghana, cotton-silk, narrow-strip weave. *Museum of Primitive Art—62.78.*

AFRICA. An indigo resist panel from Nigeria (Yoruba), made in the late 19th Century. The cotton fabric is painted with cassava paste to resist the indigo dye. The panel is made in two sections which are duplicates. The sections are then reversed against each other and sewn together. *Cranbrook Institute of Science—8922.*

AFRICA. Pile cloth from Zaire (Kuba). It is woven of raffia fiber which is then cut to produce a short pile. The cloth is sometimes known as raffia plush or velvet. This piece measures about 22″ × 28″. *Museum of Primitive Art—59.30.*

AFRICA. LEFT. Another example of raffia velvet, this one from the Bakura tribe in the Belgian Congo, late 19th Century. It is also embroidered. *Cooper-Hewitt—1957-110-3 (4636).*

RIGHT. Section of a raffia pile mat from the Congo. *Textile Museum—75.1.*

AMERICA (U.S.). ABOVE. An appliqué cotton quilt made by Harriet Powers of Athens, Georgia in 1895–98. From the M. & M. Karolik Collection. *Boston Museum of Fine Arts—64.619 (C19875).*

RIGHT TOP. Section of another appliqué quilt by Harriet Powers. This one is dated 1886 and is known as the "Bible Quilt" since it tells some of the Bible stories in cutout appliqué figures scene by scene. It begins with Adam and Eve in

the Garden of Eden and ends with Joseph, the Virgin, and the infant Jesus with the star of Bethlehem over his head.
Smithsonian: History & Technology—T.14713 (69039).

BOTTOM. One half of an appliquéd and pieced "Bride's Quilt," Weston, Vermont, 1850–60. Each block is inscribed with name of maker. Gift of Mrs. Louis P. Haller. *Chicago Art Institute—1965.379 (C30045).*

AMERICA (U.S.). ABOVE. Cotton pieced work and appliqué from Pawling, N.Y., 1850. The quilt is composed of 81 squares, each made and signed by a friend of Benoni Pearce and presented to her on her engagement. The whole quilt is 103" square. *Smithsonian: History & Technology—T. 16.323 (73-42-83).*

TOP LEFT. "Rain of Honolulu" quilt, Hawaii, 1975. *Henry Ford Museum—74.40 (B69155).*

TOP RIGHT. Simulated patchwork print, c. 1876. Gift of Millia Davenport. *Metropolitan—40.42.1 (120668).*

BOTTOM LEFT. Patchwork quilt, Glen Head, N.Y., c. 1840. Gift of Mrs. J. Hoyt Kerley. *Met—56.179 (162471).*

BOTTOM RIGHT. Pieced quilt, roller-printed cotton, c. 1835–45. *Old Sturbridge Village—26.10.71 (B2450).*

AMERICA (U.S.). TOP LEFT. Printed cotton bedspread by John Hewson, an early American printer who worked in Philadelphia 1774–1810. Gift of Joseph B. Hodgson, Jr. *Philadelphia Museum of Art—'30-100-1.*

TOP RIGHT. Embroidered blue-white blanket, Hudson River Valley, 1778. *Henry Ford Museum—(B3100).*

BOTTOM LEFT. Cotton bedcover with roller-printed floral medallion applied to quilted fabric. Dated 1830–35, 87" square. Gift of Mrs. Jennie Hodge Schmidt. *Chicago Art Institute—1965.413 (C30070).*

BOTTOM RIGHT. Table cover in a mosaic of broadcloth, embroidered about 1876 by J. Ansorge and F. Bach of New York. Gift of the Martin C. Ansorge Estate, 1968. *Metropolitan Museum of Art—68.84.1 (202901 B).*

ABOVE. The Phebe Warner coverlet, an embroidered linen masterpiece made in New York by Ann Walgrave Warner for Phebe Warner about 1800. Gift of Catherine E. Cotheal, 1938. *Metropolitan—38.59 (114977).*

AMERICA (U.S.). ABOVE. Red and white Jacquard double-woven coverlet made in 1851 at Palmyra, N.Y. *Smithsonian: History & Technology—T.16401 (73-1356).*

TOP LEFT. Overshot coverlet, New England, early 19th Century. *Old Sturbridge Village—26.19.54 (B451B).*

TOP RIGHT. Jacquard coverlet, Adams County, Pa., 1852. *Smithsonian: History & Technology—T.16961 (74-13365).*

BOTTOM LEFT. Handwoven Pennsylvania coverlet by Martin Hoke, York, Pa., 1847. Titus C. Geesey Collection. *Philadelphia Museum of Art—'55-94-57.*

BOTTOM RIGHT. Double-woven coverlet made in Pennsylvania about 1840–50. This is a detail of the "Boston Town Pattern." Gift of Mr. & Mrs. Guy E. Beardsley, 1949. *Philadelphia Museum of Art—1949.18 (138A).*

AMERICA (U.S.). ABOVE. Embroidered wool bedspread made by Mercy Post at Herkimer County, N.Y. in 1824. Gift of Mrs. Minnie E. Post. *Chicago Art Institute—1945.199 (C18393).*

TOP LEFT. Shadowgraph of quilted coverlet, 1810. Gift of Alice B. Frankenburg. *Brooklyn Museum—58.114.*

TOP RIGHT. Hooked rug, early 19th C. Gift of Emily C. Chadbourne. *Chicago Art Institute—1952.179 (C39705).*

BOTTOM LEFT. Detail of 18th C. crewelwork coverlet. Sansbury-Mills Fund. *Met—61.48.1 (172124B).*

BOTTOM RIGHT. Bed rugg, 1802, by Philena McCall, Lebanon, Conn. *Wadsworth Atheneum—1972.11 (188E).*

AMERICA (U.S.). LEFT. 18th C. resist-dyed cotton, N.Y. Rogers Fund. *Metropolitan—40.128 (122052 LS).*

RIGHT. Printed cotton, America's Cup Race, 1886. Rogers Fund. *Metropolitan—48.95.1 (141443).*

TOP LEFT. Resist-dyed cotton, 18th Century. Rogers Fund. *Metropolitan—40.131 (123332 B).*

TOP RIGHT. Lacelike printed cotton, c. 1840. Rogers Fund. *Metropolitan—48.82.1 (141245 LS).*

BOTTOM LEFT. **Stenciled coverlet made about 1830.** Rogers Fund. *Metropolitan—44.42 (132484 IF B).*

BOTTOM RIGHT. **Printed cotton made in 1870.** *Cooper-Hewitt—1916-33-238 (C11618).*

AMERICA (U.S.). TOP. Mary Wiggin's sampler, 1797. Whitman Collection. *Philadelphia Museum—'69-288-18.*
BOTTOM LEFT. **19th Century sampler.** Bolles Collection. Gift of Mrs. Russell Sage. *Met—10.125.420 (17679 LS).*
BOTTOM RIGHT. **Mary Richards' sampler, 1808.** *Cooper-Hewitt—1941-69-13 (1667).*

172

TOP. *Legend of Czar Salton*, an embroidered hanging by Mrs. Theodore Roosevelt, Jr., 1951–53. Worked in gold, silver, copper, wool, silk, glass, plastic. *Smithsonian: History & Technology—T.12177-A (59220).*

BOTTOM. **Embroidered wool picture, N.E., c. 1750. Pulitzer Fund.** *Metropolitan—39.108.1 (118715 tf).*

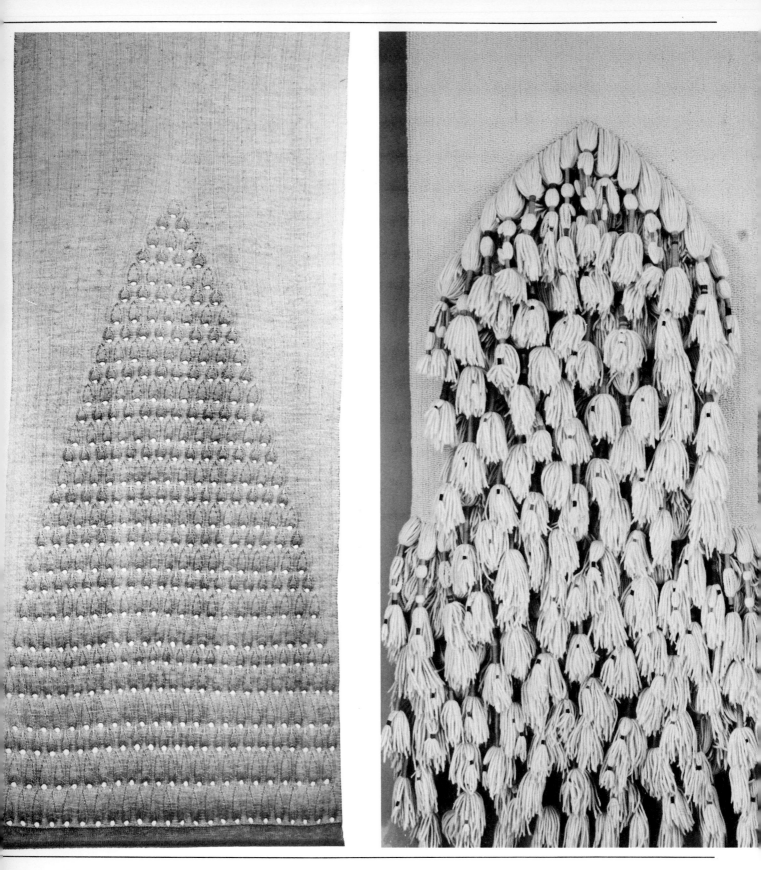

AMERICA (U.S.). LEFT. *Near East*, a hand-knitted linen wall hanging by Mary Walker Phillips, 1964. Size is 110″ × 45½″. *Museum of Modern Art—2411.*

RIGHT. *Prayer Rug* by Sheila Hicks, 1965, in wool hooked with an electric pistol using braided and wrapped pile. Size is 150″ × 40″. Gift of Dr. Mittelsten Scheid. *Museum of Modern Art—RP 1570.*

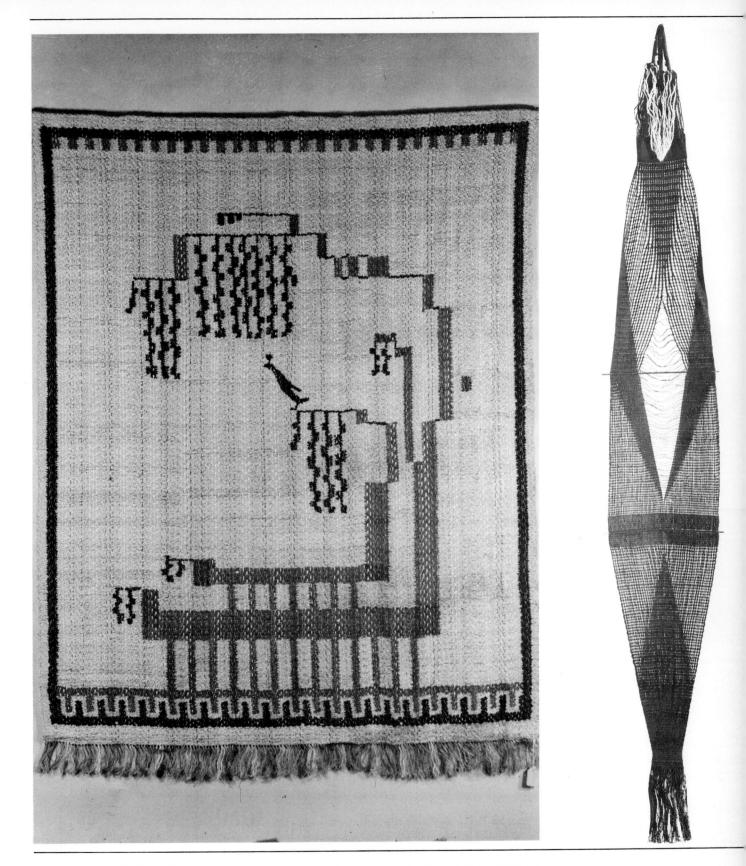

LEFT. Tapestry by Loja Saarinen, c. 1920. 45″ × 56″. *Cranbrook Academy of Art—1955.29.*

RIGHT. A woven form by Lenore Tawney, who pioneered in this art form. *Museum of Contemporary Crafts.*

AMERICAN INDIAN. TOP. Woven Chilkat blanket (Tlingit) from Stikine, Etolin Islands, Alaska. 41″ × 66″. Judge Nathan Bijur Collection. *Museum of the American Indian—23/5900 (33708).*

BOTTOM. Detail of woman's appliqué robe, Potawatomi, Wisconsin. *Field Museum—155723 (95876).*

TOP. Dance garment (blanket) in a complex twined weave made entirely of mountain-goat wool by the Tshimsian Tribe of Nass River, British Columbia, about 1840. *Royal Ontario Museum—927.37.142 (65TEX90).*

BOTTOM. Section of Salish blanket, British Columbia. *American Museum of Natural History—(311808).*

AMERICAN INDIAN. TOP. Three contemporary Navajo rugs. *American Museum of Natural History—321017.*

BOTTOM. Section of a Navajo wool saddle blanket, Arizona. *Museum of Primitive Art—62.25.*

LEFT. One half of a Navajo Chief blanket, mid-19th Century. *Cranbrook Institute of Science—592.*

TOP. Section of wool Navajo blanket. Gift of John Condon. *Brooklyn Museum—30.1068.1.*

BOTTOM. Navajo saddle throw, 29″ by 36½″. *Museum of the American Indian—21/4884 (29942).*

BELGIUM. Point de Gaze needlepoint veil, Brussels, 19th Century. *Metropolitan—47.78.1 (139300 B LS).*

Another example of Point de Gaze lace made in Brussels about 1810 for the Russian Imperial family. Gift of the Antiquarian Society. *Chicago Art Institute—1924.40 (C20223).*

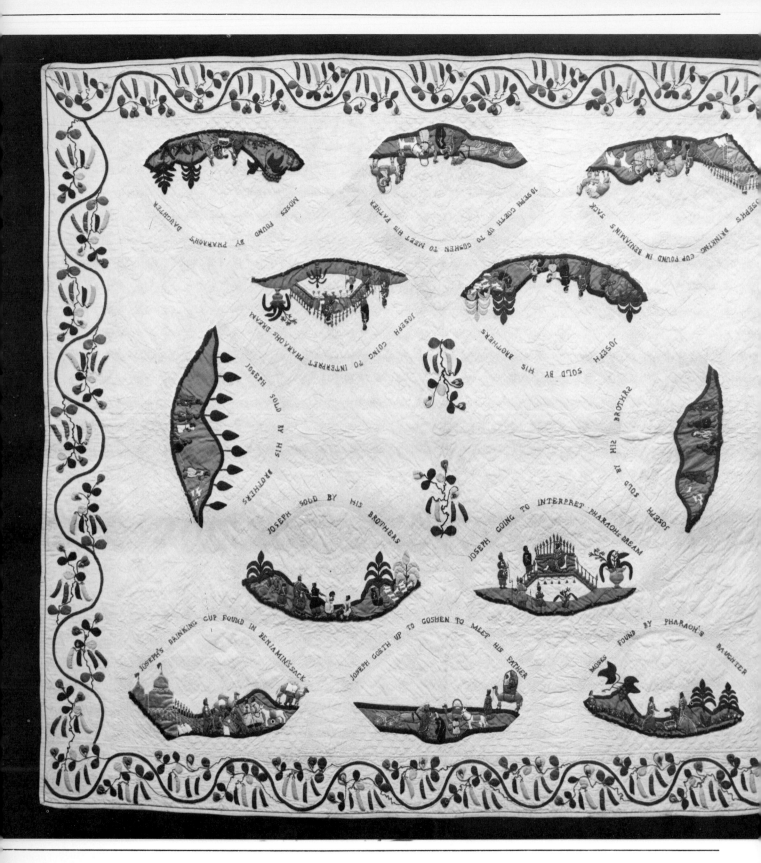

CANADA. A noted appliqué quilt made near Caledonia in Ontario during the late 1860s. It illustrates scenes from the Bible story of Joseph. Gift of Mrs. Ellen Emsley. *Royal Ontario Museum—956.151 (75TEX58).*

Enlarged section from the same quilt shows the intricate detailing of the trapunto work, the fine biblical phrasing, and the meticulousness of the quilting stitches.

CANADA. An impressive example of a pieced quilt from York County, Ontario, about 1860–75. It was made with scraps of printed cottons, and the embroidery on the central panel reads: "E. Bruels, Aged 87 years." Gift of Silas H. Armstrong. *Royal Ontario Museum—953.148 (72TEX13).*

LEFT. Coverlet from Charlevoix, Quebec, about 1835. Handwoven of cotton strips with pattern in colored wool à la planche and boutonné. Gift of Mrs. John D. Eaton. *Royal Ontario Museum—970.90.5 (64TEX9).*

TOP. A woven Quebec coverlet. *National Museum of Man—A-3375 (K74-1059).*

BOTTOM. Another example of a Quebec coverlet. *National Museum of Man—A-340 (K74-1061).*

CANADA. LEFT. Jacquard coverlet from Petersburg, Waterloo County, Ontario, 1870–75. It was handwoven by John Noll on a loom with Jacquard attachment. *Royal Ontario Museum—968.86 (68TEX158).*

RIGHT. Jacquard coverlet from Welland County, Ontario, 1856. *Royal Ontario Museum—965.24 (64TEX 360).*

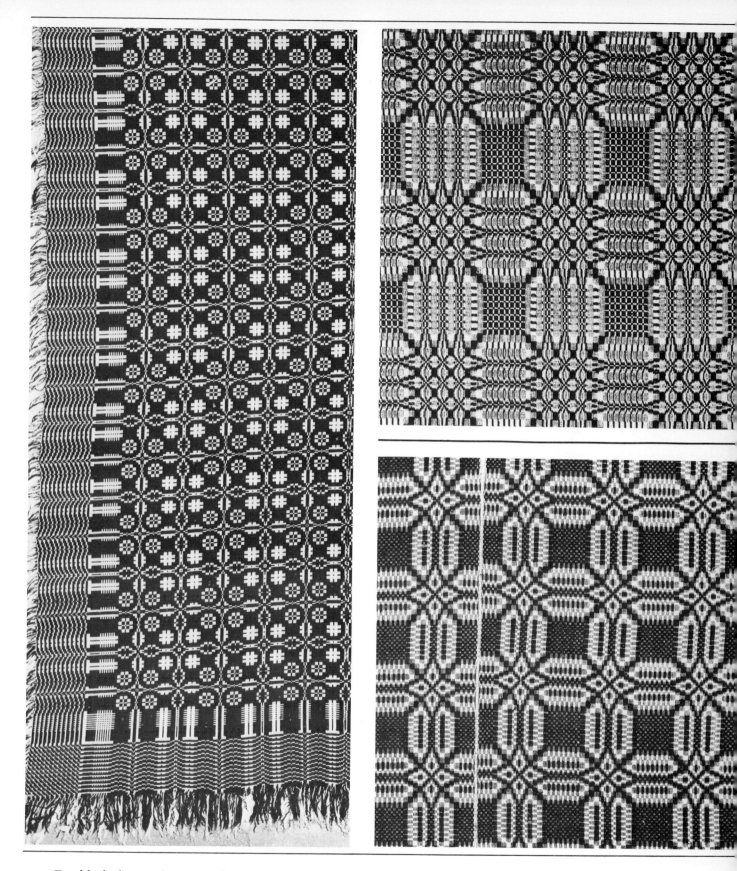

LEFT. Doublecloth coverlet, Waterloo County, c. 1850. Gift of Mrs. J. H. Crang. *ROM—949.250 (68TEX85).*

TOP. Overshot coverlet, Lincoln County, Ontario, 1860–75. Gift of Mrs. J. H. Crang. *ROM—964.19 (68TEX36).*

BOTTOM. Overshot coverlet. Gift of Mr. & Mrs. H. Burnham. *ROM—968.267.2 (68TEX351).*

CANADA. LEFT. Appliqué quilt, Simcoe County, Ontario, 1956. Designed by Ada B. Torrance and made by the Simcoe Arts & Crafts members. Gift of Toronto Star Weekly. *ROM—956.159 (IK8 57).*

RIGHT. Handwoven shawl, Dundas County, Ontario, mid-19th C. Gift of Herbert Ide. *ROM—967-69 (60TEX209).*

Braided woolen sash of the type known as "ceinture flèchée" and frequently worn by men in the fur trade. Probably made at Assomption about 1840–50. Gift of Sir Edmund Walker. *ROM—917.12 (65TEX45)*.

CHINA. LEFT. Chair cover, k'o-ssu tapestry, late 18th Century, 64½" × 21¼". Bequest of William Christian Paul, 1930. *Metropolitan Museum of Art—30.75.102 (164325).*

TOP. Fragment of 15th Century Ming Dynasty weaving. *Cooper-Hewitt—1902-1-433 (5270).*

BOTTOM. Weaving from Macao, 16th Century, Portuguese influence. Rogers Fund. *Met—12.55.4 (19744B).*

LEFT. *Reunion of the Poets in the Garden of the West*, a large k'o-ssu tapestry from the Ch'ing Dynasty, K'ang Period (1654–1722), 160" × 92". Gift of Mrs. Louis Wolf. *Indianapolis Museum of Art—62.200.*

RIGHT. Embroidered silk panel, late 18th Century, for export to Europe. *Cooper-Hewitt—1973-53-1A (12206).*

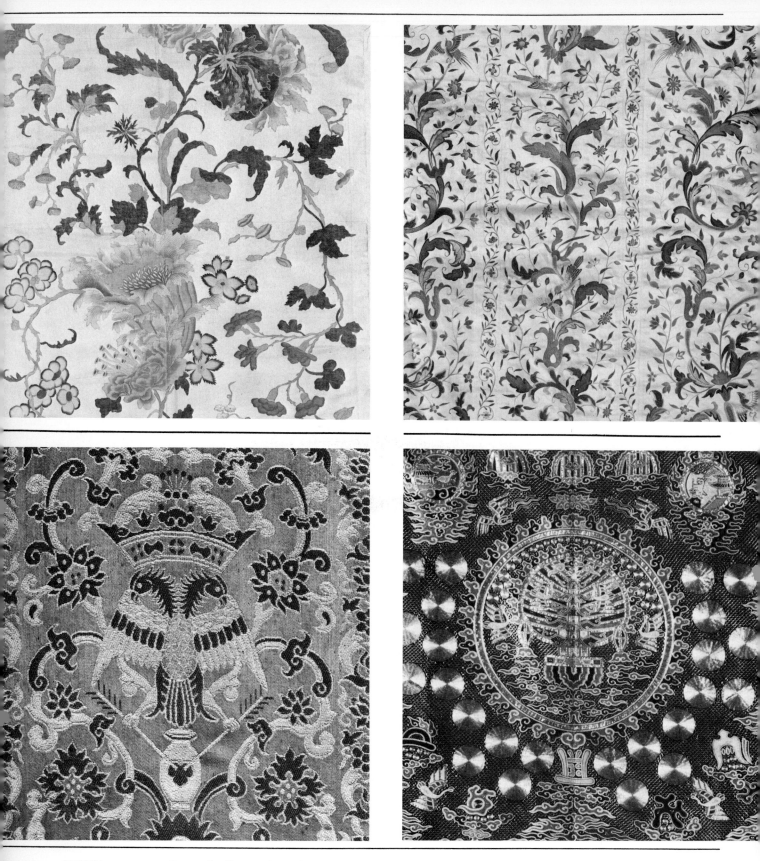

CHINA. TOP LEFT. Painted silk panel, 18th C. Costume Council Fund. *L. A. County Museum of Art—M.63.55.2.*

TOP RIGHT. Embroidered white satin chasuble, late 18th Century. Made in China for export to the European market. Condé Nast Fund & Everfast Fund. *Metropolitan Museum of Art—1973.118a (200524).*

BOTTOM LEFT. Figured silk satin, Macao, late 16th–early 17th Century. *ROM—973.422 (73TEX331).*

BOTTOM RIGHT. Detail of priest's robe, silk and gold paper, 19th Century (?). *Textile Museum—51.24.*

ABOVE. Embroidered silk Mandarin square, 19th–20th Century. 28 × 29 cm. *Textile Museum—51.52.*

CHINA. TOP LEFT. Mandarin square, fifth rank military, early 19th C. Fletcher Fund. *Met—36.65.18 (103296).*

TOP RIGHT. Informal robe of the Dowager Empress T'zu-hsi (1837–1908), about 1900. Blue silk satin embroidered in silk and gold filé. Gift of Robert Simpson Co., Ltd. *Royal Ontario Museum (ROM)—919.6.129 (72TEX116).*

BOTTOM LEFT. Tapestry table hanging, 18–19th C. Gift of Howard C. Hollis. *Cleveland Museum—62.128 (34252).*

BOTTOM RIGHT. Detail, embroidered silk coverlet, Canton, 1830–40. Everfast Fund. *Met—69.241 (192121 B).*

ABOVE. Imperial theatrical robe for warrior, 18th Century. Rogers Fund. *Met—30.76.33 (85264).*

CHINA. ABOVE. Resist-dyed and overpainted cotton hanging, probably from Kweichou province, early 20th Century, 189" × 177". Gift of Miss Aimee Kennedy. *Royal Ontario Museum (ROM)—952.138 (72TEX437).*

TOP LEFT. Detail of an embroidered cotton bed valance, late 18th or early 19th Century. Blue cross-stitch on white cotton. William C. Yawkey Fund. *Detroit Institute of Arts—49.332 (7972).*

BOTTOM LEFT. Embroidered (cross-stitch) handcloth showing a wedding procession. T'ung-ch'uan (Ssŭ-ch'uan), probably about 1930. *Field Museum—234418 (98665).*

RIGHT. Strip of indigo resist-dyed cotton, 19th Century. Seymour Fund. *Met—66.131.4 (185632 tf).*

CZECHOSLOVAKIA. Tablecloth of printed cotton with a design that simulates Czechoslovakian lacework. Made in 1839. Gift of Mr. & Mrs. A. Szekely, 1972. *Metropolitan Museum of Art—1972.241 (198738 tf).*

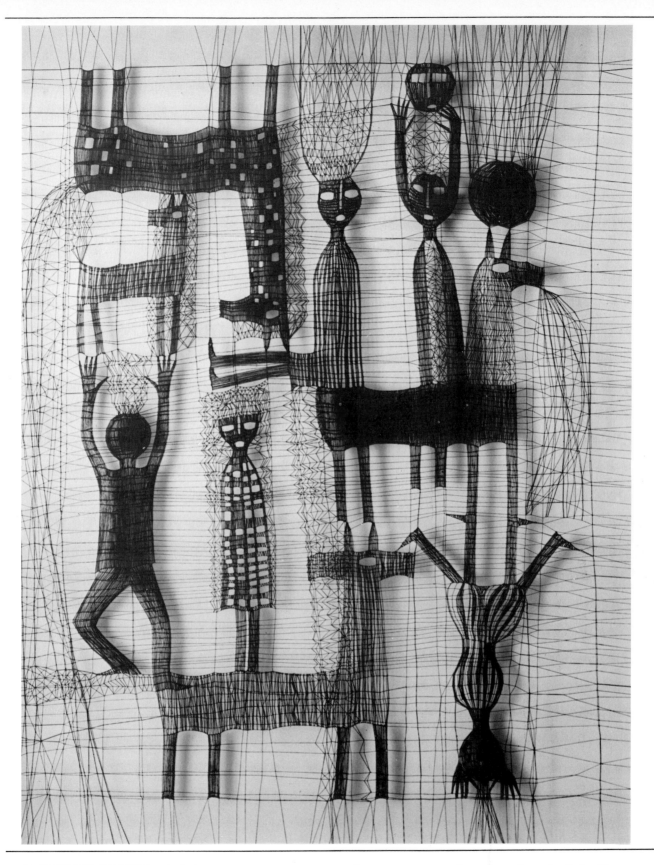

CZECHOSLOVAKIA. *Black Comet Dream*, a contemporary lace-construction hanging in linen by Luba Krejci, 1965. Gift of Mrs. Theodore D. Tieken. *Chicago Art Institute—1969.351 (C345-25).*

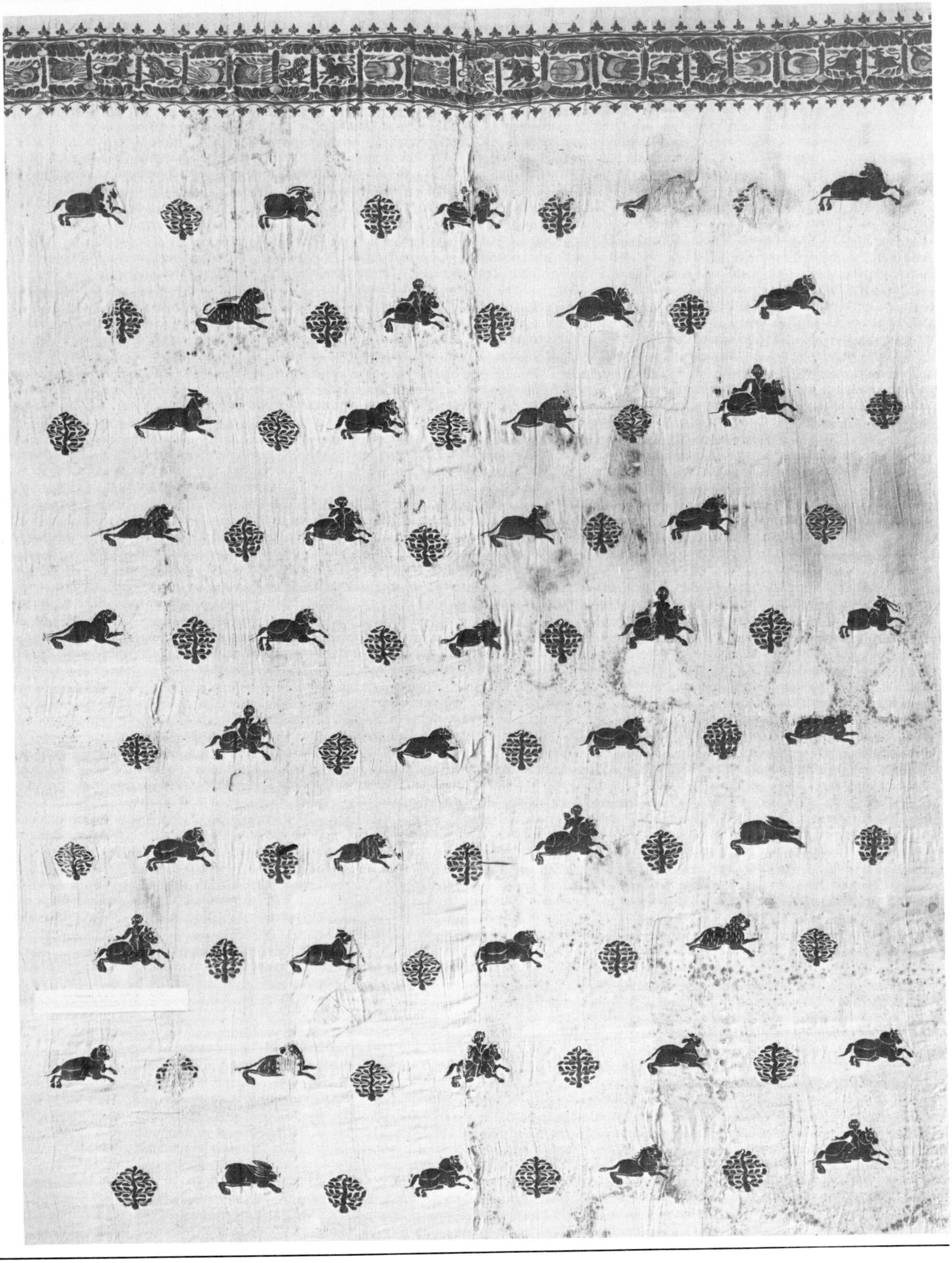

EGYPT. ABOVE. A 4th Century Coptic curtain from Akhmin. Linen with tapestry-woven wool decorations. This is one of the largest pieces of Coptic weaving in any collection. It measures 350 × 226 cm. (The Field Museum in Chicago owns a similar but smaller and more fragmentary piece.) The Walter Massey Collection. *Royal Ontario Museum—910.125.32 (ROMA 10).*

TOP LEFT. Enlarged detail of the Coptic curtain shown above.

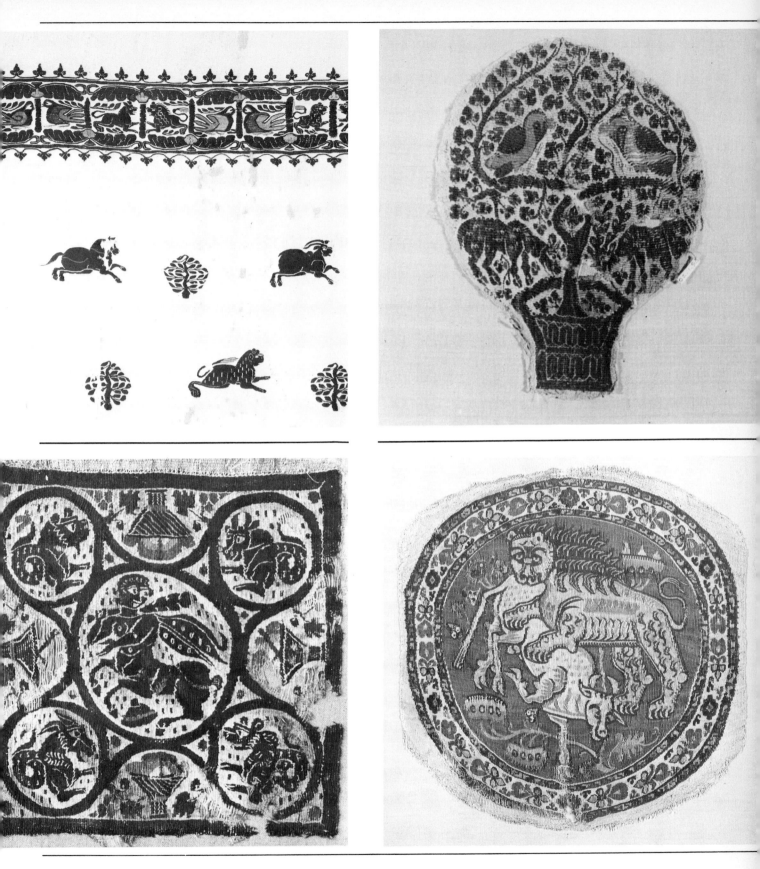

TOP RIGHT. Coptic tapestry-woven wool decoration, 4–5th Century. *Cooper-Hewitt—1902.1.34 (48).*

BOTTOM LEFT. Coptic tapestry-woven square, 3–4th Century. Subscription Fund. *Met—89.18.315 (64670 LS).*

BOTTOM RIGHT. Coptic tapestry-woven roundel, 6–7th Century. *Dumbarton Oaks—46.17 (72.150.19).*

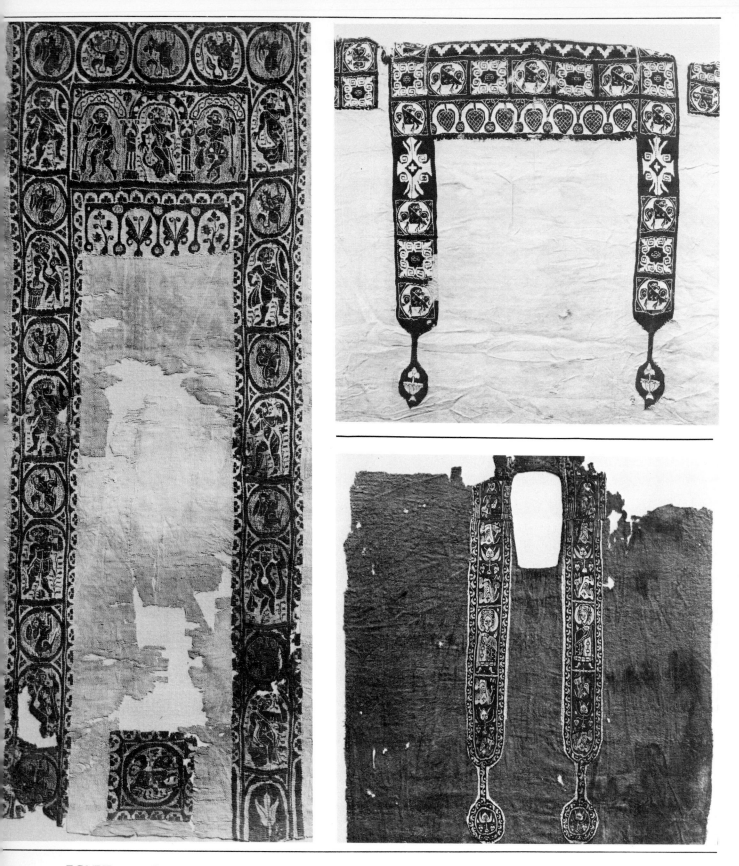

EGYPT. LEFT. Coptic tapestry-woven tunic decoration, late 7th Century. *Wadsworth Atheneum—1952.54 (162A).*

TOP. Coptic tapestry-woven clave decoration on a shirt, 5–7th Century. *Field Museum—173956 (50962).*

BOTTOM. Another example of Coptic tunic decoration, 8th Century. In this case the tunic is made of green wool, and the ornaments applied. Charles Edwin Wilbour Fund. *Brooklyn Museum—38.748 (B)*.

ABOVE. A whole Coptic tunic, probably 6th Century. The body of the tunic is linen tabby. The tapestry-woven clave decorations are in wool. Walter Massey Collection. *Royal Ontario Museum—910.1.11 (61T.93)*.

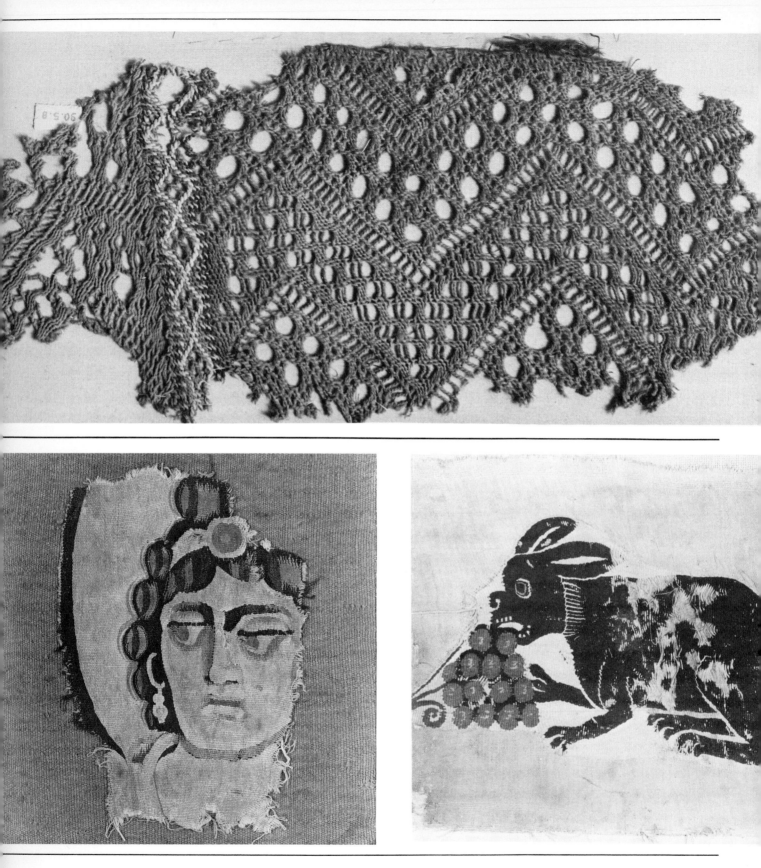

EGYPT. TOP. Coptic fragment of plaited wool, 4–5th C. Gift of George F. Baker, 1890. *Met—90.5.8 (74525tf).*

LEFT. Coptic fragment, 2–4th Century. Octavia W. Bates Fund. *Detroit Institute—35.103 (6803).*

RIGHT. Coptic fragment, 3–5th Century. Membership Fund, H. Kevorkian. *Philadelphia Museum—'22-22-108.*

EGYPT. TOP LEFT. Coptic fragment on dark blue ground, 6th Century. *Dumbarton Oaks—43.8 (74.14.8).*

TOP RIGHT. Large Coptic panel *Hestia Polyolbus*, 6th Century, 1.13 × 1.37 m. *Dumbarton Oaks—29.1 (L71).*

BOTTOM LEFT. Coptic, 4–5th C. Gift of Mrs. Theodore D. Tieken. *Chicago Art Institute—1971.643 (C37714).*

BOTTOM RIGHT. Byzantine tapestry icon, 6th C. Leonard C. Hanna Jr. Fund. *Cleveland Museum—67.144 (39276).*

EGYPT. TOP. Coptic weave, 8th Century. Charles Edwin Wilbour Fund. *Brooklyn Museum—38.664 (B).*

BOTTOM. Detail of Coptic tapestry panel, 6th Century. *Dumbarton Oaks—39.13.*

EAST MEDITERRANEAN. RIGHT. Fragments of a large hanging, probably 6th or 7th Century. Tapestry-woven wool yarns on linen, 1.84 × 0.93 m. Charles Potter Kling Fund. *Boston Museum of Fine Arts—57.180 (C26646).*

EGYPT. TOP. Fragment of a *tiraz* from the Fatimid period, reign of Mustansir (1036–1094). Tapestry band on tabby ground, linen and silk on silk. John L. Severance Fund. *Cleveland Museum—50.527 (38092).*

BOTTOM. Tapestry woven at the children's studio of Ramses Wissa Wassef, Harrania, near Cairo, 1971, 68" × 116". Gift of Mrs. Theodore D. Tieken in memory of Dr. Keith Seele. *Chi. Art Inst.—1971.686 (C39230).*

EGYPT. A large "Horse & Lion" tapestry panel, 6th Century. 1.48 × 0.78 m. *Dumbarton—39.13 (548827).*

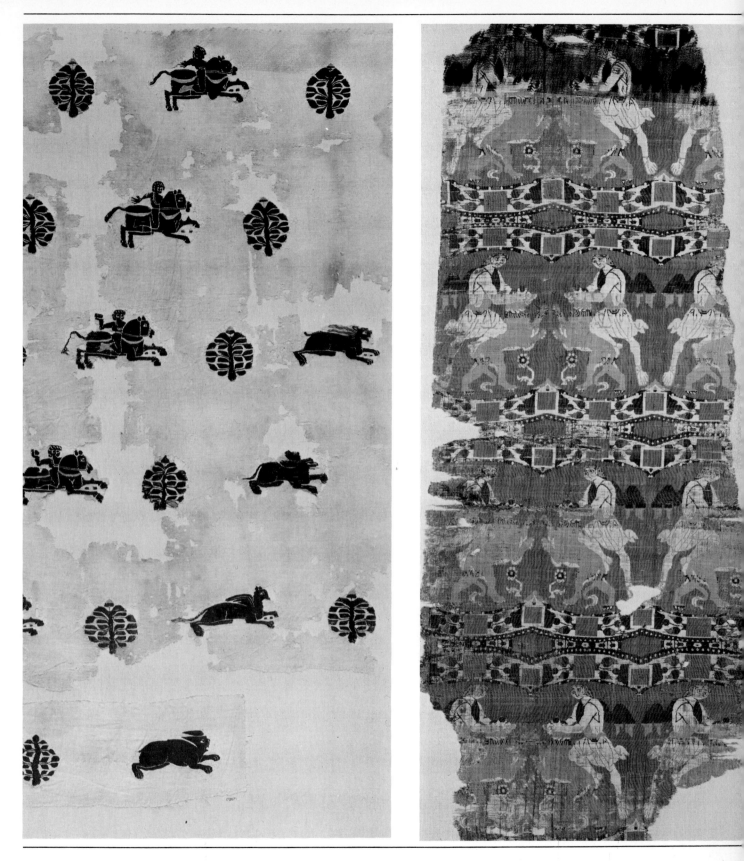

EGYPT. LEFT. Fragment of Coptic hanging, 4–5th C. Similar to one at ROM. *Field Museum—173671 (74450).*

RIGHT. The "Samson" panel, silk compound twill. Alexandria, 6–7th C. *Dumbarton Oaks—34.1 (7215039).*

ENGLAND. LEFT. Opus Anglicanum embroidered chasuble, c. 1500, 39" × 21". Silk, gold, and silver threads on silk-velvet ground. Gift of The Textile Arts Club. *Cleveland Museum of Art—70.124 (40858).*

TOP. Embroidered petit-point panel, 16th Century. *M. H. De Young Memorial Museum, San Francisco.*

BOTTOM. Embroidered casket with scenes from the Old Testament, 1668. Made by Rebecca Stonier Plaisted. Gift of Mrs. Chauncey B. Borland & Mrs. Edwin A. Seipp. *Chicago Art Institute—1959.337 (C24819).*

ENGLAND. TOP. Embroidered panel, 1650–75. Fine tent stitch in silks, padded and applied to satin ground. Gift of Mrs. H. J. Cody. *Royal Ontario Museum—937.15.2 (71TEX84).*

BOTTOM. Embroidered toilet cabinet, 17th C. Gift of Mrs. E. S. Fechimer. *Detroit Institute—48.81 (7453).*

ENGLAND. TOP LEFT. Country-life cotton bedspread, quilted, appliquéd, and embroidered c. 1830. Embroidered motto: "The Banners of England. Success to the Fleece, the Plough and the Pail. May Taxes Grow Less and Tenants near Fail." Gift of Mrs. Theodore D. Tieken. *Chicago Art Institute—1968.778 (C34121).*

TOP RIGHT. Embroidered pillow cover, 1550–1600. Marchioness of Waterford Coll. *ROM—923.4.73 (61T103).*

BOTTOM LEFT. Quilt with printed appliqué, 18th Century. Dick S. Ramsay Fund. *Brooklyn Museum—41.285.*

BOTTOM RIGHT. Pieced quilt, early 19th Century. Gift of Mr. & Mrs. R. J. Mercur. *ROM—949.259 (C64A51).*

ABOVE. Table carpet of plain-weave linen embroidered in silk, wool, and metal thread, 16th Century. Emily Crane Chadbourne Fund. *Chicago Art Institute—1968.162 (C33443).*

ENGLAND. ABOVE. Quilt with printed cotton appliqué, early 19th C. Harry Wearne Coll. *ROM—934.4.683.*

TOP LEFT. Cotton coverlet embroidered in silk and metal, early 18th Century. Rogers Fund. *Metropolitan—50.89.*

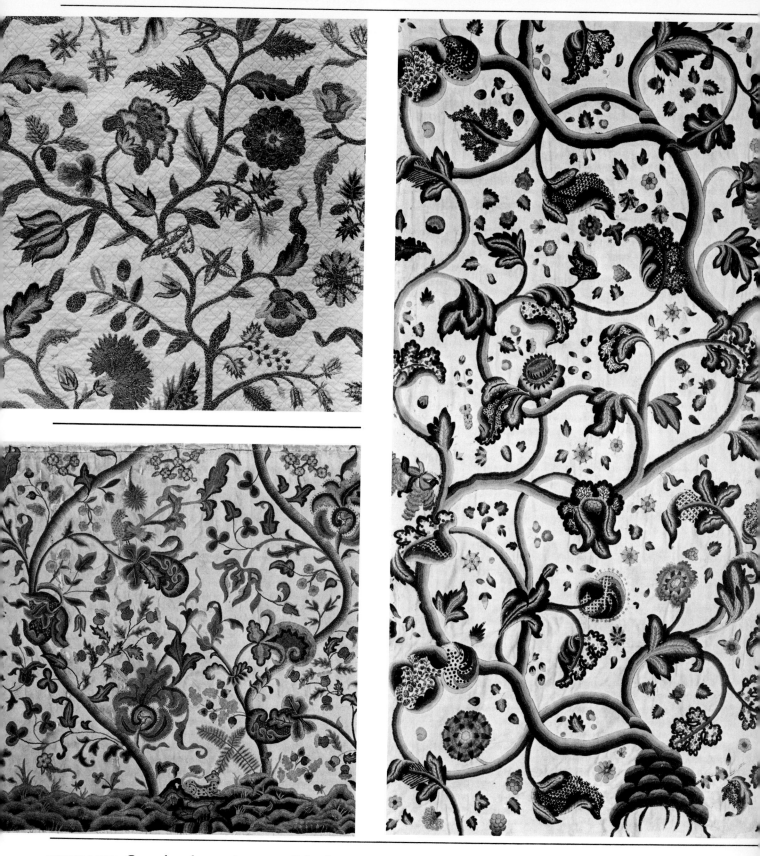

BOTTOM LEFT. Crewelwork curtain, 1699. Gift of Mrs. J. C. Watson. *Montreal Museum of Fine Arts—45.Dt.7.*

RIGHT. Wool embroidery, 17–18th C. Gift of Mrs. Chauncey B. Borland. *Chi. Art Inst.—1964.188 (C28850).*

ENGLAND. TOP LEFT. Bedspread of printed kerchiefs, 19th C. *Old Sturbridge Village—26.10.130 (B9278).*

TOP RIGHT. Simulated patchwork roller print with scenes from Gilbert & Sullivan's *H.M.S. Pinafore*, presented in 1878. Late 19th Century. Gift of Everfast Fabrics. *Metropolitan—69.59.1 (191356).*

BOTTOM LEFT. Roller-printed cotton, c. 1850. Gift of Mrs. Homer Dixon. *Chi. Art Inst.—1958.762 (C33198).*

BOTTOM RIGHT. Roller-block print, early 19th C. Gift of Robert Allerton. *Chi. Art Inst.—R48 52/23 (A6176).*

ABOVE. Roller-printed glazed cotton, 1830. *Old Sturbridge Village—26.30.118 (B6448).*

ENGLAND. ABOVE. Woven wool shawl from Paisley, 1865–70. *Royal Ontario Museum—921.16.6 (ROMA 2497).*

TOP LEFT. William Morris' *Tulip* print. Gift of Mrs. T. D. Tieken. *Chicago Art Institute—1972.390 (C38739).*

BOTTOM LEFT. Morris' *Compton* print. Gift of Mrs. T. D. Tieken. *Chicago Art Institute—1972.393 (C37914).*

RIGHT. 19th Century cotton chintz echoes Paisley design. *Wadsworth Atheneum—1928.27 (158D).*

FRANCE. TOP. Woven satin, probably early 19th Century. Bequest of Maria P. James. *Met—11.60.440 (121998 tf).*

BOTTOM. Merchant's embroidery sample, early 19th Century. *Cooper-Hewitt—1932-1-62 (5275).*

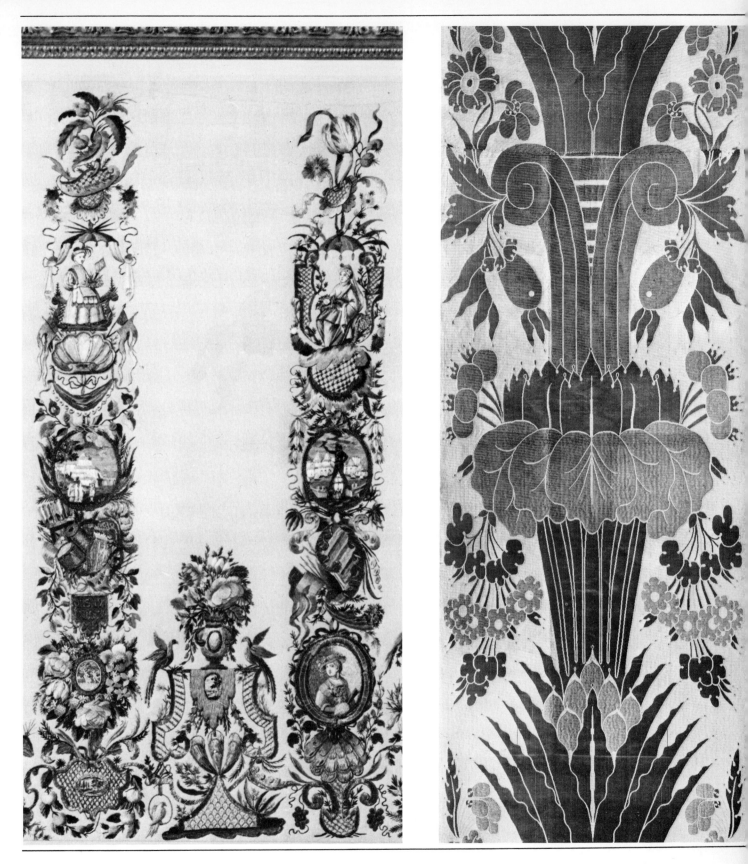

FRANCE. LEFT. Detail of embroidered panel, worked in silk and silver threads on taffeta, 18th Century. Gift of Mr. & Mrs. William J. Holliday, Sr. *Indianapolis Museum of Art—70.46.*

RIGHT. Silk brocatel, 1650–1700. Harriet Otis Cruft Fund. *Boston Museum of Fine Arts—56.878 (C17829).*

FRANCE. ABOVE. A brocaded fancy compound satin in the Louis XV style known as "Décor à Dentelle." It was made in Lyon about 1720. Fletcher Fund. *Metropolitan Museum of Art—38.30.2 (114475).*

TOP LEFT. Another example of the "Dentelle" style in a satin weave dating from the first half of the 18th Century. Bequest of Mrs. Martin A. Ryerson. *Chicago Art Institute—1937.1310 (C32759).*

BOTTOM LEFT. Point de France lace, 1700–1750. *Cooper-Hewitt—1950-121-42 (4404).*

RIGHT. Fragment of brown cut voided velvet with silk and gold metal threads. It measures about 32″ × 13″. *Chicago Art Institute—1907.482 (C32746).*

FRANCE. ABOVE. 18th Century linen toile made in France to celebrate the American Independence of 1776. Gift of Mrs. William D. Frishmuth. *Philadelphia Museum of Art—'11-32.*

TOP LEFT. Toile of coach routes to Poissy-St. Cloud, c. 1825. *Detroit Institute of Arts—69.43 (15944).*

BOTTOM LEFT. Toile, *America Doing Homage to France*, 18th C. *Detroit Institute of Arts*—54,191 (9797).

RIGHT. *Les Travaux de la Manufacture*, a copperplate toile de Jouy, 1783. By Jean-Baptiste Huet, showing processes in textile printing. Gift of Mrs. Potter Palmer II. *Chi. Art Inst.*—1953.306 (C21616).

FRANCE. TOP. Cotton reserve print, by Melet Fils, Ville Franche, late 18th Century. From the Henri Clouzot Collection (14). Gift of Mrs. Alfred Stengel. *Philadelphia Museum of Art—'29-164-21.*

BOTTOM LEFT. Indigo resist print, 18th Century. *Detroit Institute of Arts—48.224 (7601).*

BOTTOM RIGHT. Cotton block print, Jouy, c. 1775. Gift of Mrs. A. Stengel. *Philadelphia Museum—'29-164-107.*

FRANCE. TOP LEFT. *Monuments d'Egypte*, print, Jouy (Oberkampf), early 19th C. *Met—x.404 (183875tf).*

TOP RIGHT. Roller print by Huet (Oberkampf), c. 1810. Harry Wearne Collection. *ROM—934.4.528 (ROMA 3067).*

BOTTOM LEFT. Huet design for Oberkampf, c. 1810. Harry Wearne Collection. *ROM—934.4.528 (ROMA 3067).*

BOTTOM RIGHT. U.S. presidents print by Huet, c. 1810. Harry Wearne Collection. *ROM—934.4.528 (ROMA 3067).*

FRANCE. TOP LEFT. 20th Century print by Paul Poiret. Gift of Edw. C. Moore Jr. *Met—23.14.9 (51985 LS).*

TOP RIGHT. Oberkampf print, Jouy, 18th Century. From the *Jacques Martin Scrapbook of 18th Century Prints.* Gift of Josephine Howell. *Cooper-Hewitt—1973-51-134 (12311).*

BOTTOM. Printed cotton, about 1810. Gift of Edward A. Greene. *R. I. School of Design/Museum—17.131.*

FRANCE. LEFT. Block print with picotage, 1780–1800. Gift of W. M. Stone. *Newark Museum—37.560 (13915W).*

RIGHT. Block print from Oberkampf, Jouy, 1780s. Harry Wearne Collection. *ROM—934.4.179 (70TEX158).*

GERMANY. LEFT. *The Marriage of Cana.* Detail of wool tapestry woven in northern Germany in the late 16th Century. Gift of Mrs. Gustavus F. Swift. *Chicago Art Institute—1959.633 (C24901).*

TOP. Section of tapestry-woven cushion cover, 17th Century. *Cooper-Hewitt—1926-22-319 (5298).*

BOTTOM. Rhenish resist-dyed linen, blue on white, 17th Century. *Wadsworth Atheneum—1920.1014 (143).*

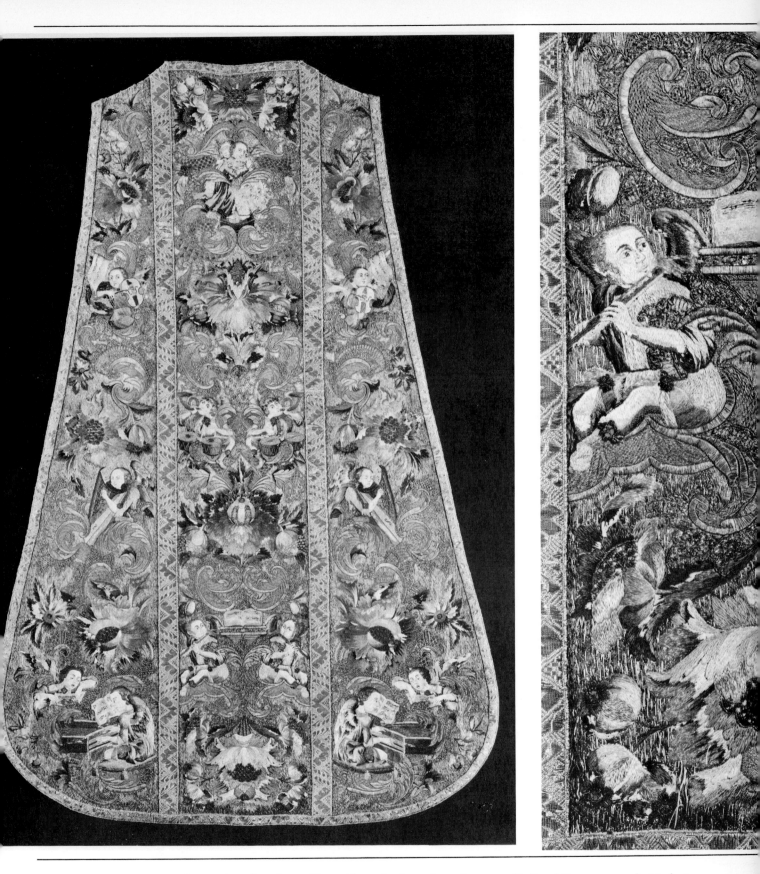

GERMANY. LEFT. Chasuble embroidered in silk, gold, and silver threads on a silk-lined linen ground. Made in Bavaria, last quarter of the 17th Century. The central pair of figures depicts Sacred and Profane Love surrounded by musical angels. John L. Severance Fund. *Cleveland Museum of Art—71.235 (42362F)F.*

RIGHT. Detail of musical angels from the embroidered chasuble at left.

GERMANY. ABOVE. Tapestry made in 1924 by Gunta Stölzl, a Bauhaus art-fabric weaver. Three-quarters of the length is shown. The width is 44". Phyllis B. Lambert Fund. *Museum of Modern Art—BAR-3240-15.*

TOP LEFT. Woven textile by Sigmund von Weech. *Busch-Reisinger Museum—1931.26.*

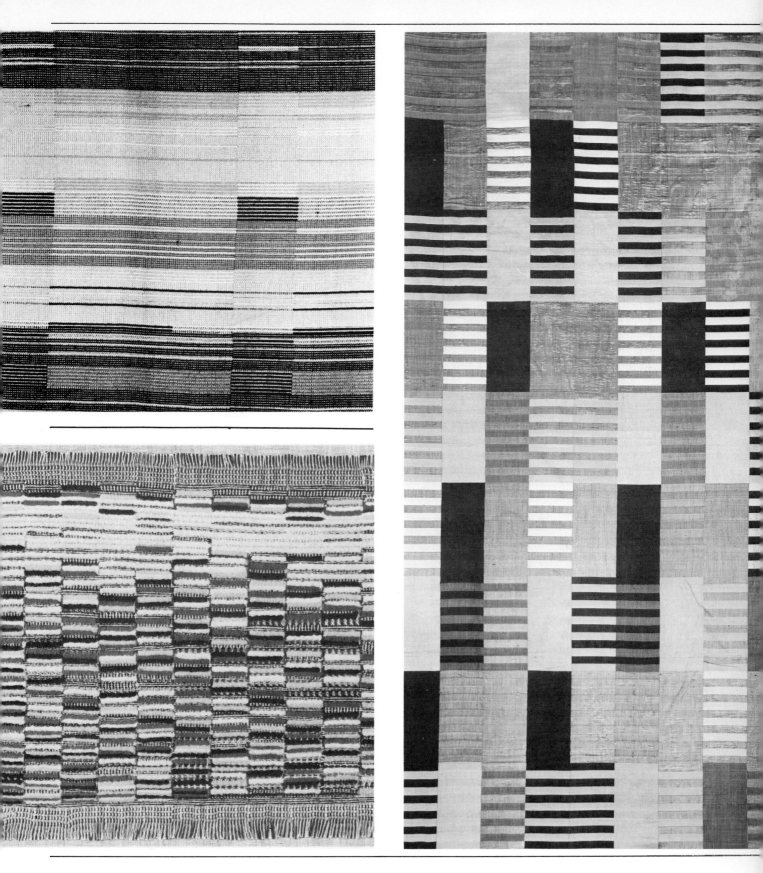

BOTTOM LEFT. Section of *Northwesterly*, a wall hanging by Anni Albers, 1957. Though made in the U.S., it also stems from the Bauhaus. Maurice D. Galleher Fund. *Chicago Art Institute—1970.346 (C35643)*.

RIGHT. Section of another Anni Albers tapestry, Bauhaus, 1926. *Busch-Reisinger Museum—1948.132.*

GREECE-MEDITERRANEAN. LEFT. Embroidered shirt front, Jerusalem, silk on linen. *Textile Museum—12.37.*

RIGHT. Greek Island embroidery, Skyros, 18–19th C. Harold N. Fowler Coll. *Cleveland Mus.—56.684 (33837).*

TOP. Embroidered pillow cover, Amorgos, Cyclades, 18th C. J. H. Wade Fund. *Cleveland Museum—27.12 (33810).*

BOTTOM. Greek Island embroidery, Dodecanese. Gift of J. W. Paige. *Boston Museum of Fine Arts—83.235 (C7904).*

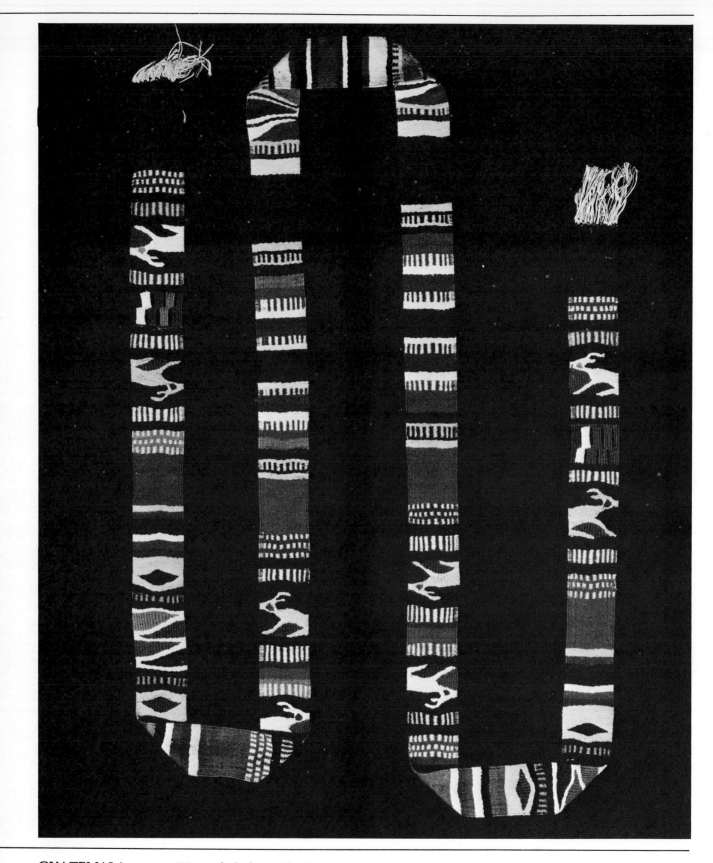

GUATEMALA. ABOVE. Woven belt from Chichicastenango. *American Museum of Natural History—(317552).*

TOP LEFT. A man's head cloth (tzute) in brocaded cotton from Nahuala. *Univ. of Wash.—60.6-65 (7183E).*

BOTTOM LEFT. Quechua Indian ikat blanket, Western Highland. *American Museum of Natural History—322150.*

RIGHT. Brocaded cotton huipil, San Antonio Aguas Calientes. *Univ. of Wash.—60.6-78 (7186D).*

GUATEMALA. ABOVE. A cotton weft ikat shawl (perraje) from Totonicapan, probably made in the early part of the 20th Century. Seattle Costume & Textile Study Center. *University of Washington—60.6-38 (7150).*

GUATEMALA. TOP. Woven cotton fabric made about 1939. *Cooper-Hewitt—1939-53-1 (386-6).*

BOTTOM. Cotton huipil, 20th C. Gift of Robert H. Tannahill. *Detroit Institute of Arts—40.124 (5500).*

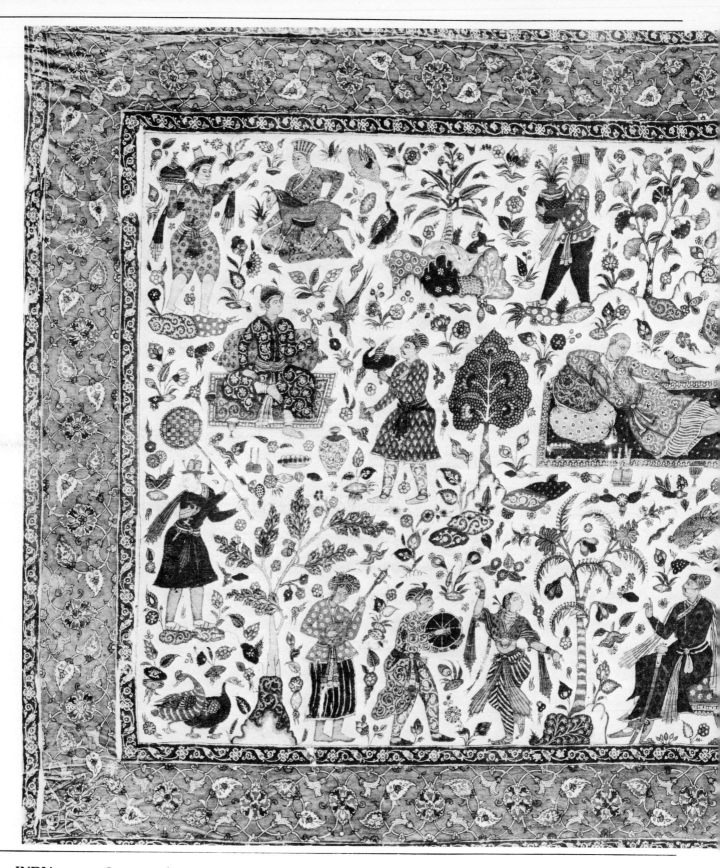

INDIA. ABOVE. Cotton cushion cover, 35" × 24½". It was handpainted and resist-dyed with mordants. It dates from the Mughal period, 1615–40, and is a superb example of the style familiar in Persian miniatures. Held by the Islamic Department. *Metropolitan Museum of Art—22.159.2 (71595).*

INDIA. RIGHT. Painted cotton curtain from Golconda or Northern Madras, dated 1630–40. It is one of seven panels originally belonging to a single curtain supposedly from the Amber Palace in Jaipur. This panel in 108″ × 37″. Museum Expedition of 1914. *Brooklyn Museum—14.719.2.*

INDIA. ABOVE. A remarkable example of India's painted and printed cotton hangings, dating from the 17th Century. It shows an Indian notable, his wife, and child surrounded by household scenes. The European figures in the lower left were introduced into this type of work about 1615–40. The inner field was painted with mordants and resist dyed; the border was printed. Gift of Mrs. Albert Blum. *Metropolitan—20.79 (121041).*

INDIA. LEFT. Enlarged detail of the hanging shown at left. *Metropolitan—20.79 (121043 B).*

RIGHT. Another enlargement of a small section 5″ from left and 1″ from top. *Met—20.79 (181336B).*

INDIA. ABOVE. Mordant-painted and resist-dyed cotton hanging or bedspread made in western India for the European market during the second quarter of the 18th Century. *Royal Ontario Museum—961.7.6 (67TEX187).*

TOP LEFT. Section of printed-painted cotton for the Persian market, late 18th C. *ROM—939.24.2 (61AA181).*

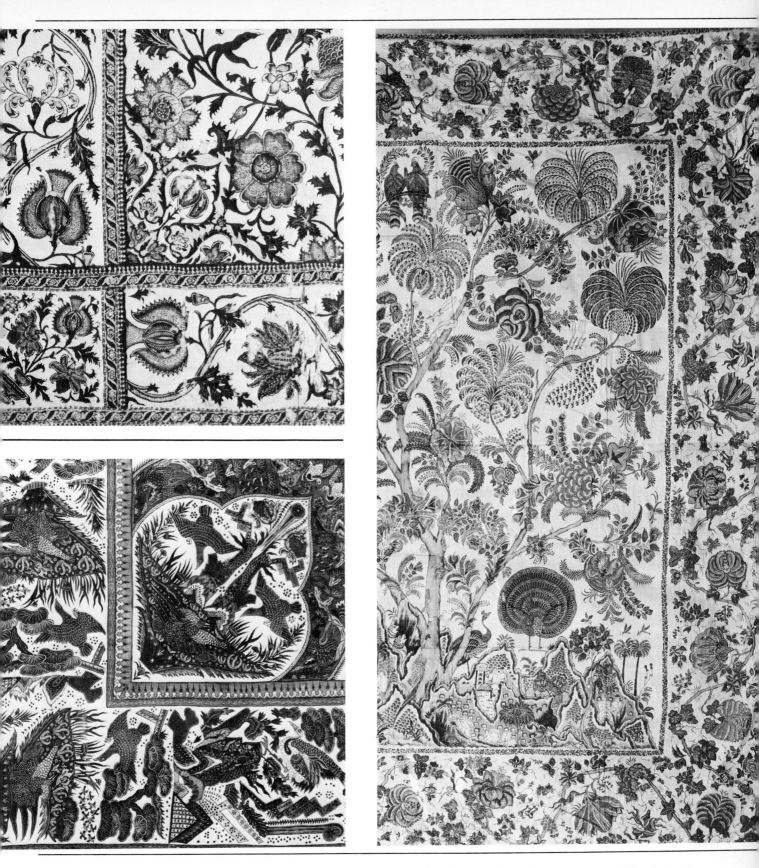

BOTTOM LEFT. Painted-and-dyed cotton from the Coromandel Coast for the Dutch market, 1700–1725. The design is influenced by Japanese motifs. *Royal Ontario Museum—963.13 (63AA92).*

RIGHT. Coromandel painted-and-dyed cotton, c. 1700–50. Harry Wearne Collection. *ROM—934.4.11 (ROMA 2088).*

INDIA. ABOVE. Tapestry-woven wool prayer mat from Kashmir, made in the second half of the 19th Century. The piece is 173 cm in length. Colors are red and green on white. *ROM—974.59.14 (74TEX85).*

INDIA. ABOVE. Brilliant example of the woven Kashmir (?) shawl, 67" × 63½", made about 1850. The museum describes it as "Indo-Persian." Gift of Mrs. John T. Watkins. *Detroit Institute of Arts—61.353 (12466).*

INDIA. TOP LEFT. Embroidered cotton hanging, Gujarat (Saurashtra), 20th C. *Phila. Mus. of Art—'65-200-8.*

TOP RIGHT. Embroidered 29" square from Kathalvar, 19th Century. Worked in silk threads and fragments of mirror glass on an indigo ground. Gift of Mr. & Mrs. J. H. Wade. *Cleveland Museum—16.1460 (33832).*

BOTTOM. Detail of embroidered woman's skirt, probably made in Cutch in the 19th Century. Worked in silk yarns on a silk ground. Ross Collection. *Boston Museum of Fine Arts—01.5817 (C2075).*

ABOVE. Kantha embroidery on cotton, East Pakistan, 1850–1900. *Philadelphia Museum of Art—'68-184-2.*

INDIA. TOP. Cutout figures appliquéd to ground. Western India, 20th C. *Philadelphia Museum—'65-200-7.*
BOTTOM. Embroidered cotton quilt, Kantha, E. Pakistan, 1850–1900. *Philadelphia Museum—'68-184-13.*

INDIA. ABOVE. Embroidered hanging, W. India, 20th C. 26″ × 37″. *Philadelphia Museum—'65-200-13.*

INDIA. Double ikat in Patola silk, 19th Century. *Cooper-Hewitt—1946-101-1 (2039).*

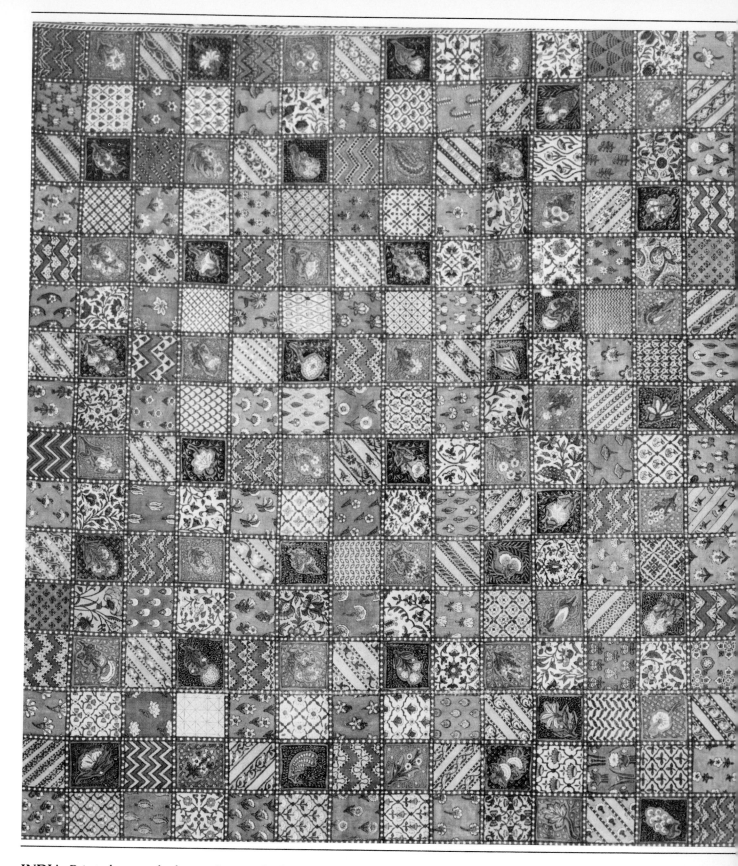

INDIA. Printed cotton bedcover from Kalimkar, dated from the 18th Century. The piece is 26″ × 40″ and contains 1,040 squares, all of which are different except one pair. *Textile Museum—6.140.*

INDONESIA. TOP. Indonesian batik sarong, 19th C. Gift of Mrs. Paul E. Vernon. *Met—58.33.9 (165837 tf).*

BOTTOM. Javanese batik sarong, possibly 18th Century. *Indianapolis Museum of Art—33.646.*

INDONESIA. LEFT. Javanese batik sarong, 19th C. Gift of Mrs. John Stemme. *Met—19.44.1 (43276 LS).*

TOP. Javanese cotton batik, 19th Century. *Cooper-Hewitt—1961-115-6 (7841).*

BOTTOM. Javanese "puppet" batik. *American Museum of Natural History—(36795).*

INDONESIA. TOP LEFT. Sumatran batik, 19–20th C. Gift of Mrs. L. S. Burchard. *Met—51.110.1 (150431 LS).*

TOP RIGHT. Indonesian batik headcloth, 19th C. Gift of Mrs. Paul E. Vernon. *Met—58.33.4 (165833 tf).*

BOTTOM LEFT. Silk tie-dyed sari, Indonesia, 19th C. *Cooper-Hewitt—1961-115-35 (7303).*

BOTTOM RIGHT. Enlarged detail of Indonesian batik. *Met—22.167.1 (51582 LS).*

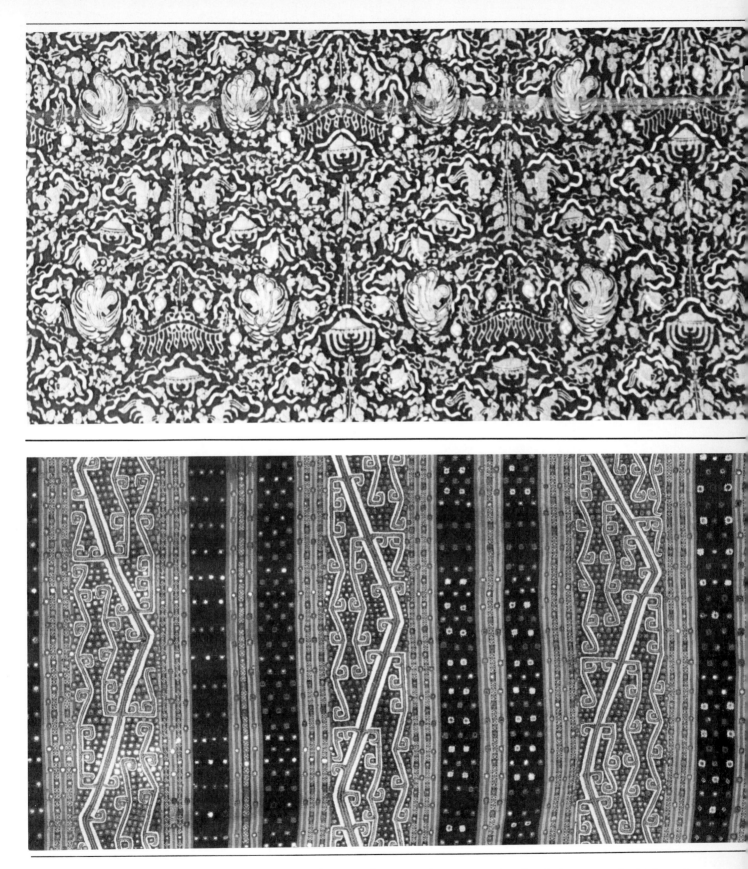

INDONESIA. TOP. Section of a large cotton batik hanging from Jogjakarta, Java, dated 19th Century. The Hobart & Edward Small Moore Memorial Collection. *Yale University Art Gallery—937.5454.*

BOTTOM. Section of an embroidered cotton sarong with mirror glass, made in South Sumatra in the late 19th Century. Costume Council Funds. *Los Angeles County Museum of Art—M.73.73.4.*

INDONESIA. ABOVE. Section of an ikat from the eastern region of the island of Sumba, near Bali. Monni Adams, who has written extensively about these unique textiles, reports that they are made entirely by women who take up to 2½ years to complete a pair of such cloths, working intermittently on a seasonal basis. She dates the example above in the 1920s when deer motifs became popular and connoted royalty, the sponsors of deer hunts in former times. *Metropolitan Museum of Art—1970.227.3 (194286).*

INDONESIA. LEFT. Another example of a Sumba ikat from the central part of the island, Kapunduk district. Each half of the cloth is a mirror image of the other half. 2.26 × 1.19 m. *Textile Museum—68.2.*

RIGHT. A double-ikat scarf made either in Bali or India during the 19th Century. The design is preplanned before weaving by tie-dyeing both warp and weft yarns. Rogers Fund. *Metropolitan—30.88.4 (80079 tf).*

INDONESIA. ABOVE. Section of a ceremonial cloth (pau) made in Sarawak, Borneo by Iban tribespeople between 1900–1925. The technique is warp ikat. Frederick Brown Fund. *Boston Museum of Fine Arts—27.474 (C6960).*

INDONESIA. TOP. Warp-ikat shoulder cloth, Tanimbar Islands. 1.45 × 0.74 m. *Textile Museum—68.11.*

BOTTOM. Detail of ceremonial cloth (Ship Cloth) from South Sumatra, 19th Century. Cotton, with supplementary weft on plain-weave background. Costume Council Funds. *Los Angeles County Museum—M.73.73.6.*

ITALY. LEFT. Woven linen-cotton towel with weft float pattern in blue and white, made in Perugia in the 15th Century. Gift of the Antiquarian Society. *Chicago Art Institute—1899.8 (A6017).*

RIGHT. 16th Century woven damask. Rogers Fund. *Metropolitan Museum of Art—50.74.1 (147462 B).*

TOP LEFT. Detail of brocaded cut-velvet panel in red silk and gold metal thread. Made in Venice or Florence in the late 15th Century. Buckingham Fund. *Chicago Art Institute—1944.403 (C22504).*

TOP RIGHT. Detail of silk satin-damask weave with brocading wefts tied in a twill weave. Dating from the early part of the 16th Century. Textile Fund. *Chicago Art Institute—1947.429 (C32742).*

BOTTOM LEFT. Detail of silk velvet with silver wires. Gift of J. W. Paige. *Boston Museum—91,178 (C346).*

BOTTOM RIGHT. Fragment of 16th Century ciselé voided velvet. *Philadelphia Museum of Art—'77-319.*

ITALY. TOP. Detail, needle-lace border, Italy or France, late 17th C. *Cooper-Hewitt—1953-143-28 (C8933).*

BOTTOM. Venetian needlepoint, 1600–1650. Chick Coll., gift of Mrs. H. D. Warren. *ROM—911.2.45 (72TEX145).*

ITALY. ABOVE. Chalice cover in linen "Punto in Aria" needle lace, latter part of the 16th Century. The size of the piece is 17" × 15". Gift of Honore Palmer. *Chicago Art Institute—1937.753 (C12541).*

ITALY. ABOVE. Enlarged section of an intricately worked "Punto in Aria" needle lace, probably made in Italy during the early part of the 17th Century, but possibly in either Spain or Portugal. *Cooper-Hewitt—1950-121-27 (2999).*

ITALY. TOP. Detail of crest from the border of a tablecloth made in Venetian Point lace. Gift of Mrs. Albert J. Beveridge. *Indianapolis Museum of Art—51.50.*

BOTTOM. Detail of needlepoint lace from Venice, 17th Century. *Cooper-Hewitt—1939-64-18 (471).*

ITALY. LEFT. Early 17th Century panel with applied and embroidered decoration. One of a pair. Gift of Robert Pfeiffer. *Metropolitan Museum of Art—69.255.1 (195770).*

RIGHT. Embroidered velvet chasuble, Florence, about 1500. *Indianapolis Museum of Art—74.114 (15491).*

ITALY. LEFT. Fortuny silk-velvet gown, handstenciled in gold. By Mariano Fortuny, Venice, 1919. Costume Council Fund. *Los Angeles County Museum of Art—M.67.20.15.*

RIGHT. Fragment of Italian cut velvet from the 16th Century. *Detroit Institute of Arts—38.83 (5430).*

JAPAN. TOP. Early Japanese embroidered silk panel, about 1665. *Detroit Institute of Arts—29.89 (1732).*

BOTTOM. Brocaded silk panel, 18–19th Century. *Cleveland Museum of Art—20.1548 (30721).*

JAPAN. LEFT. Back detail of embroidered Nō robe with gold rubbing from the early Tokugawa period, 1603–1680. Gift of Miss Lucy T. Aldrich. *Rhode Island School of Design/Museum—35.457.*

RIGHT. Another example of a Nō robe with gold rubbing, same period. *R. I. School of Design/Mus.—35.470.*

JAPAN. TOP LEFT. Stenciled and resist-dyed cotton tabby with yellow overprinting, 19th Century. Gift of Mrs. Edgar J. Stone. *Royal Ontario Museum—962.117.56 (63AA65).*

TOP RIGHT. Resist-dyed stenciled cotton, 19th C. Gift of Mrs. Edgar J. Stone. *ROM—964.57.7 (64TEX190).*

BOTTOM LEFT. Detail of ikat (kasuri) quilt, late 19th C. Gift of Mrs. E. J. Stone. *ROM—963.3.1 (63AA66).*

Painted and resist-dyed cotton, 19th C. Gift of Mrs. E. J. Stone. *ROM—967.72.14 (71TEX125).*

ABOVE. Kimono-shaped coverlet (yogi) made of indigo cotton tabby, resist-dyed and overpainted. Length is 164 cm. Late 19th Century. Gift of Mrs. Edgar J. Stone. *Royal Ontario Museum—962.117.52 (63AA63).*

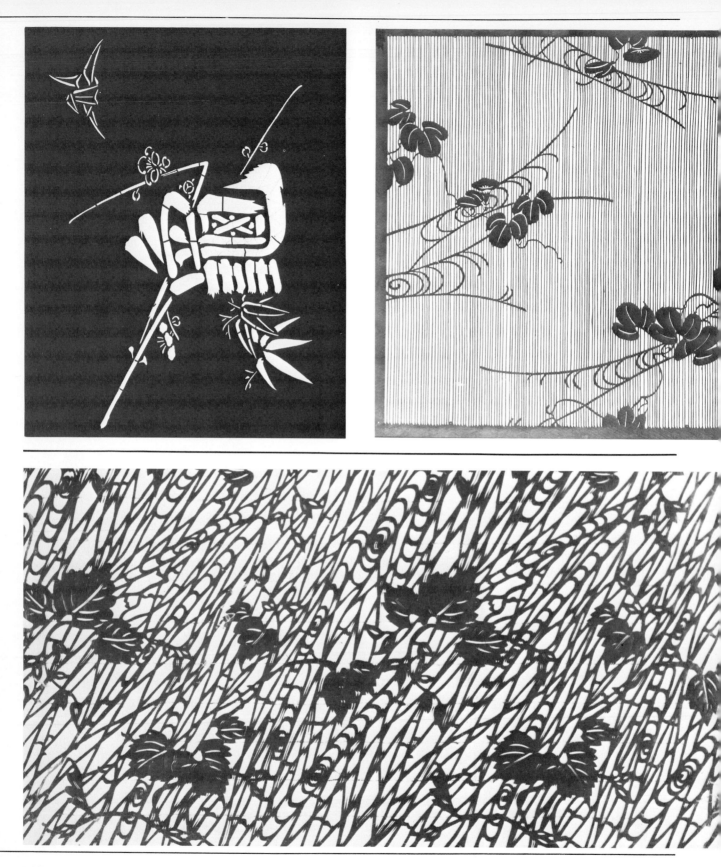

JAPAN. TOP LEFT. Printing stencil with open areas held by strands of hair. *Met—55.175.68 (160285).*

TOP RIGHT. Another stencil, one of many in the Design Lab. Probably 19th Century. *Brooklyn Museum.*

BOTTOM. This 19th C. stencil is 16″ × 12″. Bequest of Isaac C. Bates. *R. I. School of Design/Mus.—13.559.*

ABOVE. This type of stencil cutting was a Japanese folk craft. *Met—53.101.22 (155560).*

JAPAN. ABOVE. Back of a cotton coat made by the Ainu people of northern Japan in the 19th Century. This dramatic and traditional type of design is achieved with appliqué and embroidery. The length of the garment is 47½"; 51½" across the shoulders. Costume Council Fund. *L. A. County Museum of Art—M.71.87.1.*

JAPAN. LEFT. Ainu cotton kimono, about 55" long. *Museum of Primitive Art—60.146.*

RIGHT. An Ainu man's cotton coat with cotton and silk appliqué. Made in northern Honshu in the latter part of the 19th Century. Gift of Mrs. Edgar J. Stone. *Royal Ontario Museum—963.92.1 (74TEX300).*

MEXICO. LEFT. Texcoco blanket, 128" × 220". *American Museum of Natural History—(335086).*

RIGHT. Half the width of a Oaxaca blanket, 136" × 278". *American Museum of Natural History—(335081).*

MEXICO. LEFT. Half the width of a Querétaro serape woven in the early part of the 19th Century. Gift of Mrs. Paul Moore. Hobart & Edward Small Moore Collection. *Yale University Art Gallery—1958.13.22.*

RIGHT. Embroidered cotton from Cuernavaca, 26" × 17". *University of Washington (Seattle)—60.6-89 (7188A).*

MOROCCO. ABOVE. Embroidered seat cover (guelsa) from Fez, 19th Century. *Brooklyn Museum—22.1955.8.*

MOROCCO. LEFT. 18th Century woven sash in silk and metal. *Textile Museum—74.7.*

RIGHT. Appliquéd wool flannel tent squares, 19–20th C. Gift of Mrs. J. B. Whitney. *Brooklyn Museum—23.286.*

PANAMA. ABOVE. Cotton mola of medicine men, in layered appliqué, repliqué, and embroidery. Made about 1960 by Cuna Indians on the Island of Rio Sidra (San Blas Islands). The piece is about 13″ by 17″. Gift of Dr. & Mrs. F. Louis Hoover. *Cleveland Museum of Art—71.212 (41531).*

TOP LEFT. Center of another mola called "Sky Spirit," made by the same technique, with rick-rack. From the Island of Mandinga Niranjo. Gift of Mr. F. Louis Hoover. *Chicago Art Institute—1970.373 (C36575).*

TOP RIGHT. Cuna Indian mola with figures of curled worms. *Field Museum—190413 (101783).*

BOTTOM. Mola, Island of Carti Sugtupa. Gift of Dr. & Mrs. F. L. Hoover. *Cleveland Mus.—71.206 (41654K).*

PERSIA. ABOVE. A superb example of silk-velvet weaving made in Persia (Iran) during the latter part of the 16th Century. The piece measures 0.61 by 0.45 m. *Textile Museum—3.315.*

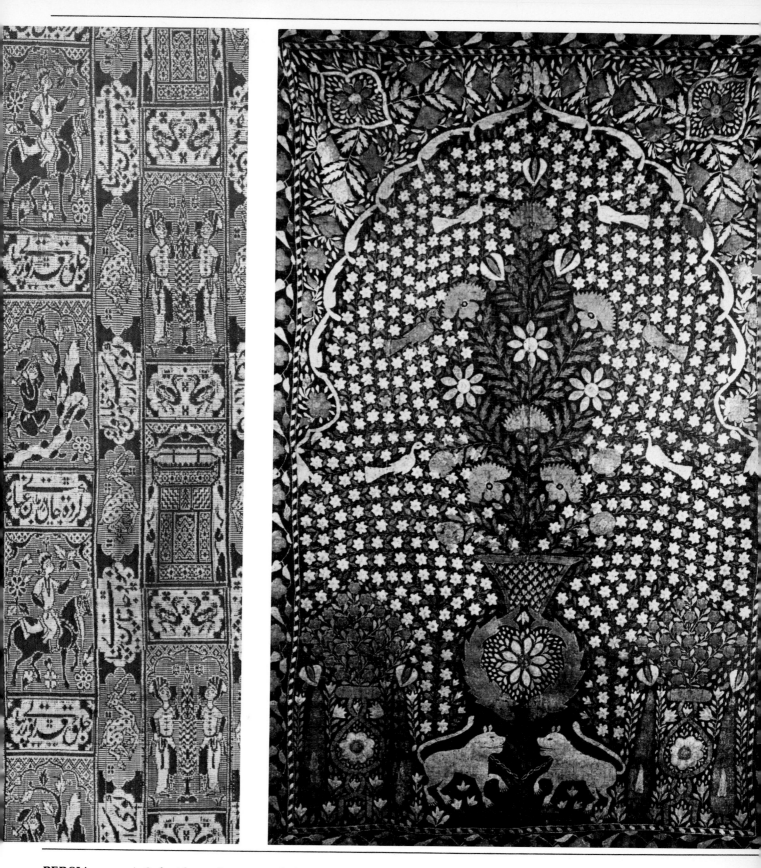

PERSIA. LEFT. A Safavid textile, reign of Shah Abbas (1587–1628). Fletcher Fund. *Met—46.156.7 (137260B).*
RIGHT. Painted cloth, 73" × 47", 18–19th C. Moore Memorial Coll. *Yale U. Art Gallery—1937.5206.*

PERSIA. ABOVE. Fragment of brocaded-silk lampas weave made during the 17th Century, Safavid period. J. H. Wade Fund. *Cleveland Museum of Art—53.17 (26384).*

PERSIA. TOP. Compound silk, 13½" × 18¾", 17th C. Gift of George D. Pratt. *Detroit Inst.—52.126 (9115).*

BOTTOM. Compound twill, tomb cover, 11–12th C. Gift of Mrs. W. H. Moore. *Yale U. Art Gallery—1937-4614.*

PERSIA. ABOVE. Printed wax resist, 18th C. Rogers Fund. *Metropolitan—25.166.2 (62288 LS).*

TOP LEFT. Detail of brocaded twill silk, 18th Century. *Textile Museum—3.159.*

TOP RIGHT. Detail of printed and painted fabric, 19th C. Gift of Carnegie Corp. *Met—30.10.14 (178544 tf).*

BOTTOM LEFT. Cut voided velvet, Kashan, early 17th C. Gift, Messrs. Archer & Huntington. *M. H. De Young Mus.*

BOTTOM RIGHT. Brocaded satin velvet with metal thread, 17th Century. *Textile Museum—3.206.*

PERSIA. LEFT. Brocaded twill, 19th C., 74" × 50". Gift of Mr. & Mrs. J. H. Wade. *Cleveland Mus.—16.1286 (31043).*
RIGHT. Silk lampas weave from Herat, early 16th C. J. H. Wade Fund. *Cleveland Museum—24.743 (29382).*

PERSIA. ABOVE. Cotton cover embroidered in silk from the Northwest Provinces of Iran. Made in the 18th Century, it measures 28" × 26". *Textile Museum—3.31.*

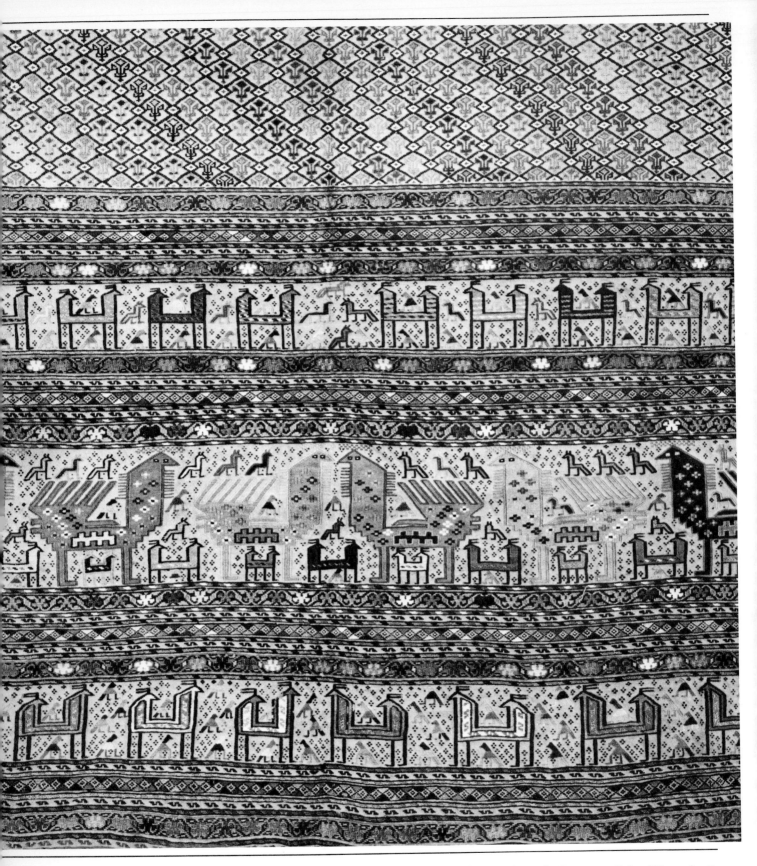

PERSIA. ABOVE. Central section of a horse cover, woven in the late 18th or early 19th Century. Gift of Dorothy F. Rolph, 1961, in memory of her sister, Helen L. Beloussoff. *Metropolitan—61.151.5 (173097 B).*

PERSIA. LEFT. Section of a printed cotton curtain, c. 1800. Gift of Jacques Martin. *Met—29.172 (75730).*

RIGHT. Silk kilim rug with metal threads, woven in Kashan for the Polish trade, probably in the early part of the 17th Century. It measures 89½" × 51½". *Textile Museum—R3.51.*

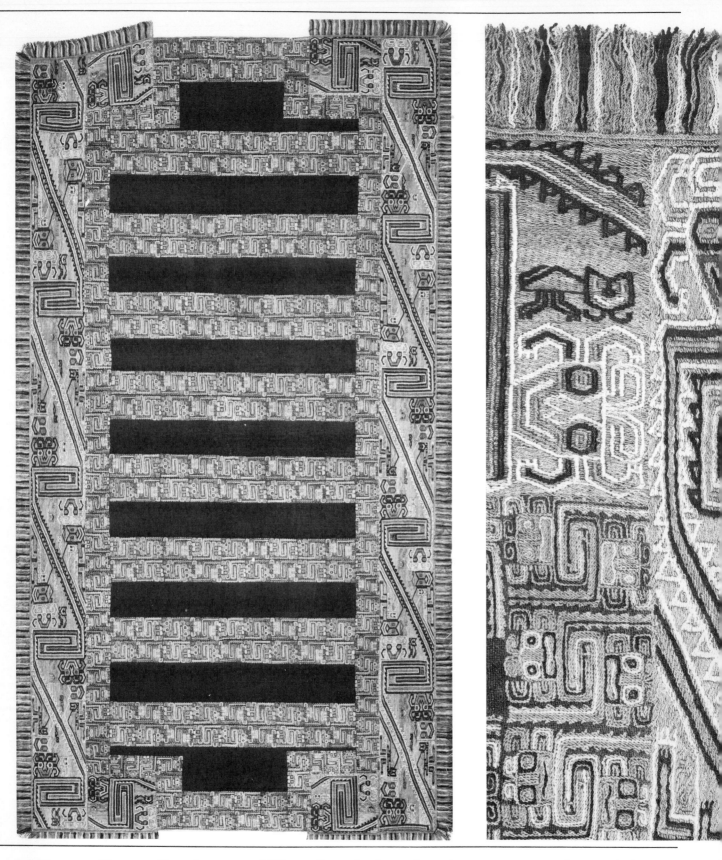

PERU. ABOVE. The magnificently preserved "Hoover" mantle, dating from the Paracas Necropolis period of 1100–200 B.C. *American Museum of Natural History—(325047).*

CENTER. Detail from the upper-right-hand corner of the "Hoover" mantle. *Negative 325043.*

RIGHT. Twined and woven reconstruction to show warp and manipulation used in Peruvian weaving between 2500 and 1300 B.C. Woven by Milica Skinner under direction of Dr. Junius B. Bird. *Am. Mus. of Nat. Hist.—(322038).*

PERU. TOP LEFT. Detail from woven Paracas mantle. Alfred W. Jenkins Fund. *Brooklyn Museum—34.1556.*

TOP RIGHT. Detail of an embroidered Early Nazca mantle from the South Coast. It may possibly come from the Paracas culture of 400–300 B.C. Wool and cotton yarns are used. *Textile Museum—91.192.*

BOTTOM LEFT. Paracas mantle detail. Alfred W. Jenkins Fund. *Brooklyn Museum—34.1553.*

BOTTOM RIGHT. Late Paracas-style weave embroidered in stem stitch. Probably from the South Coast and dating from 500–400 B.C. *Textile Museum—91.279.*

ABOVE. Embroidered wool shoulder poncho, probably from the Paracas Necropolis and dating 500–400 B.C. Size is 0.60 by 0.46 meters. Mary Woodman Fund. *Boston Museum of Fine Arts—31.496 (C27493).*

PERU. This Paracas mantle is a brilliant example of the Late Nazca style and dates from about 500 A.D. The ground is black wool and the figures are embroidered. Together with the fringe, the piece measures 50″ × 93¼″. The figures are characteristic of the style in both textiles and ceramics.

In *Mastercraftsmen of Ancient Peru* (catalog for an exhibition at the Solomon R. Guggenheim Museum in New York) this style is described thus: "The beginning of the Late Nazca style is marked by a sudden elaboration of whiskered deity motifs." *Rhode Island School of Design/Museum—40.190.*

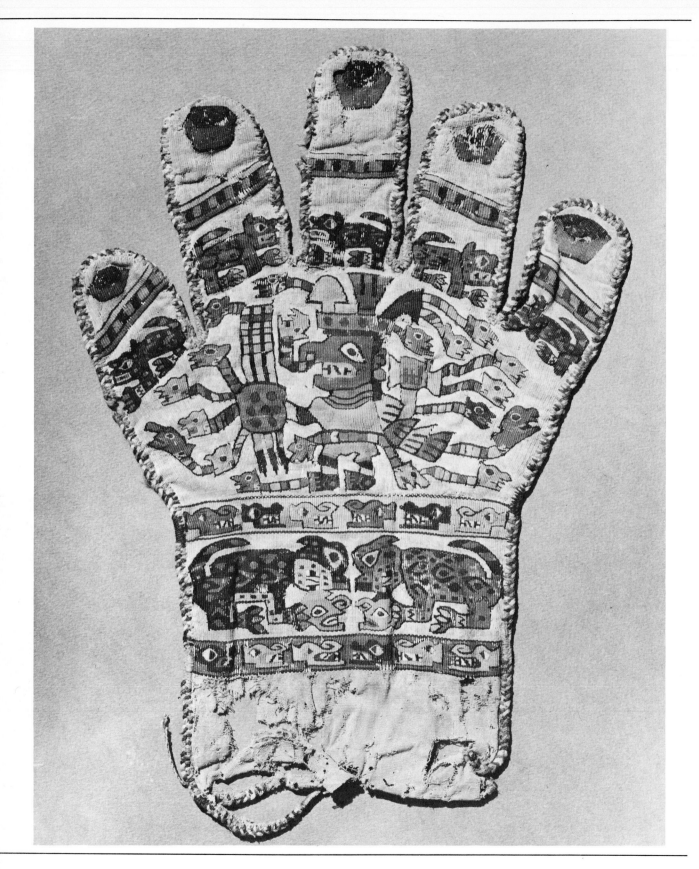

PERU. ABOVE. Embroidered textile in form of glove, Ica region. It dates from the Middle Horizon period, 600–1000 A.D. Charles Stewart Smith Memorial Fund. *Brooklyn Museum—58.204.*

TOP LEFT. Ornamental garland, 29". In *Ciba Review*, Feb., 1960 (Vol. 12, No. 136) Raoul d'Harcourt describes this type of Paracas work as "embroidered netting in a knotless or half-hitch (coil-without-foundation) technique." Gift of Henry G. Stevens. *Detroit Institute of Arts—32.3 (2705).*

TOP RIGHT. Wool-cotton coca-leaf bag, Nazca, 200–800 A.D. *Museum of Primitive Art—56.427.*

BOTTOM LEFT. Tapestry-woven wool hat from the Tiahuanaco II culture of the 9–10th Century, possibly in the Highland Region. Gift of George D. Pratt. *Metropolitan Museum of Art—33.149.101 (97554).*

BOTTOM RIGHT. Wool hat in the pile-knot technique from the Middle Period of the Coastal Tiahuanaco Culture. It is 4⅛" high without tassel. J. H. Wade Fund. *Cleveland Museum of Art—45.378 (21450).*

PERU. LEFT. Section of poncho in alpaca-cotton, Coastal Wari, 600–1000. *Mus. of Prim. Art—56.195.*

RIGHT. Woven panel, Coastal Region, Late Chimu, 11th Century. Rogers Fund. *Met—28.171.8 (72155).*

TOP LEFT. Poncho shirt, woven cotton with applied feathers, Chimu Culture, 1000–1300 A.D. It is about 33" square. Buckingham Fund. Ex coll. Dr. Edward Gaffron. *Chicago Art Institute—1955.1789 (C23243).*

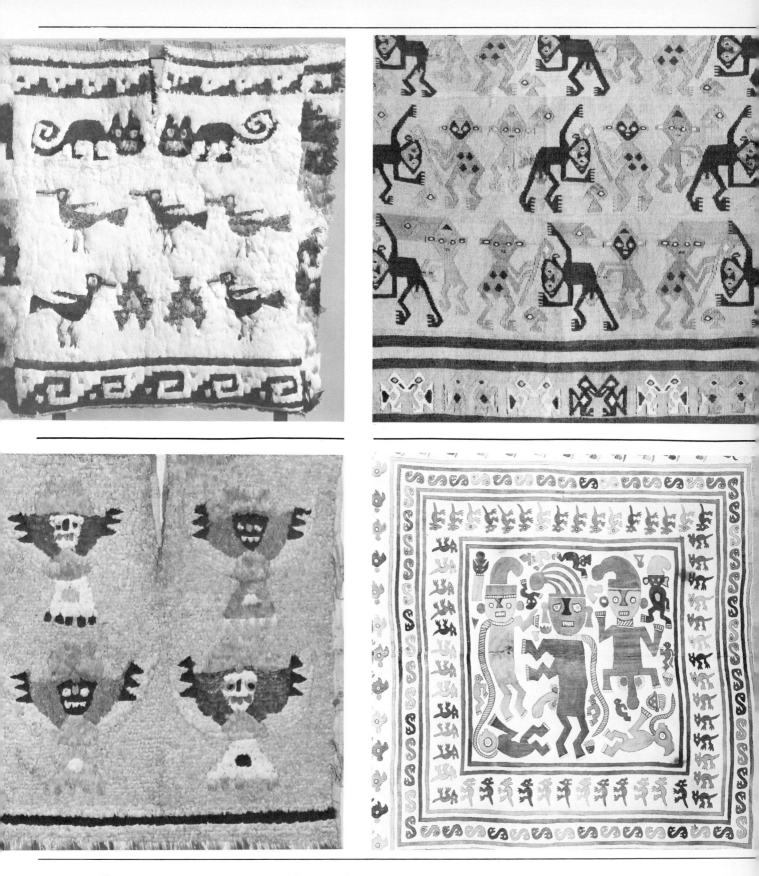

TOP RIGHT. Slit tapestry weave in cotton-wool, Central Coast, 1000–1500 A.D. Buckingham Fund. Ex coll. Dr. Edward Gaffron. *Chicago Art Institute—1955.1680 (C29023).*

BOTTOM LEFT. Poncho with featherwork, Tiahuanaco Period. Fletcher Fund. *Met—59.135.8 (169779).*

BOTTOM RIGHT. Section of painted cloth, Late Chimu, 1000–1450 A.D. *Am. Mus. of Nat. History—(325174).*

PERU. TOP LEFT. Embroidered supé-cloth, Chimu (?). Gift of Mrs. Eugene Schaefer. *Brooklyn Mus.—36.405.*

TOP RIGHT. Half of wool-cotton shirt front, Ica Culture. *Museum of Primitive Art—57.211.*

BOTTOM LEFT. Detail of wool-cotton supé-cloth from the Chimu Culture, 10–14th Century. Gift of Mrs. Jesse H. Metcalf. *Rhode Island School of Design/Museum—32.157.*

BOTTOM RIGHT. Detail of wool-cotton hanging, Chancay Culture, 1000–1470. *Mus. of Primitive Art—58.327.*

ABOVE. Section of wool-cotton shirt, Ica Culture, 1000–1470. *Museum of Primitive Art—56.431.*

PERU. ABOVE. One side of a poncho from the South Coast, Inca Culture, 1470–1532. Interlocked tapestry weave in cotton and wool. Front and back of the cloth are checkerboards of different motifs. The height is 91 cm.; the width 76.5 cm. Robert Woods Bliss Collection. *Dumbarton Oaks—B-518.PT.*

LEFT (facing page). Woven shirt fragment from the Tiahuanaco II Culture. Possibly from the 9th Century in the Highlands Region. Gift of George D. Pratt. *Metropolitan Museum of Art—33.149.92 (97549).*

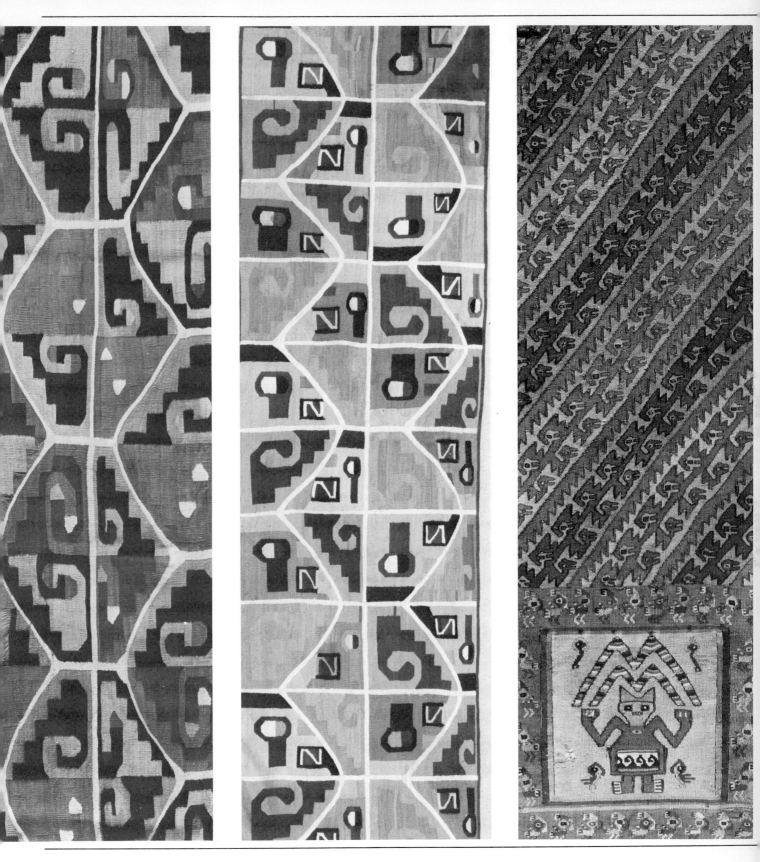

CENTER. Another example of tapestry weaving from the Tiahuanaco Period. *Am. Mus. of Nat. History—(334188).*

RIGHT. Slit tapestry weaving from the Coastal Region. It is made with a cotton warp and wool weft and is probably part of a loincloth. The piece is 23.5 cm. wide. *Textile Museum—91.257.*

PERU. ABOVE. Tapestry-woven in wool and gold metal thread, this intricate panel is only about 19″ high. No region is given and the date is listed as 16–17th Century. From the Vivès Collection, Gift of J. P. Morgan. *Cooper-Hewitt Museum of Design—1902-1-782 (5214).*

PERU. ABOVE. Horizontal decorative band on a tapestry-woven poncho with interlocked wefts. It comes from the Inca Culture, probably made during the early Colonial Period of the 16th Century. The Norweb Collection. *Cleveland Museum of Art—51.393 (25497).*

PHILIPPINES. LEFT. Warp-ikat skirt piece, Bagobo tribe, Mindanao. *Am. Mus. of Nat. History—(326076).*

RIGHT. Embroidered woman's scarf from the Bagobo tribe, Mindanao. It is worn over the right shoulder and under the left arm as a hammock in which a child is carried on the mother's hip. *Am. Mus. of Nat. History—(33464).*

PHILIPPINES. TOP. Beaded jacket with intricate lacelike design *Am. Mus. of Nat. History—33485.*

BOTTOM. Warp-ikat skirt piece of hemp, Bagobo tribe, Mindanao. *Field Museum of Natural History—(36752).*

POLYNESIA. TOP. Tapa cloth panel made in Tahiti during the middle of the 19th Century. It measures 51½″ × 75½″. Gift of Miss Marion Mellon. *Detroit Institute of Arts—35.102 (7518).*

BOTTOM. Section of a tapa-cloth panel from Samoa. *American Museum of Natural History—60690-24.*

POLYNESIA. LEFT. Two-thirds of a tapa-cloth panel from the Fiji Islands. The whole piece is 71″ long (as shown) × 49″ wide. *Museum of Primitive Art—66.8.*

RIGHT. Section of tapa cloth from Samoa, late 19th Century. *Cooper-Hewitt—1958-140-8 (10537).*

SIBERIA. ABOVE. Fine example of a decorative art form developed by the people of the Amin River region. The garment is made of fish skin, decorated with dyed deerskin appliqué. *Am. Mus. of Nat.Hist.—(101283).*

SPAIN. ABOVE. Embroidered panel made with silk yarns and metal threads. It measures 17″ square and is dated at about 1600 A.D. Gift of Mr. & Mrs. David Beecher Hudnut. *M. H. De Young Memorial Museum—70.14.*

SPAIN. LEFT. Woven-silk scarf, 15th Century. Section shown is about 14" high. *Textile Museum—84.11.*

RIGHT. Hispano-Moresque weaving, about 1470. Fletcher Fund. *Metropolitan Museum—46.156.12 (137333 B).*

SPAIN. LEFT. Fragment of silk twill with plain compound warp in the Hispano-Moresque style, dating from the 14th Century. Shown: about 35 cm. high. J. H. Wade Fund. *Cleveland Museum of Art—27.378 (8014).*

RIGHT. 16th Century Hispano-Moresque woven hanging. Pulitzer Bequest Fund. *Met—52.20.14 (152085 B).*

SPAIN. LEFT. Silk damask with gold thread, woven in the 18th Century. The fragment is 22" high. Arthur Byne Collection. *Montreal Museum of Fine Arts—40.Ea.74.*

TOP. Fragment of 17th Century silk damask. *Indianapolis Museum of Art—50.60.*

BOTTOM. Fragment of plain compound satin and brocaded silk in colors of cream, green, and peach on a red ground. From a wedding dress of 1781. Gift of Robert Bonniwell. *Philadelphia Museum of Art—'36-8-5.*

SPAIN. TOP. Hispano-Moresque (Mudejar) weaving, 15th C. Gift of Herman van Slochem. *Met—11.23 (10070 B).*

BOTTOM. Embroidered velvet altar frontal of the mid-16th Century, 41″ high. It was made by Marcos Covarrubias at the order of Charles V for the Church of San Juan de Los Reyes in Toledo. Gift of the Frederick Talbot Estate. *M. H. De Young Memorial Museum.*

TIBET. TOP. Section of a cotton tent roof with appliqué design in cotton and woolen broadcloth. Elaborately decorated tents are used for ceremonial purposes in Tibet. This piece dates from about 1930. Thomas L. Raymond Bequest. *Newark Museum—59.71 (8097W).*

BOTTOM. Woven wool monk's mat from East Tibet, 20th Century. *Field Museum—235324.*

TIBET. TOP LEFT. Central section from a painted napkin. *American Museum of Natural History—327661.*

BOTTOM LEFT. Apron of a Lama dancer, 18–19th Century. It is made of silk with appliqué in silks and gilt leather. Size is 30″ × 32½″. Harry E. Sutter Endowment Fund. *Newark Museum—69.29 (15779A).*

RIGHT. Temple banner in mosaic of Chinese silks, 18th Century. The Tibetans imported woven silks from China for this type of work. *Detroit Institute of Arts—29.241 (1893).*

TURKEY. ABOVE. Cut silk-velvet hanging made in the 16th Century. The piece measures 1.085 by 0.65 meters. *Textile Museum—1.54.*

TURKEY. ABOVE. Cut silk-velvet hanging made in the 16th Century. The piece measures 1.085 by 0.65 meters. *Textile Museum—1.54.*

TURKEY. ABOVE. Velvet panel from Brusa, 17th Century. *Metropolitan—09.99 (6090 B).*

MEDITERRANEAN. TOP LEFT. Embroidered cover detail, 19th Century. It is worked in silk yarns on a linen or cotton ground. Ross Collection. *Boston Museum of Fine Arts—03.1310 (C5423).*

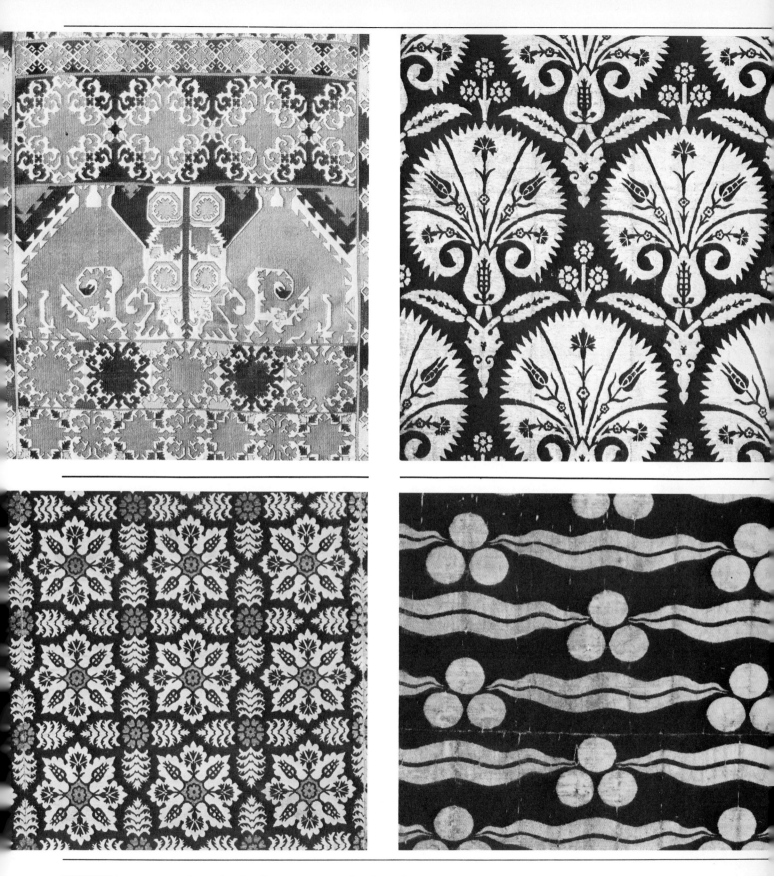

TURKEY. TOP RIGHT. Length of velvet woven with silk and metallic yarns and dating from the 17th Century. The section shown is 0.62 m. wide. Gift of Martin Brimmer. *Boston Museum of Fine Arts—77.271 (C4850).*

TURKEY. BOTTOM LEFT. Section of brocaded velvet made in the 16th Century for Andrea Doria throne hanging. Gift of Mr. & Mrs. Eugene H. Welker. *Detroit Institute of Arts—48.137 (7496).*

TURKEY. BOTTOM RIGHT. 16th Century silk velvet with metallic threads. *Textile Museum—1.78.*

UKRAINE. TOP LEFT. Woman's woven shirt fabric, Volyn region, 1870. *Ukrainian Arts & Crafts Museum.*

TOP RIGHT. Wedding-towel embroidery, Central Ukraine, 1900. *Ukrainian Arts & Crafts Museum.*

BOTTOM LEFT. Woven wool bed throw, "Hutsul" region, Carpatho-Ukraine, 1900. *Ukrainian Arts & Crafts Museum.*

BOTTOM RIGHT. Woman's sheepskin jacket embroidery, Bukovina, 1880. *Ukrainian Arts & Crafts Museum.*

UKRAINE. TOP. "Nyzenka" embroidery stitch, Carpatho region, W. Ukraine. *Ukrainian Arts & Crafts Museum.*

BOTTOM. "Poyas" detail of woman's woven sash, Bukovina, W. Ukraine, 1880. *Ukrainian Arts & Crafts Museum.*

RIGHT. Reverse side of Sluts'k sash, about 1780. *Ukrainian Cultural & Educational Centre, Winnipeg.*

U.S.S.R. (CAUCASUS). 18th Century embroidered cushion cover from Daghestan, silk yarns on cotton, 37" × 28". Gift of Mr. & Mrs. J. H. Wade. *Cleveland Museum of Art—20.528 (33825).*

U.S.S.R. (CAUCASUS). Ghiordes-knot carpet from Azerbaijan, 1890. Wool and cotton, 49¾" × 62". Florence & Charles Abel Oriental Rug Collection. *Cleveland Museum of Art—61.383 (32860).*

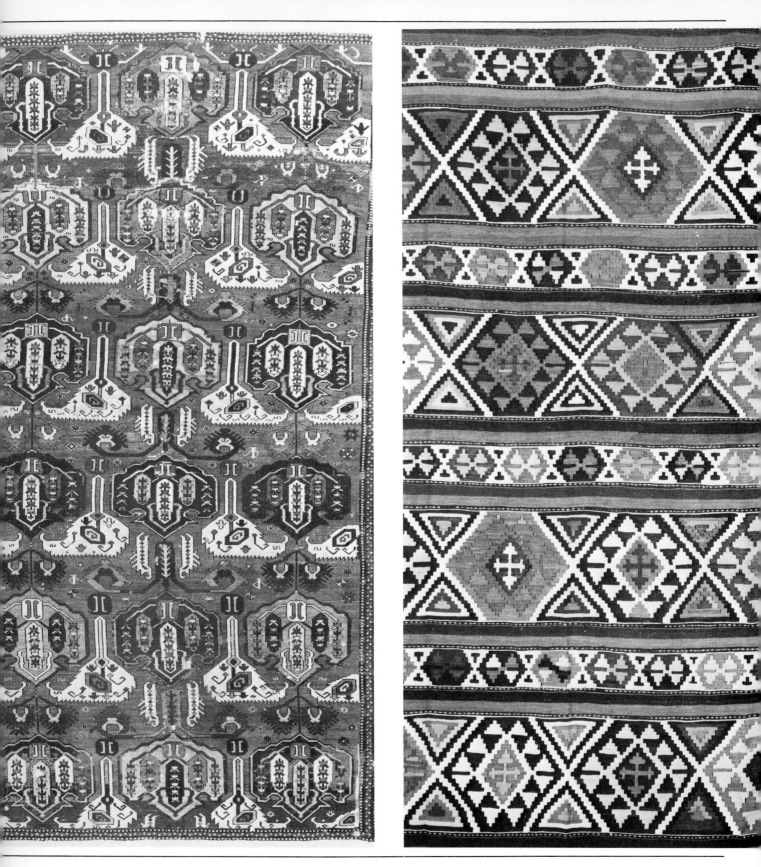

U.S.S.R. (CAUCASUS). LEFT. Knotted carpet, 1800–1850. *Royal Ontario Museum—910.95.7 (68TEX165).*

RIGHT. 19th Century Caucasian tapestry-woven rug. *Royal Ontario Museum—959.105.23 (74TEX34).*

U.S.S.R. (CAUCASUS). A superb example of Turkman embroidery. This is a Turkman woman's coat (kurti) of white cotton tabby embroidered in multicolored silks. It comes from the Merv Region of Western Turkestan and was made in the 19th Century. *Royal Ontario Museum—972.124.2 (72TEX173).*

INDEX

335

1